Make It Easy, Make It Light

BY
Laurie Burrows Grad

SIMON AND SCHUSTER
New York

Designed by Irving Perkins Associates
Illustrations by Norman Sevigny
Manufactured in the United States of America
3   5   7   9   10   8   6   4

Library of Congress Cataloging-in-Publication Data
Grad, Laurie Burrows.
Make it easy, make it light.

Bibliography: p.
Includes index.
1. Low-calorie diet—Recipes.   2. Low-fat diet—Recipes.   I. Title.
RM222.2.G68   1987   641.5′635   87-4363
ISBN: 0-671-62538-1

Portions of this book have appeared in Los Angeles *magazine.*

This book is dedicated
in loving memory to
my father, Abe Burrows,
whose love and appreciation
of food was second only
to his love and appreciation
of the written word.

CONTENTS

Fruits with Port
Light Banana Freeze
Frozen Strawberry-Banana Yogurt
Hot Strawberry Soufflé
Raspberry Applesauce
Crisp Apple Tart
Italian Lemon Cheesecake
Yogurt Cheesecake
Papaya Broiled with Orange-Ginger Glaze

Acknowledgments

To my editor, Carole Lalli, for her support and wisdom.

To my chief recipe tester, Anne Natwick, who helped me again and again, and again. . . .

To Elaine Markson, my agent, for her faith in both me and my projects.

To Millie Loeb, for her tireless research efforts into nutritional exploration.

To Mary Carey, for her loyal friendship and assistance.

To my testers and friends and relatives who all lent a hand: Marta Brannan, Catherine Bergstrom-Katz, Linda Burrows, Ruth Burrows, Sandra Carter Collyer, Lucinda Dyer, Betsy Halpern Castenir, Ashby Chadburn, Peter and Barbette Hunt, Nancy Kalish, Midori Kawamura, Susan Klein, Barbara Rhoades Orenstein Jane Raidin, Irene Ramirez, Karin Richman, Fred Roberts, Barbara and Stacy Tenenbaum, Diane Rossen Worthington, Leslie Zinberg.

And . . . once again to my very special husband, Peter, and my wonderful son, Nick, for tolerating my culinary madness.

FOREWORD

Finally! A cookbook you can enjoy without guilt, all of whose 200 delicious recipes you can safely savor to your heart's delight (pun definitely intended). This is not a book you will need to hide from your doctor. He is apt to approve of it as enthusiastically as I do. There are no gimmicks here. The author does not pit her "personal experience" against solid scientific evidence. There is no one who can argue with the wholesomeness of these recipes and their ingredients.

Laurie Burrows Grad is more than a great chef. She knows a whole lot about sound nutrition. Perhaps most important, she really cares about what people eat. She takes very seriously the recommendations of the American Heart Association and those of your own doctor, and translates them into mouth-watering dishes which will delight you and which you can prepare for your family and friends with pride and in good conscience.

In addition to the many delicacies you will learn to make in your own kitchen in easy-to-follow steps, you will also garner a great deal about nutrition—not about fads or crash diets, but solid facts which reflect what we *really* know about healthy eating. If you wonder about the difference among the various kinds of fat—poly, mono or fully saturated—this is where to look. If you have been titillated by the promise of the Omega-3 fatty fish oils, that subject is also explored. And after you have eaten any of these dishes, as I have, you will find it hard to believe they are low in calories, sugar, and salt and rich in fiber, fresh herbs, and spices.

Enjoy—with my blessing. But, be prepared to have your family and friends tell you they are "too tired" to eat out!

—Isadore Rosenfeld, M.D., F.A.C.P., F.A.C.C.

INTRODUCTION

I feel fortunate to live in a time when the explosion of information about good nutrition can be combined with my particular specialty—"Make-It-Easy" cooking, which combines fresh ingredients and simplicity for healthful cooking. This happy marriage has led to what I call *Make It Easy, Make It Light*, an approach toward cooking and eating that helps to keep me slim —no simple feat since food preparation is my profession—satisfied with the amount I eat, and delighted with the variety and tastes in my diet.

The impetus for this book, like my others, *Make It Easy in the Kitchen* and *Make It Easy Entertaining*, came from my readers and viewers. Those who watch me each week on "Hour Magazine," or read my column in *Los Angeles* magazine, or who have enjoyed the previous books, have written letters asking for a specific kind of help. You wanted to know how I keep my figure with all the cooking I do, and how you might do this in a healthful manner without spending hours on complicated preparation or retreating to the 1980s' version of the diet TV dinner. Could the Make-It-Easy approach be applied to those who wanted to change their eating habits and lifestyles? Can this approach accommodate the realities of today's busy lives, and what we now know about what's good and what's not good for us?

I had already begun this process in my previous books, especially in recipe variations. I have always looked for ways to cut calories without sacrificing quality. However, this challenge took me on a new path. I read just about every diet and nutrition book on the market and turned to experts all over the country.

My conclusion was that there is an enormous amount of information, almost too much for anyone to take in, but there was a need for a cookbook that put it all together. I wanted to provide quick, delicious, and healthful recipes that could be learned easily, prepared in just minutes, and thereby integrated into the new "light" lifestyle being adopted by millions of Americans who care just as much about their longevity as they do about their looks.

Your letters told me you had misgivings about the fancily packaged, dietetic frozen meals—all under 300 calories—that most resemble airline cuisine. I personally have found them to be tasteless; and *Consumer Reports* warns, in addition, that many are high in sodium, MSG, cholesterol, or fat, and none really offers the kind of balanced diet most experts advise. What's more, they're expensive—anywhere from $2 to $4 apiece; and for that kind of money we can purchase small portions of the best fish, strawberries out of season, or any number of treats that are as nutritious as they are satisfying.

So I decided to take the challenge—to invent, collect, test, and assemble recipes that could be cooked after a day of work (or beforehand and reheated), food that would be both party perfect and soul satisfying after a long day. Most important, these recipes all had to meet certain criteria: They had to be relatively *light* in calories, *light* in fat, *light* in sodium, and especially *light* in processed sugar. They also had to be the kind of recipes one would include in a balanced diet. They had to be made from the kinds of ingredients doctors and nutritionists are urging us to eat—lots of chicken and fish, fresh fruits and vegetables, whole-wheat flour, oat bran, brown rice, barley—the kinds of complex carbohydrates and fiber we need.

Adding, in this case, means subtracting; you won't find too many recipes for red meat—and the ones you will find use only the leanest cuts—or heavy cream sauces or decadent desserts. That doesn't mean we can never have another piece of chocolate cake "with pleasure and freedom," to quote Julia Child. As an everyday routine, however, these recipes are designed to help you maintain your weight or to lose, depending on how you use the book. I am convinced that a good diet and good habits can also mean good, even great food, and I offer this collection of recipes as a testament to that fact.

As many of you know, I am neither a nutritionist nor a diet expert so you won't find any strict regimens here. *This is not a diet book!* In fact, most experts are now suggesting that most of us don't need to learn how to diet. Anyone who has ever lost ten or twenty or more pounds already is a diet expert. But the sad fact is that 75 to 85 percent of Americans put back the weight they lose on diet programs. What's more, if you need to lose weight, more than a few pounds, I recommend seeing your doctor, first for advice and then to remain under his or her watchful attention while you lose. I should also note that if you have a specific medical problem that calls for a special diet, your doctor is your first line of defense. With his or her advice, you may find many recipes here that are appropriate for your needs.

However, I wrote this book for a more general audience, for people who want to learn how to cook and eat in a way that is both pleasurable and health-enhancing. That means it is possible to lose three or thirty pounds, or whatever your goal is, or simply to do as I have done, which is to maintain my weight as I have shifted to a more healthful way of eating.

There is nothing faddish or complicated here. I won't tell you to eat kiwis on Tuesdays and watermelon on Fridays or to cut protein out of your diet, or carbohydrates; nor will I tell you to combine this and that. On the contrary, for some foolproof results, the light approach represents a return to what I consider balance and common sense, to the basic food groups that made up our menu before processed and fast foods became an integral part of our way of life. Nor will you hear me preaching extreme strictness or deprivation. I believe that for healthy people this approach leads to a kind of hidden hunger that makes you think about running for the nearest Twinkie.

However, if your diet is now very high in one or more of what many consider the big, bad three—fat, sodium, and processed sugar—there will be a period of transition while your taste buds adjust. Very few people can shift easily overnight from a love of steak, marbelized with fat, baked potato and sour cream, vegetables dripping in butter, and gooey desserts to this lighter way of life. But it can be done gradually; and the rewards, from both a physical and culinary point of view, may be enormous. After a period of no more than six weeks I had retrained my taste buds so that I now *prefer* food prepared the ways described in this book. I no longer add even salt to taste, though I'll leave this one up to you since the experts disagree more about sodium than about fat or sugar. Perhaps, like me, you will no longer yearn for sweet concoctions and you may even come to dislike oily and buttery food. Instead, I enjoy the tastes and textures of foods in their natural state. For example, I love crunchy steamed vegetables with a sprinkling of fresh herbs or a bit of lemon. I still eat normal amounts because I have a healthy appetite, so you will find the portion sizes in this book satisfying—comparable to the portions in my previous books, unless otherwise noted. Only the ingredients and the cooking techniques have changed.

SHOPPING FOR THE LIGHT LIFESTYLE

Some tips concerning grocery shopping are so often repeated they hardly bear mentioning. For instance, how many times have you been advised to stay away from the market if you are hungry? Still, we all fall into this trap occasionally; and when I do, I head immediately for the apples, polish one as best I can, take another of similar size so I can pay for the one I've munched while avoiding the junk food that is no longer quite so tempting.

I assume your time for grocery shopping is more limited than mine, but I still suggest a minimum of two trips a week since a diet based on cooking primarily fresh ingredients tastes considerably better when those ingredients really are fresh. To save money, I shop at more than one store since my neighborhood is a cook's heaven; but you may not be as fortunate. If so, you might consider a monthly trip to the nearest inexpensive supermarket to stock up on staples that are easily stored over a long period of time. There is something depressing about paying top price for items like paper towels, club soda, or tomato juice. This monthly outing, if well planned, allows your biweekly grocery visits to be brief and restricted to the purchase of high-quality produce, fresh herbs, meat, and poultry.

I didn't mention fish because, if possible, I suggest getting to know your local fishmonger. In my neighborhood he has a wider selection, his selection is fresher, his prices are a bit lower than at surrounding supermarkets, and, at no extra fee, he will perform time-saving and helpful services, like shelling and deveining shrimp, grinding fish for fish loaves, and finding me the best of the catch. He also has a storehouse of information about clever ways to prepare fish and seafood. I have been especially grateful when he introduced me to the many new varieties of fish (like John Dory, orange roughy, and monkfish) that are more and more readily available, at least on the West Coast. Your local fishmonger may be able to recommend other types more easily available where you live.

But back to the supermarket. Never before, for those who wish a healthful, light diet, has the phrase *caveat emptor* (Let the buyer beware!) been more appropriate. Manufacturers have caught on to the fact that we want to eat more lightly, taking in less calories, fat, cholesterol, sugar, and sodium. So they have plastered the word "light" or "lite" on everything from crackers to beer. A study of those items so labeled is both (no pun intended) enlightening and depressing. Many, if not most, are not what they might appear.

The Food and Drug Administration has rules dealing with "low-calorie" or "reduced-calorie" foods. Under FDA's regulations, a food can be labeled "low calorie" only if a serving supplies no more than 40 calories and contains no more than 0.4 calories per gram. To be labeled "reduced calorie," a food must be at least one-third lower in calorie content than a similar food in which calories are not reduced, and it must not be nutritionally inferior to the unmodified food.

At the moment, however, there are *no* federal standards defining what "light" or its alternative misspelled "lite" means. In the case of some products, "light/lite" refers to the color, or the texture. Some are lighter in sodium but higher in calories. Others are lighter in cholesterol but higher in calories. For example, the tofu ice cream—like products fit this mold—no fat but high calorie content. One congressman, Jim Cooper of Tennessee, is sufficiently annoyed by these attempts to fool you and me to have introduced the Lite Food Labeling Act (H.R. 4269). If this bill passes Congress (and it will take considerable consumer support for this to happen), foods called "light/lite" must have at least one-third fewer calories, half the fat, or three-quarters less sodium than the same product without the reduction. Processed meats could be labeled "lean" only if they have less than 10 percent fat by weight. Right now at one of my local markets, the ground sirloin is labeled "lite" with a 15 percent fat content. The Cooper bill would also require that "light" beer have no more than 100 calories per twelve-ounce serving. One so-called light beer, according to the Center for Science in the Public Interest *Nutrition Action Healthletter*, has more calories in a twelve-ounce serving than regular beer. I have written to my congressman and urged him to sign on as a cosponsor of H.R. 4269 and suggest you do likewise if you want to see this legislation pass. (Write to your local congressperson care of U.S. House of Representatives, Washington D.C. 20515).

Until then, our best recourse is to read and study labels with great care. We can also avoid certain products, like bottled salad dressings. Even the low-calorie and "light" varieties are often high in sodium. In fact, the less processed food we purchase, the better off we seem to be.

Even so, many markets are offering new forms of temptation. The convenient salad bars in many markets as well as restaurants are probably the most dramatic example. Again, a little knowledge about nutrition and common sense should be your guide. I have followed people who have literally stuffed 1,500 to 2,000 calories into those pretty plastic containers or those deep salad plates. I advise you to avoid the bacon bits, the croutons, the nuts, the cheese, the stuffed pasta, the pasta salads slathered with mayonnaise, the olives, the avocado, the herring in cream sauce, and those other items you wouldn't consider under other circumstances. I also avoid the salad bar salad dressings, even those labeled "reduced calories," since the manufacturer's definition and mine may bear little resemblance.

On the other hand, I'm not suggesting you never go near a salad bar. After a very busy day, if you are willing to pay a higher price than if you made the salad at home—and you restrict yourself to the spinach and genuinely low-calorie vegetables—buying at the salad bar can free up time to do other cooking.

As someone who loves kitchen gadgets and equipment, I'm happy to report that manufacturers are offering a number of products essential to light cooking. Of course, the granddaddy of them all is the frying pan with a nonstick or Teflon surface. About twenty-five years ago these magical pans first appeared in American kitchens, allowing even inexperienced cooks to make perfect omelets. Discovered by chance by a Du Pont chemist, this easy-to-clean surface, requiring neither butter nor oil, can now be found on just about everything we cook in and on—for example, bread and cake pans, muffin tins, springforms, egg poachers, griddles. It is important to have a skillet and saucepan, and, if you can afford one, the new cast-iron nonstick-lined pots, which are sturdier when used with higher temperatures, last for many more years than the lightweight skillets.

Given what medical authorities suggest about lowering fat and cholesterol, there has probably been no more important discovery in the area of equipment than this nonstick surface. Recipes that once took ½ cup oil can now be made with 1 tablespoon. The Vegetarian Chili on Angel Hair Pasta is just this kind of adaptation.

In terms of low-fat cooking, grilling is the best way to achieve flavor and burn off fat at the same time. If an outdoor grill is unavailable, or it's inconvenient on a cold, snowy night and a broiler is not as satisfying in flavor, try one of these new indoor electric grills, which produce low-fat results with satisfying flavor. If these indoor grills are too expensive, look for a cast-iron pan with a grid on the bottom and coat it with vegetable cooking spray before pan grilling—remember, however, to spray the pan before heating. As an alternative, a light rubbing of olive, peanut, or vegetable oil, using a paper towel dipped in the oil, will prevent the food from sticking without adding extra calories.

Many people have discovered those inexpensive metal steamers that fan out and can fit in a variety of pot sizes. If you don't own one, I urge the modest investment since you can easily steam most vegetables so they are crunchy and delicious.

And the water can be collected for nutritious vegetable stocks.

I am also partial to the vertical roaster (I use a Spanek, but a number of other brands are available), which allows you to cook chicken in such a way that the natural juices are trapped and the fat drips away. The vertical position cuts down cooking time and simplifies carving.

"Light" cooks are also discovering the virtues of terra-cotta clay pots. Instead of basting with fat, steam seals in the flavors. The Chinese Chicken Cooked in Clay is evidence you never need to baste again.

A nonstick double meat loaf pan also reduces the amount of fat in the final product. This inexpensive item (I saw one in a catalog recently for under $7) is really a pan within a pan. The inner pan has holes in the bottom so fat can drip away. The outer pan can also do double duty for breads and other baking.

I use the new gravy and soup strainers too. These plastic devices do a great job of separating fats and oils from gravies, sauces, stews, and soups when you don't have time to refrigerate overnight. The gravy strainer is a pitcher with the spout based at the bottom. The soup or gravy is poured into the pitcher, the fat quickly rises to the top, the liquid is poured off from the bottom, and the fat remains in the pitcher.

I almost neglected mentioning the immersion blender, an amazing little machine that turns nonfat milk into something that resembles whipped cream. (I almost forgot about it because I lent mine to a friend who wanted to lose thirty pounds.) To use it, you take a small amount of very cold nonfat milk, about ½ cup, and add it to a puree of unsweetened fruit (fresh or unsweetened frozen fruit, thawed and pureed in the food processor or blender). Remember that the fruit must have a very sweet, natural flavor, as with strawberries or peaches. You then immerse the blender, whipping this concoction for just a few minutes until you have enough to add whipped dollops to baked pears, or plain berries or any fruit to which you would add whipped cream. I must admit I find the result vaguely medicinal. However, my friend who is using the blender reminds me that there is something psychologically satisfying about the consistency, which is very similar to the real thing. It is also a low-calorie way to get some calcium, and cooks at many of the best spas use immersion-blended whipped "cream" as part of their standard dessert fare. Whether you care for this concoction or not, it must be served immediately after preparation as it will convert back to liquid in a matter of minutes.

The issue of weighing and measuring what you cook is a personal matter and clearly more important if you are on a reducing rather than a maintenance regime. Nevertheless, I am glad I own a kitchen scale that measures portions in ounces since using it for two or three months accustomed my eye to distinguishing between even a three- and a four-ounce portion of fish or chicken.

I also like the new pasta measures that allow you to tell exactly how much you are preparing, essential for anyone interested in portion control.

Perhaps my most specialized gadget is my hot air popper for popcorn, a real favorite in our house. According to a recent article in the *Los Angeles Times*, you can save 100 calories in two cups of popped corn without butter or oil using such a device (approximately 50 calories versus 150). It is these 100 calories here and 100 calories there, especially when they are in the form of unnecessary fat, that make the difference.

I hesitate to say much about microwave ovens since I have and enjoy using mine to defrost and reheat food and know others love and depend on them. However, I don't use mine to create light cuisine because I favor more traditional forms of cooking. I recognize the speed with which you can bake a potato, but I don't like the taste or texture of a microwaved potato. And the time difference between steaming and microwaving fresh vegetables seems too negligible to switch to the microwave method.

On the other hand, I have left for last a piece of equipment I consider essential for the creation of Make-It-Easy light cooking —my food processor. Designed for the preparation of fresh ingredients, just the ingredients that are the heart of this new style of cooking, it speedily slices, chops, and purees such as in my Creamy Carrot Soup. The processor, therefore, makes cooking light a pleasure rather than a drudgery.

Obviously, it is what you eat that really counts, but these kitchen aids make the challenging transition to a healthier and still tasty diet much easier and even fun.

COOK IT LIGHT AND EASY

There are scores of cooking techniques and choices of ingredients you can make to remove unwanted calories, fat, sugar, and sodium without sacrificing quality and often with tasty results that are similar to the original. As you begin to add many of these methods to your repertoire, over six months or a year's time, family members may discover they have slowly lost those pounds that never previously would come off. Some of the suggestions below are best suited to dieters (e.g., always remove the skin from chicken before cooking it), but for those who wish to maintain their weight, this can be an occasional technique. At any rate, all these ideas are part of a lighter regime for those in pursuit of good health and trim bodies.

- When a recipe calls for sautéing ingredients in butter, margarine, or oil, substitute chicken, beef, or vegetable broth alone or with a fraction of the amount of fat you would have used in the past.
- Use dry vermouth as you would broth, as described above. Just make sure the alcohol has burned off before adding your other ingredients.
- Instead of butter, margarine, or oil, use vegetable cooking sprays such as Pam or Mazola. Butter and oil run 100 to 120 calories per tablespoon. There are only 4 calories per 1¼ seconds spray.
- Substitute plain low-fat yogurt for sour cream. There is a 275-calorie saving in just 1 cup.
- Use nonfat or low-fat milk and cottage cheese instead of their whole-milk counterparts. You reduce both calories and fat. Evaporated skimmed milk will whip after it has been thoroughly chilled. Of course, the taste will differ from real whipped cream by a wide margin.
- Stop all deep frying! Potato skins roasted or broiled in the oven taste just as good.
- Buy only the leanest cuts of meat; trim away all visible fat and

then roast or bake on an oven rack or barbecue so that the fat drips away.

- Instead of using cornstarch at 30 calories per tablespoon, thicken sauces by letting them reduce naturally. As you boil the sauce down, some of the liquid evaporates and the sauce becomes more concentrated and more flavorful.
- If you do want to use a thickener use arrowroot powder, the lightest of the starches with the most neutral taste. Since arrowroot is slightly stronger than cornstarch, use 1 teaspoon arrowroot for every 1½ teaspoons cornstarch.
- If possible, prepare soups and stews a day ahead and refrigerate. The fat will rise to the top, congeal, and can be removed easily. Or, alternatively, use the fat or gravy strainers described in the equipment chapter.
- Chill canned chicken broth in the refrigerator overnight. Fat congeals and can be easily removed. If possible, use the low-sodium broths, which are readily available at supermarkets.
- Use cooked and pureed vegetables instead of conventional thickeners for soups and sauces.
- Purchase canned tuna packed in water, not oil. You can save 300 calories in just 1 cup. However, beware of the tuna packed in oil with the label "lite." This tuna is not "lite" in oil but "lite" in sodium.
- Cook *en papillote* (in paper packets). All the flavors and juices remain sealed inside the parchment paper, no extra fat is needed, and there is drama to the opening of the packets at the table. This kind of preparation is simple. Most recipes can be prepared hours ahead of time and placed in the oven just before serving. Parchment paper, which is available at supermarkets, has been specially treated with silicone for nonstick cooking and baking.
- Stick to skim milk, low-fat cheeses such as Parmesan, mozzarella, and hoop cheese. Use even these sparingly.
- Use mustard, especially the grainy variety, in place of butter, margarine, mayonnaise, or dressing. It's delicious on sandwiches, a steamed artichoke, or even a baked potato.
- Use fresh lemon juice, garlic, herbs, and pepper as flavor enhancers, especially in place of salt.
- Use low-sodium soy sauce rather than the regular variety.

Read package information carefully since "light" on soy sauce may refer to its color. If Worcestershire sauce can be substituted, do so since it is even lower in sodium.

- Add salt to taste only after tasting! It may not be necessary, particularly if adding canned chicken broth or mustard, both of which have added salt.
- Place a large chunk of a peeled potato in canned chicken broth and bring to a simmer. The potato will absorb some of the sodium and can later be discarded.
- Purchase no-salt-added canned tomatoes and vegetable or tomato juices. Avoid canned diet fruits and vegetables and opt for fresh instead. The taste is better and the price is generally lower. I also avoid frozen vegetables except for frozen chopped spinach, which I find too convenient to pass up.
- Substitute Mexican salsa for ketchup to avoid the sugar and salt in most bottled ketchups.
- While cooking, taste with the back of the spoon. That way you just "taste" rather than get a full sample.
- Help your family get accustomed to eating less meat by including it in stir-fried dishes to which you have added additional vegetables.
- Serve healthy portions of complex carbohydrates (such as brown rice, pasta, whole-wheat pizza, baked potatoes, etc.) and lots of vegetables as you cut down on the size of protein portions.
- Offer new toppings for baked potatoes to replace the usual butter or sour cream—for example, snipped chives, yogurt, salsa, mustard, small amounts of low-fat cheese.
- If possible, remove the skin from chicken before cooking. White meat portions are lower in calories and fat than the dark meat.
- On an ounce-for-ounce basis, fish and poultry typically have less calories and a lower fat content than beef, lamb, or pork. Of the meats, veal has the lowest fat and caloric count although it is higher in cholesterol than lean beef or lamb.
- Make your own salad dressings. You can control the contents, and the taste will be infinitely better.
- If you haven't already, consider trying tofu (or bean curd). It is low in fat and high in protein. I use the firm Chinese variety.

See Tofu Dip, page 65, for instructions about removing water from the softer Japanese tofu.

- Whenever possible, serve food that takes a long time to eat, like artichokes or cracked crab. Slice everything you possibly can into uniform, small slices. It takes much longer to eat an apple sliced this way than to munch on a whole piece of the fruit.
- Purchase whole-wheat or whole-grain breads. Again, read labels carefully. Make sure the bread is sliced very thin. This may even be worth a trip to the bakery if you have the time.
- Avoid artificial sweeteners. So far, according to the experts, all the available choices have limitations in terms of health.
- Use frozen apple or orange juice concentrate, white grape juice, or cooked carrots as a sweetener, depending on the recipe. Or use a little bit of the real thing—brown sugar, honey, molasses, or pure maple syrup. Avoid dietetic maple syrup, which generally contains additives, preservatives, and is tasteless and watery. The difference in calories cannot be compensated by the lack in taste or preponderance of unhealthful substances.
- In fact, avoid all "'dietetic" candy, cookies, and ice cream. Sometimes their calorie count is as high as regular sweets.
- Use phyllo (or filo) pastry. It is paper thin and even with a light brushing of butter or margarine is lower in calories than traditional crusts. See the Crisp Apple Tart in the Dessert chapter.
- For the most part, offer fresh, baked, stewed, or poached fruit for dessert.
- Use monounsaturated oils in cooking (olive oil, peanut oil, or the newly popular avocado oil), but remember small amounts will do. See the ingredients chapter for the reasons why the experts are recommending these over the polyunsaturated oils.
- If time permits, save all the vitamin-rich water from steaming and boiling vegetables for use in rice, soups, and stews. Also, save asparagus peelings and broccoli stems for use in stocks.
- Whatever you do, do not overcook vegetables! Like pasta, they are best and most nutritious when cooked al dente, a bit crunchy to the tooth. Some families hate vegetables because they have never really tasted them properly cooked.

• Take a few moments and read, or reread, the equipment chapter. You can literally save thousands of calories by using the proper equipment (and *every* 3,500 calories equals one pound).

MAKE IT LIGHT—MAKE IT PLEASANT

Appearances do count, especially when it comes to food. Those who have specialized in light or Spa cuisine have learned some simple—and complicated—tricks to make meals more aesthetically appealing. Since my philosophy is predicated on a Make-It-Easy approach, I won't be recommending you learn to carve like a sushi chef, making birds out of apples or flowers out of oranges. These are wonderful chef's tricks but not truly necessary.

But garnishing *is* necessary. Two or three sprigs of fresh dill or one little flower on a plate make dinner an event. I use just about every fresh herb imaginable (mint in summer is especially wonderful), nontoxic flowers from my garden, or even just a cherry tomato on one small leaf of white kale.

I pay very special attention to color since we all respond to striking combinations. Look for the unusual and the beautiful in the produce section. You may find an exquisite purple cabbage or a special fruit in season, like blood oranges. One or two such oranges, sliced and offered as an edible garnish, can dramatize a simple chicken dish.

I would also consider occasionally using smaller plates so portions appear larger. If you are planning to purchase a new set, if possible select plates with a decorated border or design on them. Yes, there can be some sleight of hand in feeling well fed on less food, especially if you are on a reducing regime or serving heavier fare.

Making light dinners a pleasant experience can involve changing a number of ingrained habits. Some of what has worked in our family may work for yours too. Step number one was to stop serving meals family-style. We were eating seconds and sometimes thirds because the food was there right in front of us.

We make dinner a special time. I even do this if I am alone. The TV is off and phone calls are returned afterwards. So many people eat while watching TV that I think it is worth reiterating how harmful a habit this can be. I can't see how the mayhem on the evening news could help one's digestion or mood. And, even if you are watching something more entertaining, one of the best ways to be reintroduced to your taste buds is to turn away from the distraction of TV and refocus on your food and the company at hand.

It takes no more than two or three minutes to set a table properly and attractively. This simple investment in gracious living is the factor that can make the new light lifestyle work. It is a bit like treating yourself as if you are as important as company.

Some people make it a habit to take a stiff drink or two at the end of the day. Beverly Hills nutritionist Hermien Lee calls these "empty" or "nonnutritional" calories and explains that they whet the appetite because of the sugar content in alcohol. Instead she suggests *one* glass of wine or a wine spritzer (wine and sparkling water) for those on maintenance regimes who love wine with their dinner, and preferably no alcohol whatsoever for those who wish to shed pounds. Since I like a little wine with dinner, I follow Hermien's advice. It works.

I have also given up caffeine entirely although I did so slowly. For the past four or five years the only coffee I have had is water-processed decaffeinated. I avoid the other kinds because of the chemicals used in the decaffeination process. I have also stopped drinking soft drinks, even the diet variety, since many contain sodium, caffeine, or chemical sweeteners. Instead, I begin my day with herbal tea and then drink filtered or sparkling water spruced up with a slice of lemon, lime, or orange. I recognize that giving up some of the habits I am describing here is just as difficult as cutting fat or sugar from your diet, but to really switch to a light lifestyle involves drinking as well as eating in a healthful manner.

Although I am no expert on the subject of exercise, I think that it is an integral part of a light lifestyle. I find that brisk walking is not only beneficial for fitness but also relaxes and eliminates stress. I do low-impact aerobics two or three times a week, which I greatly enjoy, and find that my body is tighter and more fit while my mind is clearer and sharper.

THE INGREDIENTS OF A LIGHT DIET

By now most of us realize that the new light way of cooking and eating is a delicate and balanced combination of behaviors, ranging from the use of proper equipment to presenting meals as pleasing to the eye as to the palate. Therefore, it is worth reviewing the previous section on cooking tips since its emphasis is on the reduction of fat, sugar, sodium, and excess animal protein. But this is just the beginning.

I know I had scores of questions when I started this book and assume you do as well. So I will attempt a quick rundown here on the most up-to-date information on ingredients from fish (oily and otherwise) to cruciferous vegetables, and I will sort out some of the most important facts about cholesterol and fiber. However, at the end of the book, you will also find a bibliography listing several of the most respected consumer and medical nutrition newsletters written for the public, a number of them from major universities. This bibliography includes national organizations, such as the American Heart Association, where you can find additional information on nutritional topics.

I also want to say a word of thanks to Jane Brody for her pioneering work in this area. In her books and *New York Times* columns she has documented how out of balance the typical American diet is. She describes in detail how our bodies weren't made for the way too many of us eat. I am one of the people she has inspired; and, therefore, you will find that the recipes in this book are richer in complex carbohydrates (more about them in a moment), meeting Ms. Brody's criteria for a "healthier diet that more closely resembles our biological destiny."

TOO MUCH FAT

When we begin to examine our typical diet, there appear to be more villains than in an average murder mystery, though no would-be perpetrators attract more negative attention than fat and cholesterol. The issue isn't fat itself, for as we will see in a moment, there is more than one kind of fat and we all need some fat in our diets. The problem is that experts estimate that between 40 and 45 percent of our typical (and by typical, I don't mean light) diet is made up of fat calories. Many of these are hidden, sometimes in foods you would not suspect (see the chart on pages 36–37).

Our problem with fat appears to be closely connected to our overconsumption of animal protein. Today the experts are guessing that most of us consume about twice as much protein as we need, making our bodies work much harder than they should. Worse, our favorite protein foods tend to be red meat, cheese and other dairy products, eggs, poultry, and fish. The latter two, especially if the chicken is skinless, are generally seen in a positive light.

Most doctors today are suggesting that it is better to be safe than sorry. While there are some people whose cholesterol level is unaffected by diet, many others can reduce this substance that clogs our arteries by eating a diet that is more fat-free and by choosing monounsaturated fats. According to Jane Brody, we could have all the fat we need if we consumed the equivalent of one tablespoon per day instead of about eight times that amount. (You can visualize eight times one tablespoon if you think of it as a stick of butter.) We have to be especially careful to avoid those fats that are highly saturated. The worst offenders are coconut and palm oil because they are inexpensive, used in processed food, and do not turn rancid easily—this is another instance where you must read labels very carefully.

Until recently, polyunsaturated fats such as corn oil were the darlings, but a series of new studies suggests that olive oil, peanut oil, or the new and very expensive (and delicious) avocado oil (all monounsaturates), used in small amounts in cooking and salad dressing can actually *lower* the cholesterol levels for many people.

There just is nothing more fattening than fat! This sounds nonsensical until we look at the calorie count of a gram of fat compared to a gram of protein (without fat) or a gram of sugar. Fat has more than twice as many calories (9 versus 4), and its only close competitor is alcohol at 7 calories per gram. Considering that most doctors view fat as a factor in both heart disease

| Where Your Fat Comes From | | | |
Food	Serving Size	Grams of Fat (and Types)*	Percentage of Calories from Fats
DAIRY & EGGS			
Swiss or Cheddar cheese	1 oz	9 (S)	69%
Cottage cheese	1 cup	10 (S)	39%
Cottage cheese, low-fat	1 cup	2 (S)	12%
Whole milk	1 cup	8 (S)	48%
Low-fat milk (2%)	1 cup	5 (S)	37%
Skim milk	1 cup	.4 (S)	5%
Half-and-half	1 cup	28 (S)	80%
Yogurt, low-fat	8 oz	2–4 (S)	10–25%
Ice cream	4 oz	10–20 (S)	50–65%
Butter	1 tbsp	11.5 (S)	100%
Egg	1	6 (MS)	75%
MEAT & FISH			
Beef, pork, or lamb, cooked,			
with visible fat	3 oz	12–25 (SM)	50–70%
all visible fat trimmed	3 oz	5–12 (SM)	30–50%
Sausage, pork, cooked	3 oz	36 (SM)	85%
Frankfurter, beef	1	15 (SM)	79%
Chicken, roasted			
dark meat, with skin	3 oz	13 (MS)	55%
light meat, no skin	3 oz	4 (MS)	23%
Fish, fresh, broiled	3 oz	4–8 (P)	20–35%

and certain forms of cancer, the only reasonable conclusion would appear to be an immediate reduction of our fat intake.

But wait! There is yet new research suggesting that one kind of fat—the oil in fish—may actually have a salutary effect, protecting us from heart disease; and I will explain the results of those studies in the section below on fish.

First, I want to return to the theme of the book, moderation and balance. I agree with Ms. Brody that we all have eaten too much fat, but that doesn't mean you can never have another egg or a small portion of red meat. Instead of offering your family or guests soufflés rich in eggs, use the egg recipes in this book: The Spinach Tart uses three eggs but serves at least six to

Where Your Fat Comes From			
Food	Serving Size	Grams of Fat (and Types)*	Percentage of Calories from Fats
FRUIT & VEGETABLES			
Avocado	1	37 (M)	90%
Others	1	0–1 (—)	0–8%
NUTS			
Peanuts	½ cup	36 (MP)	75%
Pecans	½ cup	42 (MP)	90%
GRAINS			
Bread	1 slice	1 (MP)	13%
Spaghetti, cooked	1 cup	1 (—)	5%
Rice, cooked	1 cup	—	—
MISCELLANEOUS			
Coconut or palm oil	1 tbsp	14 (S)	100%
Other vegetable oils	1 tbsp	14 (PM)	100%
Margarine	1 tbsp	11.5 (PM)	100%
Potato chips	10	8 (PS)	62%
Doughnut	1	6 (MS)	54%
Chocolate bar, milk	1 oz	9 (S)	56%
Mayonnaise	1 tbsp	11 (PMS)	99%

* The letters after the number of grams of fat stand for the primary types of fatty acids in the food: S = saturated, M = monounsaturated, P = polyunsaturated fatty acids. Reprinted permission of: *University of California, Berkeley Wellness Letter*, P.O. Box 10922, Des Moines, IA 50340. © Health Letter Associates, 1986.

eight as a satisfying appetizer, while the Terrine of Chicken with Mustard Sauce Coating uses one whole egg plus one egg white to serve twelve.

I personally eat no more than three eggs per week. I have also shifted to scrambling eggs with one whole egg and a second white. The white has very few calories and no cholesterol. For added flavor, I add vegetables that have first been cooked in broth until soft, and I have heard no complaints from my family.

While on the subject of fat, I must mention the controversy surrounding margarine. According to a January 20, 1986 article in *U.S. News & World Report* on "America's Diet Wars," the perception in America is that margarine "is the top substitute for butter to lessen arterial clogging." But, the article continues, the reality of the situation is that "new studies cast doubt on its [margarine] cholesterol-cutting effectiveness; plus, polyunsaturates are linked to cancer in animal tests. Olive oil may drop cholesterol danger more."

My rule of thumb again is moderation. I use a very small amount of either butter or margarine in my recipes, but I do make sure both are the unsalted variety to reduce sodium and because the addition of salt in butter can often camouflage a poor or rancid taste.

One more word about margarine. I must mention my dislike for diet margarine. I particularly object to the added water and how it affects a recipe. I similarly dislike diet or so-called light mayonnaise. I am not fond of the taste, or in many cases, the extra additives and preservatives. So instead I use the real thing and reduce the amounts used. Instead of 2 teaspoons of light mayonnaise, I will use 1 teaspoon of regular mayonnaise. In the diet varieties what you are getting and paying for is lots of air and water.

HOW SWEET IT ISN'T

According to Jane Brody, 20 to 25 percent of our daily caloric intake—if we are a statistically average American—comes from processed sugars added to our food. The *Nutrition Action Healthletter*, published by the Center for Science in the Public Interest, says that about 40 percent of this sugar comes from soft drinks and sweets. The remainder comes in less visible forms. These sugar calories, like the fat calories previously discussed, are nutritionally empty.

The connection between sugar and health, or more properly stated, between sugar and disease, is somewhat controversial. The only direct link that has been established is between sugar and tooth decay. However, as a subject of abuse, sugar has been accused of causing a range of problems from heart disease to hypoglycemia. While some of the research may be questionable, there are enough people who report that once they begin eating sugary junk food, they have trouble stopping. They often describe mood swings and, as one might guess, weight gains. If you have this kind of problem, I advise seeing your family physician to work out a diet in which the sugar you eat comes primarily from fresh fruit. Many women report this craving for sweets as part of a premenstrual syndrome. In that case, I would see your gynecologist.

When I spoke with nutritionist Hermien Lee, she explained that a good proportion of the people who come to her for help are sugar addicts. When they remove the processed sugar and alcohol from their diets, they often experience a range of withdrawal symptoms, from headaches to moodiness. She explains that these can last up to six or eight weeks; but once the bond to sugar is broken, the desire for it goes away.

I have stated it before but I think it is worth repeating: I am strongly opposed to all currently available artificial sweeteners since there are too many unanswered questions about each one. I am especially concerned about the enormous volume of diet drinks being consumed, especially by children and adolescents.

The whole idea of "light" as a way of life is to wean a person away from his or her traditional sweet tooth, fulfilling this need instead with sweet, ripe fruit. The use of artificial sweeteners makes this more difficult.

Perhaps one day we will have the ideal artificial sweetener— relatively inexpensive, water soluble, stable within a range of temperatures, and, most important, nontoxic. So far nothing on the market absolutely meets these criteria for the general public. So what you will find in the recipes in this book are small amounts of real sugar, pure maple syrup, molasses, and unsweetened fruit concentrates and juices.

Over and over I will be urging you to read labels carefully. Regarding sugar, this is especially important. Foods such as ketchup, cereals (and I don't mean the devious offenders such as Fruit Loops and Cocoa Puffs), and canned goods can be filled with hidden sugar. Recently, I saw dextrose (a form of sugar) listed as an ingredient in a national brand of oxidized salt.

Finally, according to Ms. Brody, more than 10 percent of the American population is at least sensitive to a high-sugar diet. Twenty million alone will develop high levels of blood fats—

called triglycerides—on this kind of diet. Triglycerides is the technical term for fats and oils. The body's fat stores are triglycerides. The level of these fall quickly once sugar is removed from the diet.

Now that I have said all this, let me add some balance. For the majority of people, something sweet now and then prevents a feeling of deprivation, and that's why you will find some sweet treats in the dessert chapter of this book. However, even in these, an attempt has been made to make them as appealing as possible with the least amount of sugar.

SALT TO TASTE

I only add salt to taste in those rare instances when a recipe would be ruined without it. I assume that most of us already get more than an adequate amount of sodium (salt is 40 percent sodium) in the food we normally eat.

There are differences of opinion on the safe or necessary daily range for sodium intake, but the Food and Nutrition Board of the National Academy of Science recommends 1,100 to 3,300 milligrams a day. That translates into ½ to 1½ teaspoons. But the average American eats at least twice that amount.

Sixty million Americans suffer from high blood pressure, and study after study appears to suggest a connection with salt intake. Admittedly, however, reducing sodium intake once one's blood pressure is elevated only helps about one-third of this population.

Nevertheless, logic dictates we reduce our sodium consumption. From an evolutionary point of view, our diet was low in sodium and high in potassium until recently. Potassium is a mineral found in fresh fruits and vegetables that appears to protect against high blood pressure. With the rise in sodium intake, we saw a decrease in potassium. Most experts suggest the reason for this rise was the increased number of processed foods in our diet—from canned products to processed meats or fast-food meals. What we stopped eating were fresh fruits and vegetables.

See the following chart for the sodium content of various popular seasonings. And remember that eating *light* promotes consuming foods in the form nature provides, which is low in sodium.

Sodium Content of Various Seasonings*

The following U.S. Department of Agriculture figures illustrate the sodium content of the more popular "extras."

	Amount	Sodium (mg.)
Condiments/Relishes		
Garlic powder	1 tsp.	1
Garlic salt	1 tsp.	1,850
Horseradish, prepared	1 tbsp.	198
Ketchup	1 tbsp.	156
Meat tenderizer	1 tsp.	1,750
MSG (monosodium glutamate)	1 tsp.	492
Mustard, prepared	1 tsp.	65
Olives, green	4	323
Onion powder	1 tsp.	1
Onion salt	1 tsp.	1,620
Pickle, dill	1–2 oz.	928
Pickle, sweet	1½ oz.	128
Relish, sweet	1 tbsp.	124
Salt	1 tsp.	1,938
Sauces		
Barbecue	1 tbsp.	130
Chili	1 tbsp.	227
Soy	1 tbsp.	1,029
Tabasco	1 tsp.	24
Tartar	1 tbsp.	182
Teriyaki	1 tbsp.	690
Worcestershire	1 tbsp.	206

*Values for specific foods vary according to brand.

Reprinted with permission, *Tufts University Diet & Nutrition Letter*, December 1985, 475 Park Avenue South, 30th fl., New York, NY 10016.

A FEW WORDS ABOUT CALCIUM

One of the greatest problems health authorities are facing is how to get enough calcium into our diets once we reach adulthood. Clearly, its major source, dairy products, tend to be high in fat unless we choose them carefully. And the calcium amounts in vegetables are not enough to take care of daily needs.

The problem is the link between calcium deficiency and osteoporosis, the condition that leads to more than one million bone fractures a year, especially in middle-aged and elderly women.

The scientists agree on a few things. First, they believe that all children, adolescents, and young adults up to age thirty should get more calcium to increase bone mass and skeletal structure. Unfortunately, most agree that there is little evidence that calcium supplements *alone* after age thirty will slow bone loss unless combined with regular exercise or estrogen therapy. Since estrogen therapy is itself controversial and not appropriate for all women, doctors are recommending the supplements, exercise, and the low- or nonfat versions of those foods that do contain calcium.

THE NUTRITIONAL ESSENCE OF COOKING AND EATING LIGHT

So far we have been focusing on what to remove from your diet. I'm happy to say that the light approach substitutes lots of good, hearty food for the fat and sugar and sodium removed. This regimen is lower in animal protein and higher in complex carbohydrates. It is a diet that includes potatoes, brown rice, and pasta, and is one on which people actually lose weight if they are careful about what they add to these starches.

There appear to be a number of logical reasons why this way of life works. First, the starches, fresh fruits, and fresh vegetables that are its mainstay are relatively low in calories. Also, complex carbohydrates, in contrast to simple carbohydrates such as sugar, are sufficiently filling so one doesn't experience the kind of hidden hunger that leads to bingeing. And, up to one-third of complex carbohydrates (again, in contrast to the simple sugary kind) is not digested and instead is excreted unabsorbed.

This is a diet that favors fish and poultry over red meat, so again it is lower in calories and fat. And the emphasis on fresh as against processed foods gives you, the cook, genuine control over what you and your family will be eating.

There is also no reason why this kind of cuisine can't be Make-It-Easy. My other books emphasized fresh-ingredient cooking, and so it is here—with perhaps more emphasis on clever cooking techniques and the ingredients chosen. It is worth your time being knowledgeable about some of these ingredients.

THE BENEFITS OF EATING FISH

According to three new studies published in the *New England Journal of Medicine*, eating fish regularly, even fatty fish—at least a couple of times a week—may protect us from heart disease, high blood triglycerides, and cholesterol, and may even have positive implications for people who are prone to arthritis.

It is the oil in fish, known as Omega-3 fatty acid, that appears to be the secret ingredient. (See the chart on the next page.) This fat provides the protection, but since healthy people appear to need very small amounts, it's not necessary to stick with the oily varieties of fish, such as salmon, trout, or mackerel, according to the *Tufts University Diet & Nutrition Letter*.

Dr. Beverly Phillipson, the principal investigator in one of these studies, suggests if you have a special medical problem with high cholesterol or triglycerides that you be monitored closely by a physician and nutritionist as you experiment with fish that previously may have been restricted on your diet. For the rest of us, Dr. Phillipson warns us to avoid fish oil supplements from the health food store; eat the real thing.

There is also good news for those who love shellfish. According to the same *Tufts University Diet & Nutrition Letter*, new analyses demonstrate that the cholesterol values for shellfish are far lower than previously thought. According to the new U.S. Department of Agriculture tables even shrimp, thought highest in cholesterol among the shellfish, is well within the American Heart Association's safe level. Lobsters, clams, oysters, scallops, and mussels are even lower. These foods are all the more desirable since they are low in fat and calories. And if the portions you are serving are small, they may be well within your budget.

Species (italic indicates fish with at least one gram of Omega-3 fatty acids.)	Percent of Calories from Fat	Omega-3 Fatty Acids (grams per 4 oz.)
Haddock	7	0.2
Cod	8	0.3
Pollock	9	0.6
Northern Pike	9	0.2
Sole	9	0.3
Tuna, light in water	10	0.2
Scallop	11	0.4
Crab	11	0.5
Red Snapper	11	0.4
Lobster	11	0.3
Shrimp	12	0.5
Flounder	13	0.3
Turbot	13	0.3
Tuna, white in water	14	0.5
Rockfish	14	0.6
Halibut, Pacific	17	0.4
Clam	17	0.2
Striped Bass	19	0.9
Squid	20	1.0
Mussel	21	0.8
Ocean Perch	23	0.5
Whiting	26	N.A.
Porgy	27	N.A.
Channel Catfish	30	0.7
Rainbow Trout	31	1.2
Oyster, Pacific	31	1.0
Carp	33	0.3
Oyster, Eastern	34	0.5

One fish that clearly is within most of our budgets is the new "imitation" crab product called by a variety of names in the supermarket. This flaked fish is really surimi and comes from the white fish Alaskan pollock. I am told it will soon be available also as imitation shrimp and scallops. I am not crazy about surimi,

Species (italic indicates fish with at least one gram of Omega-3 fatty acids.)	Percent of Calories from Fat	Omega-3 Fatty Acids (grams per 4 oz.)
Salmon, Atlantic	35	0.4
Salmon, Pink	36	2.2
Salmon, Sockeye, canned	36	1.8
Whitefish, Lake	37	1.0
Herring, Atlantic	43	1.3
Salmon, Coho, canned	45	1.8
Mackerel, Atlantic	52	2.5
Lake Trout	54	N.A.
Salmon, Chinook, canned	57	3.3
Salmon, Chinook	59	2.4
Sablefish	68	1.7
American Eel	71	1.9
For Comparison:		
Chicken breast, no skin	19	0.03
Round steak, lean	29	trace
Ground beef	64	trace

N.A. = Not available

All values are for cooked fish, meat, and poultry.

Sources:
Estimated from raw values in:
USDA Handbook #8.
J. Amer. Diet. Assoc. 71:518, 1977
J. Amer. Diet. Assoc. 69: 243, 1976
(Values for tuna estimated, in part, from data supplied by Chicken of the Sea.)

Reprinted from *Nutrition Action Health Letter*, September 1984, which is available from the Center for Science in the Public Interest, 1501 16th Street, N.W., Washington, D.C. 20036, for $20 for 10 issues, copyright 1986.

and there is considerable variety from store to store, but as a product it is not inferior in nutritional content. Three and one-half ounces is about 90 calories, making it a good, low-fat protein source with little cholesterol. The only catch is that it has a fair amount of sodium.

If your family is not used to eating fish, the new health benefits may motivate them to try some of the recipes you will find in this book. You might start with the Japanese Grilled Fish Steaks or the Grilled Swordfish with Spinach Pesto and perhaps graduate to the Grilled Fish Escabeche.

FABULOUS FIBER

Probably no word is more associated with the new nutrition or eating light than fiber. It has been called everything from roughage to nature's broom, but there is a certain amount of confusion about what fiber is and why it is essential to our diets.

Most simply defined, fiber is that portion of our diet that cannot be broken down by digestive juices. After the small intestine absorbs the protein, carbohydrate, fat, vitamins, and minerals from the food we eat, most of the remaining *plant* material is passed on to the large intestine and is called dietary fiber. It is in this part of the body, before being expelled, where fiber does its important work.

Fiber comes in two varieties, insoluble and soluble. Water-insoluble fibers make up the structural parts of plant cell walls, and water-soluble fibers, which really aren't fibrous in nature, are resistant to human digestion. To clarify further, insoluble fibers include cellulose, among others, and are the predominant fiber types in whole-wheat products, wheat bran, and fruit and vegetable skins. Soluble fibers include pectins, from fruits and vegetables, gums, primarily used as additives, and the fibers in dried beans and oats. Medical experts believe both kinds of fiber are essential to our health though they have no nutrient value. And, in fact, there is no RDA (recommended daily allowance) from the federal government as there are for those food categories, vitamins, and minerals with nutrient value.

So what's all this fuss about fiber? About fifteen years ago, two well-respected British doctors who had devoted long careers to working in Africa published a book, *Diseases of Civilization*, in which they recorded their observations that the Africans they studied who tended to eat very high-fiber diets had low incidences of heart disease, obesity, diabetes, and common gastro-intestinal disorders. Their conclusion was that the Africans' high-fiber diet was a protection against these diseases. Since then, other studies have suggested that this sort of diet may also provide protection against certain forms of cancer, especially colon cancer. All these hypotheses are still being tested, and the medical community has come to no final conclusions.

There are a number of reasons why these conclusions are considered speculative. One is that people on high-fiber diets also tend to consume less fat, which some doctors believe may be more closely related to the prevention of some of these maladies, especially colon cancer and heart disease. In addition, people on high-fiber diets tend to eat more vegetables, and some authorities think certain vegetables, or certain vitamins found in both fruits and vegetables, may contain cancer-preventing substances. (That old theory of an apple a day has become a carrot a day in some circles.) Or a high-fiber diet's connection to weight control may be a factor. These foods tend to require a fair amount of chewing. Therefore, it takes a bit longer to eat them, and one feels satisfied more easily. Obviously, there are a number of variables; but what all this suggests is that, for whatever reason, increasing one's fiber intake is worthwhile.

However, it is clear that most Americans are eating less fiber than they did many years ago, while simultaneously the incidences of these diseases have increased. In fact, according to the *Tufts University Diet & Nutrition Letter*, medical experts suggest we "shoot for between 25 and 50 grams of dietary fiber per day, compared to the average American intake of 10 to 20 grams a day." See the following tables for the fiber content of a number of foods.

High-fiber foods include *whole-grain* versions of bread, cereal, and pasta (including wheat, oat, and rye products), brown rice, fruits, vegetables, dried beans (legumes), nuts, and seeds. On an ounce-for-ounce basis, vegetables and fruits have less fiber than whole grains because of their high water content; and some fruits and vegetables offer more fiber than others. Lettuce, for instance, has very little.

Cooking seems to have no effect on decreasing the fiber con-

Dietary Fiber Content of High-Fiber Foods

Legumes: about 9 grams per serving, cooked

kidney beans	½ cup
lima beans	½ cup
pinto beans	½ cup
lentils	1 cup

Vegetables: about 5 grams per serving, cooked

corn	½ cup
peas	½ cup
spinach	½ cup
broccoli	¾ cup
Brussels sprouts	1 cup

Fruit: about 3 grams per serving, raw

apple	1 medium
banana	1 medium
pear	1 medium
strawberries	1 cup
raisins	5 Tbsp

Nuts: about 5 grams per serving

almonds	1 ounce
peanuts	2 ounces
pecans	2.5 ounces

Adapted with permission from *Plant Fiber in Foods* by J. W. Anderson, W. L. Chen, and B. Sieling. © 1980, published by HCF Diabetes Research Foundation, Inc., Lexington, KY 40502.

Reprinted with permission, *Tufts University Diet & Nutrition Letter*, July 1985, 475 Park Avenue South, 30th fl., New York, NY 10016.

---

tent in food, but peeling these foods can decrease their fiber content—a good reason to own a good vegetable scrubbing brush. In general, processing food—canning, freezing, or freeze-drying it—doesn't lower its fiber content. But when vegetables or fruits are turned into juices, most of the fiber is lost. This explains why nutritionists advise us to eat an orange rather than drinking orange juice. There are caloric benefits with this approach as well.

People's systems are highly individual, so the amount of fiber you need, especially for regularity, is also individual. Certainly, if you have gastrointestinal problems, you are best advised to seek the help of a specialist in the field.

As important as fiber is, experts do warn that for the average person there can be too much of a good thing. Once again, our

Dietary Fiber Content of Cereals

Cereal	Serving size	Sugar (gms)[1]	Fiber (gms)[2]
Cereals containing approximately 10% sugar or less			
Oatmeal Oats	½ cup, cooked	-	2.9
Puffed Wheat	¾ cup	-	3.4
Shredded Wheat	1 biscuit	-	2.8
Ralstons	½ cup, cooked	1	2.1
Cheerios	1 cup	1	2.5
Chex, Corn	⅔ cup	1	2.6
Chex, Wheat	½ cup	1	2.0
Corn Flakes	⅔ cup	1	2.6
Grape Nuts	3 Tbsp.	1	2.7
Nutri-Grains	½ cup	1	2.0
Corn Bran	½ cup	2	4.4
Grape-Nuts Flakes	⅔ cup	2	2.5
Oat Bran	¼ cup	2	5.3
Total	¾ cup	2	2.5
Wheaties	¾ cup	2	2.6
Cereals containing approximately 10 to 30% sugar			
40% Bran Flakes	⅔ cup	4	3.0
Bran Chex	½ cup	4	4.1
Most	⅓ cup	4	3.0
All-Bran	⅓ cup	5	9.0
Honey Bran	⅔ cup	5	2.4
Frosted Mini-Wheats	2½ biscuits	5	1.3
Cracklin' Bran	⅓ cup	5	3.0
Raisin Bran	¾ cup	8	3.0
Cereals containing approximately 30 to 40% sugar			
Wheat and Raisin Chex	½ cup	6	2
Bran Buds	⅓ cup	8	8

[1]Source: USDA Nutrient Composition Laboratory of the Nutrition Institute. Human Nutrition Center, Beltsville, MD. *Journal of Food Science* 45 (1): 138–141, 1980.
[2]Sources: Anderson, J.W., *et al.*, *Plant Fiber in Foods*, HCF Diabetes Research Foundation, Inc., Lexington, Kentucky: Kellogg's: Ralston Purina.

Copyright 1983, the American Diabetes Association. Reprinted with permission from *Diabetes Forecast* May-June 1983.

themes of moderation and common sense emerge. Yes, you can get too much fiber. If so, it may bind minerals such as calcium, iron, and zinc. One should especially avoid those high-fiber breads that use wood cellulose as an additive. The experts at Tufts warn that these breads appear to have an adverse effect on iron, copper, zinc, and magnesium metabolism. And the doctors and nutritionists there agree that taking fiber in naturally through food is much safer than taking the fiber pills now available on the market.

However, if you eat a well-balanced diet in reasonable proportions, those same Tufts experts believe you won't have problems with mineral metabolism when you increase your diet's fiber content. They do suggest making the increase slowly, over a period of weeks rather than overnight, in order to avoid a range of discomforts, and to drink plenty of liquids (I advise water) and to consume a variety of foods at the same time.

It also helps to beware of the fact that some manufacturers of processed foods have caught on to the fact that we want to increase our fiber intake. Certainly not all, but a few prey on our fears and lack of information. So don't be fooled by the name of a product, advertising claims (the FDA may not have caught up with them yet), or its color. Especially with bread, we tend to equate dark with good and health-enhancing; but this is not always so.

Since wheat bran is the best source of insoluble fiber (one of those two varieties I mentioned before), when buying bread, check to see if the *first* ingredient listed on the package is "whole-wheat flour." At best, this should be the only kind of flour in the bread. Similarly, cereals made from 100 percent wheat bran are the highest in total fiber.

However, if you are one of those people allergic to wheat or you just don't like wheat bread or cereal, there are other unrefined grain products rich in fiber. Buckwheat groats, oat groats, and rolled oats are in this category, as are rye and wheat berries.

Fiber experts are also extolling the virtues of oat bran. Like wheat bran, some preliminary medical studies suggest oat bran may be helpful in tackling heart disease by lowering cholesterol levels and may also have a role in preventing colon cancer. However, the research here is as preliminary as the research described above.

Unlike wheat bran, oat bran is rich in soluble fiber. It can be used in baking (as in my Oat-Bran Muffins), or cooked as a hot cereal. But, because it has become so trendy, the price is up and, again, you have to be careful to read the small print on packages, especially cereal packages. One of the nation's largest cereal producers makes an oat bran product that retails for almost $3 per pound, and each serving includes approximately two teaspoons of sugar and as much fat as one ounce of butter. That's not a huge amount of fat, but it is about four times the amount as in other cereal except granolas. Since cereal brands, like rabbits, seem to proliferate on grocery shelves, I have settled on purchasing a nonsugar brand from the health food store.

VEGEMAGIC!

In the midst of this nutritional revolution, perhaps the most interesting fact is that our mothers were right—vegetables are good for us, and not just for their fiber content.

One group especially, the cruciferous variety, has been singled out in a special report called "Nutrition and Cancer: Cause and Prevention," prepared by the American Cancer Society. Though the wording of the report is cautious—no one is making any promises—there is the suggestion that eating these vegetables regularly may reduce the risk of cancer, particularly of the gastrointestinal and respiratory tracts.

Let me begin by naming them: green and red cabbage; broccoli; cauliflower; radishes; watercress; collard, mustard, and turnip greens, kohlrabi; brussels sprouts, rutabagas; and Chinese vegetables, such as bok choy. Obviously, some of these are more familiar than others. But if they are not a part of your diet, it may be because, to quote food writer, Nancy Harmon Jenkins, they "have suffered from an undeservedly evil reputation ...overcooked...too often their sulfurous aromas evoking images of grim kitchens in Orwellian rooming houses."

Her description is a bit overdramatic and literary; but it is true that in general our parents' generation did not prepare vegetables with as much sophistication and subtlety as we do today. Nor were vegetables available in the kind of profusion we have today. In fact, the Make-It-Easy approach has helped to rescue vegetables from the kind of oblivion Jenkins describes. They are cooked for a shorter period of time, often steamed and dressed with herbs, lemon juice, a bit of grainy mustard, or soy sauce.

They are used in Chinese cooking methods, especially in stir-fried dishes and, in the case of cauliflower, cabbages, watercress, and broccoli, find their way into our salads, raw. Sometimes they are pureed alone, or in combination. In the hands of a creative cook, they are a marvelous addition to his or her repertoire.

I am not suggesting you restrict your preparation of vegetables to the cruciferous variety. We are aware that the beta carotene in carrots is also touted as potentially good for our longevity. It's just that these cabbagelike vegetables have been truly maligned and neglected and are quite wonderful if properly cooked.

In fact, the nutritional advice I was asked to pass on to you from a number of professional sources was to vary your diet as much as possible when it comes to both fruits and vegetables. In any week's time, serve as many kinds as possible, remembering to vary the colors. Some experts feel this approach is helpful in avoiding the development of food allergies or sensitivities. And it is why I advised earlier at least two trips to the market each week so you can purchase the freshest and most seasonal varieties. Invariably, they are the most delicious and the least expensive.

CHANGING TO A LIGHT LIFESTYLE

Only you know yourself and your family well enough to determine the best way to make the changes described in this introduction. To suggest an analogy, there were some smokers who read the U.S. surgeon general's report and quit smoking that same day. Most people, however, could not change their ways so simply and did so only by fits and starts.

My guess is that you are already motivated to change and perhaps have already adopted some or all aspects of the "light" lifestyle. So, if you have not yet made the complete switchover, you might select one new habit to improve and pursue that goal for a number of months until the new eating behavior becomes as familiar as the old. Then move on to the next. If you are doing this on your own, you may wish to list your own order of change; or if you are cooking for more than one, the family might meet to make these decisions. By the end of a year, you can reduce the big bad three—fat, sugar, and sodium, and replace them with a healthful diet and exercise regime. This is a major shift. When you have made it, odds are you will look and feel wonderful.

LOSING WEIGHT THE LIGHT WAY

Many people lose weight without even trying when they adopt the habits described here. But to lose weight even when eating light there are a few special rules you can follow. First, select those recipes in the book that are lower in calories. For example, stick with the chicken dishes made with the skin removed before cooking. Use fish that is lower in fat. Restrict yourself to red meat no more than once a week and watch your portion size carefully. Eat fresh fruit rather than the more caloric desserts when you want something sweet. In addition, fork-dip your salad dressing, a trick advised by Beverly Hills nutritionist Hermien Lee. Instead of placing the dressing directly on the salad, place the dressing in a small bowl by your plate and dip your fork gently in to get just a bit of taste.

Be careful to eat well and not skip meals when losing weight, in order to avoid becoming ravenous. For myself, I don't lose quickly. And this is no instant diet. But the pounds I shed stay off, seem to come off in all the right places, and tend to stay off with normal maintenance.

EATING OUT—EATING LIGHT

While this is a cookbook, designed for eating at home, your family may be like mine—in restaurants at least a few times each week. So it seems worthwhile to discuss how to maintain all those good "light" habits while confronted with about every temptation possible.

Again much depends on whether you are on a maintenance or losing regime. Nutritionist Hermien Lee has a number of excellent suggestions if you are trying to shed a few pounds. She herself has tried a wide selection of restaurants, chosen a few favorites, and knows their menus. She decides what to order before she walks in the door, avoiding all that tempting reading. She also suggests that people speak up to ask that meals be prepared in a light manner—without cheese, without fat, or with only a minimum amount; and that vegetables be steamed. She also asks to have the bread and butter removed from the table immediately after being seated. I have a favorite fish restaurant that grills my fish deliciously with mustard and garlic, and without any fat. With more and more restaurants becoming savvy about changing eating habits, these requests are met much more warmly today than ever before.

In fact, many restaurants now have specialty menus of lighter offerings. You can contact your local Heart Association for a list of approved restaurants in your area. The little red heart by a menu item in those establishments suggests that the dish is nutritional, light fare. You might follow the restaurant columns in your local newspaper. At least in mine, places offering lighter dishes are reviewed. I clip these stories, place them in a folder to which I turn when we are looking for a new place to try.

I frequently find myself on the charity or speaking circuit, eating banquet food in hotels. Then there are all those weddings and other kinds of major celebrations. I have solved it by always asking for the vegetarian plate. I make every attempt to do this in advance as it tends to guarantee my success in receiving it. At worst, I have been presented with fresh fruit and cottage cheese; and, on occasion, I have had lovely plates of steamed vegetables. When this alternative is not available, I ask for a piece of broiled or poached fish; and again I have been pleased. Even if the fish is in a cream sauce, I simply scrape it away and eat the fish and the accompanying vegetables.

If you fly often, as I do, you surely face a food problem. I have decided that the best way of dealing with airline food is to not eat it at all. I carry my own picnic, to be consumed at 30,000 feet, often to the envy of my neighbors in the seats around me. On planes I eat lighter than usual and consume enormous amounts of water. This may mean a few extra trips to the bathroom, but the experts say that the best ways to reduce jet lag are to eat lightly, avoid alcoholic beverages, drink lots of water, and do as much exercising as possible during the flight. If I am unable to take along a picnic, I just eat the vegetables or ask if there is a fruit plate available. It definitely beats the mystery meat entrées so often served in the sky.

Most people tell me that eating ethnic—Italian, Chinese, Mexican, French, Indian, Thai, or whatever—is their real undoing. I admit when I am losing a few pounds I try to keep away from some of these, especially those cuisines high in fat or sugar. But if you eat reasonable portions and order carefully, all you have to remember is which foods are high in fat, sugar, and sodium. For example, I will order Mexican food but ask that it be served without sour cream or guacamole. And I ask that the predinner chips be removed from the table. At an Italian restaurant I now order a chicken dish instead of pizza or I may look for a pasta dish with vegetables and no cream sauce. And at a Chinese restaurant I tend to order a clear soup, a spicy shrimp dish, and lots of vegetables, with a small portion of steamed white rice.

For those of you who can't avoid fast-food establishments, I would opt for those that offer salad bars (remembering the dangers I discussed in an earlier chapter) and would select a hamburger rather than anything fried.

With the proliferation of carry-out restaurants, I would visit the new ones in my neighborhood to find the best in light food. But actually, my advice is to avoid these places, despite the pleas of children. In fact, my advice is more for the children's sake since experts suggest that food habits are established early in life.

LAURIE'S LIGHT LARDER

In my second book, *Make It Easy Entertaining*, I included a brief list called "Laurie's Low-Calorie Larder," which included all those special ingredients I have discovered to shave off just a few more calories. This current list is an expanded form of ingredients I keep on hand in my kitchen for the *Make-It-Easy* light lifestyle. Remember to read the ingredients list on the package carefully before purchasing any canned, dried, or frozen foods. I make it a point to avoid those products listing sugar, salt, or MSG as a primary ingredient.

Seasoning Enhancers:
Fresh lemons
Fresh limes
Vinegars (cider, red wine, white wine, Japanese rice, raspberry, etc.)
Fresh herbs (I purchase when available, chop, and freeze in small plastic bags or containers)
Dried herbs and spices (replenished annually)
Freshly ground black and white pepper
Worcestershire sauce
Reduced-sodium soy sauce
Tabasco sauce
Grated prepared horseradish
Grainy and regular Dijon mustard
Variety of tasty mustards
Fresh garlic (chopped all at once in a food processor and kept in a small jar in the refrigerator for several weeks)
Shallots
Scallions
Onions
Fresh ginger

On the Shelf:
Canned chicken, beef, and vegetable broth without MSG
Canned tomatoes (if watching sodium intake, use no-salt varieties)
Tomato paste (I find the tube easiest to use)

Canned green chilies

Canned salsa or salsa packed in jars(although I prefer the fresh salsa, preferably without sodium, sold in the refrigerated section of the market)

Canned water chestnuts

Dry vermouth or dry white wine

Dry sherry(for stir-frying)

Capers

Cornichons(sour pickles)

Ketchup

Mayonnaise

Olive oil

Peanut oil(for stir-frying)

Corn or safflower oil

Toasted sesame oil(for Asian dishes)

Vegetable cooking spray

Raisins

Honey

Molasses

Brown sugar

Pure maple syrup

Vanilla extract

Almond extract

No-sugar jams sweetened with juices

Unsweetened apple butter

Unsweetened apple sauce

Unsweetened juices

No-salt tomato juice

Whole-wheat flour

Buckwheat flour

All-purpose flour

Unprocessed bran

Oat bran

Stone-ground cornmeal

Unsweetened cold whole-grain cereals

Cream of Wheat, Wheatena, and oatmeal cereals

Arrowroot (in place of cornstarch for thickening)

Active dry yeast (I prefer quick rise)

Whole-wheat, spinach, or other varieties of pasta

Buckwheat noodles (soba)

Brown, white, and basmati rice
Wild rice
Bulgur (cracked wheat)
Barley
Lentils
Sun-dried tomatoes, in cellophane packages (not the variety
 packed in oil)
Dried mushrooms
Pine nuts
Nonfat dry milk
Canned evaporated skimmed milk
Tuna, packed in water
Herbal tea
Salt-free sparkling water

In the Refrigerator:
Nonfat and low-fat milk
Buttermilk
Low-fat cottage cheese
Nonfat and plain low-fat yogurt
Part-skim ricotta cheese
Part-skim mozzarella cheese or other low-fat cheeses
Parmesan cheese
Salsa
Unsalted butter or margarine
Whole-grain breads (keep a supply in the freezer)
Corn and flour tortillas
Variety of raw vegetables for crudités: carrots, celery, radishes,
 broccoli, cauliflower, etc.
Variety of steamed or cooked vegetables: to munch on cold
 topped with mustard, or to reheat, or to turn into cold or hot
 soups
Variety of fresh fruits: apples, pears, oranges, tangerines, and
 bananas in winter; melons, nectarines, peaches, plums, ber-
 ries, apricots, and grapes in summer

In the Freezer:
Frozen chopped spinach
Phyllo pastry
Apple and orange juice concentrates (once opened and thawed,
 store in a jar in the refrigerator for several weeks)
Whole-grain breads

AND, IN CONCLUSION

I do not see all the emphasis on nutrition today as a fad, despite some faddish elements. We have before us an explosion of information, some of it contradictory or unclear; but the main thrust, that what we eat and how it is prepared affects our general well being, is undisputed.

Eight general guidelines emerge:

1. Reduce fat.
2. Reduce sodium.
3. Reduce sugar.
4. Increase fiber intake.
5. Eat more fresh fruits and vegetables (especially from the cabbage family).
6. Avoid simple carbohydrates; eat the complex variety.
7. Eat smaller portions of animal protein.
8. Include an exercise regime in your life.

Since we each have individual body chemistries and the same rules may not hold for all of us, it seems sensible to implement this entire program to the best of our abilities. The recipes that follow are a reflection of what can be done with food, in a Make-It-Easy manner, so that living light can be a delicious experience. Since what we are talking about here may involve profound change in the way you live your life, I wanted each recipe to be as emotionally satisfying as it is healthful. My family was ready to make this transition. I will bet yours is too.

PLEASE NOTE

Calorie values have been calculated for each recipe that follows. Bear in mind that the variations offered for some recipes may change that count.

APPETIZERS

Crudités are crisp, fresh raw vegetables often served with a dip. They are crunchy, satisfying, and when attractively arranged in a basket, provide the perfect appetizer for any dinner. The Make-It-Easy trick to cutting up crudités is to select those vegetables that need as little work as possible.

There are some gadgets that help in the preparation of crudités such as a radish decorator or serrated knife. These tools shorten preparation time and make the vegetables look more appealing without additional effort.

The following is a list of vegetables that can easily be cut and organized as crudités, in a basket, bowl, or prettily arranged on a plate. Remember to select vegetables in season which are the freshest, best looking, and least costly.

Asparagus: Very thin asparagus can be eaten raw. Simply wash well, break off fibrous stem ends, and serve. Thicker asparagus should be parboiled for 1 to 2 minutes, drained, run under cold water, and drained again.

Broccoli Florets: Wash broccoli and cut off the florets. (The stems can be reserved for another use.)

Belgian Endive: Belgian endive, not to be confused with curly endive, is a compact, white, cigar-shaped vegetable. Separate the leaves and, if necessary, wipe with a damp towel. Belgian endive should not be soaked in water or it will become too bitter.

Bell Peppers: Green, Red, Yellow, or Purple: Wash, remove the seeds, and cut into thick slices.

Carrots: Peeling and cutting carrots or celery is often time-consuming. Best to do lots of carrots and keep them in a container in the refrigerator, covered with water. Change the water every other day.

Cauliflower Florets: Wash cauliflower, break into florets, and discard stems.

Celery: Best to do lots of celery at one time and keep in a container in the refrigerator, covered with water. Change the water every other day.

Cherry Tomatoes: Wash, but leave the stems on—they look prettier and most guests do not mind.

Cucumbers: Use "European" hothouse cucumbers, which need no peeling or seeding, or unwaxed American cucumbers, found at local produce stands, which need seeding. Wash and slice into spears or circles using a serrated slicer if available.

Daikon (Oriental Radish or Icicle Radish): Peel off only a thin layer of skin with a vegetable peeler and slice with a serrated knife into strips or circles.

Fennel: Florentine fennel, also called finocchio, resembles a pregnant bunch of celery. Cut off the feathery tops at bulb level. Remove the tough outer stalks, wash, cut off the hard base, and cut with the grain into slices.

Green Beans: Wash, break off the tips, if desired, and serve.

Jicama: A crunchy Mexican vegetable with a sweet taste, similar to a fresh water chestnut. Peel, and cut with a serrated knife into sticks that resemble french fries, or slice into thin pieces. Jicama can also be cut with cookie cutters into a variety of shapes.

Kohlrabi: Also called "cabbage turnip." Select small kohlrabi, trim the tops, pare the outside, and slice into strips.

Mushrooms: The easiest way to clean them is to dip a mushroom brush or paper towel into lemon juice and brush or wipe away any dirt, which will also prevent the mushrooms from discoloring. Trim a small piece off the bottom of the stem and serve whole or cut in half.

Red Radishes: Wash and remove the ends. Use a radish flowering tool, if desired, for a pretty presentation. White radishes should be scrubbed with the ends removed.

Scallions: Slice off the root ends, wash, and retain the greens.

Snow Pea Pods or Sugar Snap Peas: Wash, and if possible, remove the strings by pulling from the top down the sides.

Summer Squash: Pattypan, Yellow Crookneck, or Zucchini: Wash and slice into spears or circles with a serrated slicer if available. The new miniature varieties, sometimes called courgettes, can be left whole.

Turnips: Peel and slice.

THREE DIPS FOR CRUDITÉS

Curried Yogurt Dip	SERVES: 6 CALORIES: 77 per serving PREPARATION TIME: 10 minutes

This spicy dip is prepared with low-fat yogurt, and yet still has a creamy consistency and flavor.

1 cup plain low-fat yogurt
3 tablespoons mayonnaise
½ teaspoon curry powder or to taste
⅛ teaspoon grated fresh ginger, or pinch of ground
Pinch of sugar
Salt and freshly ground white pepper to taste

1. Place all the ingredients in a food processor or blender and puree until smooth.
2. Place in a covered container and chill until ready to serve.

COOK NOTE: Curry powder is actually a blend of spices usually containing cardamom, cloves, coriander (cilantro), cumin, dill, fenugreek, ginger, mace, pepper, and turmeric. Taste varies from brand to brand, so try out several to find the one you like best.

VARIATION:
* The dip can be used as a salad dressing or even a topping for cold fish or vegetables.

Yogurt-Dill Dip

SERVES: 8
CALORIES: 48 per serving
PREPARATION TIME: 10–15 minutes

In place of rich sour cream, this dip is prepared with low-fat yogurt and a touch of mayonnaise. Besides crudités, serve this tangy herb dip with cold poached fish, or use it as a creamy salad dressing.

1 cup plain low-fat yogurt
2 tablespoons mayonnaise
2 tablespoons minced scallions (green and white parts included)
1½ tablespoons freshly snipped dill, or ½ teaspoon dried
2 teaspoons lemon juice
2 teaspoons capers, drained
½ teaspoon Dijon mustard
Pinch of sugar
Salt and freshly ground white pepper to taste

1. Fold the ingredients together in a large bowl.
2. Serve immediately or chill in a covered container until ready to use.

VARIATIONS:
* The dip can be pureed in a food processor or blender, but much of the texture will be lost.
* Chopped fresh basil, tarragon, parsley, or a combination of all three can be added.

MAKE-IT-EASY TIP:
* When fresh dill is abundant, chop and freeze extra quantities in small containers to have on hand to add to sauces, soups, or other dishes. Fresh dill, chopped and frozen, is preferable to the dried variety.

Tofu Dip	SERVES: 8
	CALORIES: 74 per serving
	PREPARATION TIME: 10–15 minutes

Tofu or bean curd cake is a wonderfully inexpensive source of protein. If possible, use Chinese tofu, which is firmer and less watery than other varieties. Serve this dip with crudités.

1 1-pound package refrigerated Chinese tofu (bean curd),
   drained and patted dry on paper towels (see Notes)
2 tablespoons roasted sesame seeds
2 tablespoons lemon juice
1½ tablespoons Japanese rice or white wine vinegar
1½ tablespoons reduced-sodium soy sauce
2 teaspoons finely minced fresh ginger
2 teaspoons toasted sesame oil
1 teaspoon sugar
1 teaspoon finely minced garlic
Salt and freshly ground white pepper to taste
Garnish: minced scallion greens

1. In a food processor or blender combine the dip ingredients and process until smooth; refrigerate until ready to serve.
2. Serve the dip chilled topped with scallion greens and surrounded by crudités.

COOK NOTES: Tofu is available in 1-pound or occasionally in 14.2-ounce packages. Either size will work in this recipe.

If only Japanese or soft-variety of bean curd is available, you can press the water from the curds to make them firmer. To press, wrap each bean curd cake (or slice the whole cake into 2″ horizontal lengths) in cheesecloth and place in a large dish; place a 2- to 3-pound weight on top (a large book or several cans will do). After 1 hour, unwrap the bean curd and proceed with the recipe.

VARIATION:
* Use tofu dip as a salad dressing for any type of greens.

Celery Root Remoulade	SERVES: 8 CALORIES: 131 per serving PREPARATION TIME: 10–15 minutes CHILLING TIME: 1 hour

Celery root, also called celeriac or celery knob, is a turnip-rooted celery used extensively in France for flavoring much as we use celery. Celery Root Remoulade, traditionally prepared with a rich mayonnaise sauce, is the most familiar dish for this vegetable. This light version is prepared with low-fat yogurt.

1 1-pound celery root, peeled (see Notes)

Remoulade
1 cup plain low-fat yogurt
2 tablespoons mayonnaise
2 tablespoons grainy-style Dijon mustard
1 tablespoon finely chopped fresh chives
1 tablespoon capers, drained
2 teaspooons lemon juice
½ teaspoon crumbled dried tarragon
Salt and freshly ground white pepper to taste

Garnish
Lettuce leaves
Thin crackers

1. Grate the celery root in a food processor or cut by hand into julienne strips.
2. In a small bowl whisk the remoulade sauce until smooth. Pour over the celery root and toss until coated. Chill for 1 hour.
3. Serve on a lettuce-lined platter accompanied by thin crackers.

COOK NOTES: Select medium-sized firm celery roots with green tops.

Do not let the cut celery root remain standing or it tends to discolor. If it must stand for any length of time, place in acidulated water, a combination of lemon juice and water, to prevent discoloring. Drain well and proceed with the recipe.

VARIATION:

* Celery root remoulade is most often served as a first course, but it is also a lovely accompaniment to roast poultry or a garnish for leafy salads.

Oysters on the Half-Shell with Salsa	SERVES: 4 CALORIES: 97 per serving PREPARATION TIME: 10 minutes

Oysters are a low-cholesterol seafood. They are best in flavor from September through April, when they are not spawning. Fresh oysters should have a fresh seaweed aroma with perhaps just a hint of iodine, while any that have a strong, sharp odor should be avoided. Oysters served on the half shell should be alive when opened.

Fresh seaweed or shredded daikon (Japanese radish)
1 dozen medium fresh, plump oysters, shucked
⅓ cup Mexican Salsa (page 82)

1. Arrange the seaweed or daikon in a nest on 4 plates.
2. Make sure the muscle attaching the oyster to its bottom shell is severed and place 3 oysters, in their shells, on each of the plates.
3. Top each oyster with salsa and serve chilled.

VARIATION:

* Serve plain oysters with a sprinkling of lemon or lime juice on a bed of fresh dill.

MAKE-IT-EASY TIP:

* Most fish markets will shuck the oysters and provide seaweed upon request.

Spinach Tart	SERVES: 10
	CALORIES:142 per serving
	PREPARATION TIME: 20–25 minutes
	COOKING TIME: 40–45 minutes

This quichelike appetizer is made with phyllo pastry, paper-thin sheets prepared from flour, water, cornstarch, and vegetable oil. Phyllo (or filo) is used in many Greek, Middle Eastern, and eastern European recipes, and can be purchased fresh or frozen at Middle Eastern groceries or many supermarkets. This light and crisp crust needs only a light brushing of butter or margarine on the layers and is consequently lower both in calories and fat than a traditional butter or oil pastry.

Filling:
1 teaspoon olive oil
2 scallions, finely chopped (green and white parts included)
½ cup frozen chopped spinach, thawed and squeezed dry
¾ cup part-skim ricotta cheese
¾ cup low-fat milk
2 ounces Neufchâtel or light cream cheese
3 eggs, separated
¼ cup grated part-skim mozzarella cheese
1 tablespoon grated Parmesan cheese
2 tablespoons chopped fresh basil, or ½ teaspoon crumbled dried
1 teaspoon finely minced garlic
1 teaspoon grated lemon rind
¼ teaspoon grated nutmeg
Salt and freshly ground white pepper to taste

4 sheets phyllo pastry (see Notes)
1½ tablespoons unsalted butter or margarine, melted

1. Preheat the oven to 375°F. Generously coat a 9″ pie plate with vegetable cooking spray.
2. In a small nonstick skillet heat the oil and sauté the scallions over medium heat for 6 to 7 minutes, or until just softened,

stirring occasionally. Add the spinach, and continue to stir until well-mixed.

3. With an electric mixer (or food processor pulsating) combine the ricotta, milk, Neufchâtel, egg yolk, mozzarella, Parmesan, basil, garlic, lemon rind, nutmeg, and salt and pepper; beat until smooth. Add the spinach mixture and continue to beat until well-mixed but not pureed. Whip the egg whites until stiff and gently fold into the spinach mixture with a spatula.

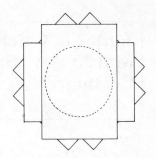

4. Place the 4 sheets of phyllo pastry in the prepared pan, crisscrossing them on the bottom (see illustration) and brushing each lightly with butter or margarine. Trim the pastry to leave a 2″ overhanging edge.

5. Place the filling in the pan, roll the outer edges of the overhanging pastry toward the filling, tucking it in and rolling to create a rim. Brush the edges lightly with the remaining butter or margarine. (See illustration.)

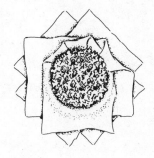

6. Place the pan on cookie sheet, place in the bottom third of the oven, and bake for 35 to 40 minutes, or until set.

7. Allow the quiche to cool slightly and serve warm, or at room temperature, cut into wedges.

COOK NOTES: Phyllo pastry tends to dry out quickly. Do not open the package of phyllo until the filling is prepared, as the leaves will dry out and become difficult to work with. Once opened, place the contents of the package on a dry flat surface and keep covered with plastic wrap and a dampened tea towel as you assemble the dish.

If the phyllo dough is frozen when purchased, thaw it overnight in the refrigerator prior to use. Also it's best left at room temperature, unopened, for 1 to 2 hours before using.

Unused phyllo leaves can be rerolled in waxed paper, and replaced in the original plastic cover, sealed securely, and stored in the refrigerator. Once thawed, the leaves should not be refrozen or they will become crumbly.

VARIATION:

* The quiche filling can be baked without the crust, topped by sliced tomatoes, and served as a side dish.

Terrine of Chicken with Mustard Sauce Coating

SERVES: 10
CALORIES: 133 per serving
PREPARATION TIME: 25 minutes
COOKING TIME: 1 hour
CHILLING TIME: 4–6 hours or overnight

This pâté makes a beautiful presentation when frosted with a mustard coating prepared with low-fat yogurt and topped with chopped tomatoes. The pâté can be prepared 1 to 2 days in advance and refrigerated until serving time. This sauce also makes a good dip for crudités.

Pâté:
12 leaves spinach (about ½ bunch), washed, stems removed
1 pound boneless, skinless chicken breasts, cut into 1" pieces
1 egg
1 egg white
2½ tablespoons olive oil
1 leek, finely chopped (white part only)
1 tablespoon grainy-style Dijon mustard
2 teaspoons capers, drained
1 teaspoon finely minced garlic
1 teaspoon white horseradish
1 teaspoon Worcestershire sauce
1 teaspoon finely chopped fresh tarragon, or ¼ teaspoon crumbled dried
Salt and freshly ground white pepper to taste

Mustard Sauce:
½ cup plain low-fat yogurt
1½ tablespoons mayonnaise
2 teaspoons grainy-style Dijon mustard
1 tablespoon chopped fresh chives or scallion greens
Salt and freshly ground white pepper to taste

Garnish:
1 large tomato, peeled, seeded, and chopped
Watercress sprigs

1. Preheat the oven to 325°F. Coat an 8"-×-4"-×-2" loaf pan with vegetable cooking spray.
2. In a large skillet place the spinach and allow to wilt for 1 to 2 minutes over medium heat; drain on paper towels.
3. In a food processor or in a blender in batches process the chicken with the remaining pâté ingredients until just smooth.
4. Place half the chicken mixture in the bottom of the prepared pan, smooth with a spatula, cover with a layer of the spinach leaves, and top with the remaining chicken mixture. Cover with a piece of aluminum foil, place in a roasting pan with hot water coming halfway up the sides of the loaf pan, and bake for 1 hour.
5. Remove from the oven, allow to sit for 15 minutes, and then unmold the pâté onto the platter top side down, discarding any accumulated liquid that has collected during cooking. Cover and chill for 4 to 6 hours or overnight.
6. In small bowl combine the sauce ingredients together and whisk until smooth. Chill.
7. At serving time, frost a terrine with sauce, top with the to-mato, and surround with watercress sprigs.

COOK NOTES: Spinach is wilted first to release most of the mois-ture.

All types of horseradish, other than the dried variety, should be kept tightly sealed in the refrigerator, and used fairly soon or there will be a loss of flavor and often a bitter taste.

VARIATIONS:
*   Scallions may be substituted for the leek.
*   Regular Dijon mustard may be substituted for the grainy vari-ety.
*   Chopped carrots may be substituted for the spinach.
*   Mexican Salsa may be substituted for the tomato topping.

Chinese-Style Chicken Wings	SERVES: 12 CALORIES: 61 per serving PREPARATION TIME: 5–10 minutes COOKING TIME: 25–30 minutes MARINATING TIME: 4–6 hours or overnight

Chicken drumettes are chicken wings with the tip end removed at the joint so that they resemble mini-drumsticks. If drumettes are unavailable, substitute regular chicken wings and remove the tips yourself.

24 chicken drumettes

Sauce:
6 tablespoons reduced-sodium soy sauce
6 tablespoons chicken broth
3 tablespoons Japanese rice vinegar
3 tablespoons dry sherry
1½ tablespoons Worcestershire sauce
1½ tablespoons lemon juice
1½ tablespoons toasted sesame oil
1 tablespoon finely minced fresh ginger
2 teaspoons finely minced garlic
Freshly ground pepper to taste

1. Arrange the chicken in a single layer in a shallow dish.
2. In a small saucepan place the sauce ingredients, bring to a boil, and cook for 1 to 2 minutes. Pour over the wings, cover, and refrigerate for 4 to 6 hours or overnight, turning once.
3. Preheat the oven to 375°F. Coat a roasting pan with vegetable cooking spray.
4. Drain the marinade from the chicken and set aside. Arrange the drumettes in the prepared pan and bake for 10 minutes. Turn, and bake for an additional 10 minutes, basting often with the reserved marinade. (Whole wings need 5 to 10 minutes longer to cook.)

5. Turn the heat up to broil and brown the wings for 2 to 3 minutes, or until crisp on both sides.
6. In a small saucepan bring the remaining marinade to a boil and cook over medium-high heat for 4 to 5 minutes. Place in a bowl and serve as a dipping sauce along with the wings.

VARIATIONS:
* Wings can be placed in a hamburger grill basket and grilled outdoors.
* 2 tablespoons minced scallions can be added to the marinade.
* Use the marinade with 8 to 10 chicken thighs, cook for 30 to 40 minutes, and serve as a main course or chill for a picnic.

MAKE-IT-EASY TIP:
* Collect wing tips and save in a plastic bag in the freezer to use for making chicken stock.

Grilled Eggplant Appetizer	SERVES: 6 CALORIES: 53 per serving PREPARATION TIME: 10–15 minutes COOKING TIME: 8 minutes

Eggplant is generally sautéed in lots of olive oil to get it crisp. The vegetable is porous, like a sponge, and therefore needs lots of the oil in order to brown. By grilling the eggplant, you only use a tablespoon of oil to achieve the same browned results.

1 medium eggplant, washed and dried
1–2 tablespoons olive oil
2 tablespoons balsamic or red wine vinegar

1. Preheat the broiler to high.
2. Slice the eggplant horizontally ¼" to ⅛" thick. Place in a single layer in a broiling pan, brush lightly with half the oil on one side, and broil for 3 to 4 minutes, or until golden. Turn, brush with the remaining oil, and broil as before.

3. Remove, slice into thin strips, place in a bowl, toss with the vinegar to coat, and allow to stand for 5 to 10 minutes.
4. Serve at room temperature.

COOK NOTE: Eggplant is quite perishable and should be used as soon as possible. Store in a plastic bag in the refrigerator to retain moisture as long as possible.

VARIATION:
* Small Japanese eggplants, called nasu, are easily adapted to this recipe.

MAKE-IT-EASY TIP:
Broiled eggplant can be stored in a covered container for several days. Bring to room temperature and serve.

Moroccan Carrot Salad	SERVES: 8 CALORIES: 46 per serving PREPARATION TIME: 15 minutes CHILLING TIME: 4–6 hours or overnight

This spicy salad, redolent of cilantro, contains only 1 tablespoon of peanut oil in a quantity to serve 8 people.

¼ cup chopped fresh parsley
2 tablespoons chopped fresh cilantro (coriander)
1 clove garlic, finely minced
2 tablespoons lemon juice
1 tablespoon peanut oil
1 tablespoon tomato paste
1 teaspoon chili powder
1 teaspoon ground cumin
½ teaspoon paprika
Pinch of cayenne
Salt to taste
1 pound carrots, shredded

1. In a food processor, blender, or by hand, combine the parsley, cilantro, and garlic and process until finely chopped. Add the lemon juice, peanut oil, tomato paste, and seasonings. Process just until all the ingredients are well-combined.
2. Place the mixture in a large glass or ceramic bowl, top with the carrots, and toss until the carrots are coated. Cover the bowl and refrigerate for 4 to 6 hours or overnight.
3. Adjust the seasonings and serve chilled or at room temperature.

COOK NOTE: Never store carrots with apples in the refrigerator. Apples release a gas that gives carrots a bitter taste.

VARIATION:
* The salad can be prepared using half carrots and half shredded jicama.

MAKE-IT-EASY TIP:
* Tomato paste is available in squeeze tubes, which are easier to use than canned paste. Simply squeeze out the required amount, replace the lid, and refrigerate until the next use.

Steamed Clams in Flavored Broth	SERVES: 6 CALORIES: 101 per serving PREPARATION TIME: 10–15 minutes SOAKING TIME: 20–30 minutes COOKING TIME: 8–10 minutes

Steamed clams need not be served with buckets of butter. Here they are steamed in a flavored broth, the broth is strained, and the clams are served along with the delicious clear juices.

Serve the clams as an appetizer course or double the recipe and serve to 4 as an entrée.

4 dozen steamer clams
1 tablespoon cornmeal
2 cups chicken broth
⅔ cup dry vermouth
3 shallots, finely minced
2 cloves garlic, crushed and peeled but still intact
2 slices lemon
2 sprigs of parsley
Salt and freshly ground white pepper to taste

1. Place the clams in a large bowl, fill with cold water, and sprinkle with cornmeal. Allow to soak for 20 to 30 minutes. Rinse, place in a covered container, and chill until ready to cook.
2. In a large kettle, place the remaining ingredients; bring to a boil, cover, and cook over medium heat for 5 minutes. Add the clams and continue to cook for 3 to 5 minutes, or just until they open. Then remove them immediately or they will become tough.
3. Put all the ingredients through a strainer. Place the clams in a warm serving bowl and discard the vegetables.
4. Strain the broth through a strainer lined with 2 layers of cheesecloth to remove the sand. Serve the clams in deep soup plates with individual bowls of broth for dipping.

VARIATIONS:
* Steamer—or soft-shell clams—are best for this dish but the hard-shell variety, littlenecks or cherrystones, can be substituted.
* The white part of scallions can be substituted for the shallots.

Baked Corn Tortilla Chips	SERVES: 6 CALORIES: 55 per serving PREPARATION TIME: 5 minutes COOKING TIME: 12 minutes

Corn tortillas make excellent crisp, light chips when baked instead of frying. Serve with Mexican Salsa.

4 corn tortillas
½ teaspoon chili powder
Salt to taste
Accompaniment: 1 cup Mexican Salsa (page 82)

1. Preheat the oven to 400°F.
2. Cut the tortillas into 8 wedges. Place on a baking sheet, sprinkle with chili powder and salt, and bake for 12 minutes, or until crisp and lightly golden.
3. Allow to cool slightly and serve.

COOK NOTE: Store fresh tortillas in plastic bags in the refrigerator for several days. Tortillas can also be frozen, each tortilla placed between a sheet of waxed paper, and then sealed in a plastic bag. Thaw before baking.

VARIATIONS:
* For those watching their sodium intake, a nonsalt herb seasoning can be substituted for salt.
* Flour tortillas can be substituted.

Salmon Slices Marinated with Lime Juice and Basil	SERVES: 8 CALORIES: 200 per serving PREPARATION TIME: 15 minutes MARINATING TIME: 4–6 hours

It is important to use fresh basil in this recipe. If fresh basil is unavailable, substitute fresh dill or parsley and avoid dried herbs. Serve this dish accompanied by thin pumpernickel bread.

1 pound salmon fillets with skin on, preferably from the tail end

Marinade:
½ cup lime juice
2 tablespoons finely chopped fresh basil
1 teaspoon sugar
Salt and freshly ground white pepper to taste

Garnish:
Basil leaves or sprigs of watercress

1. Lay the fillets, skin side down, on a washable cutting board. With a very sharp knife slice the salmon thinly. Discard the skin and cut larger pieces in half.
2. Arrange the slices in a shallow dish. Combine the marinade ingredients in a small bowl, stir, and pour over the salmon. (The salmon should be covered with the marinade.) Cover and allow to marinate in the refrigerator for 4 to 6 hours, turning occasionally.
3. When ready to serve, arrange the salmon slices attractively on a platter and drizzle with some of the marinade.

VARIATION:
* Halibut fillets can be substituted for the salmon.

MAKE-IT-EASY TIP:
* Before cooking with salmon, or any other fish, feel the flesh with your fingertips for any small bones. Remove any bones with a tweezer.

Halibut Tartare

SERVES: 6
CALORIES: 137 per serving
PREPARATION TIME: 15 minutes
CHILLING TIME: 2 HOURS

This recipe is a variation of Diane Rossen Worthington's Salmon Tartare from her wonderful book *The Cuisine of California* (J.P. Tarcher, 1983). Serve with thin crackers.

1 pound fresh halibut fillets, cut into 3" pieces (see Note)
¼ cup coarsely chopped cornichons (French baby pickles)
¼ cup plus 1 teaspoon lemon juice
2 tablespoons grainy-style Dijon mustard
2 tablespoons chopped fresh parsley
2 teaspoons mayonnaise
1 tablespoon plus 1 teaspoon capers, drained and rinsed
⅛ teaspoon Tabasco sauce
Salt and freshly ground white pepper to taste

Garnish:
Sprigs of parsley

1. In a food processor pulsate the halibut into coarse pieces only.
2. Place the fish in a medium-sized bowl and add the cornichons, lemon juice, mustard, parsley, and mayonnaise. Mix well. Gently add the capers, Tabasco, and salt and pepper. Spoon into a serving container, cover, and refrigerate for 2 hours to intensify the flavors.
3. Serve chilled, garnished with sprigs of parsley, and accompanied by thin crackers.

COOK NOTE: Be certain that the fish you purchase has not been previously frozen. Ask the people at the fish store or in the supermarket to allow you to smell the fish and avoid any that has a "fishy" aroma—it surely is not fresh.

Marbled Tea-Steeped Eggs	YIELD: 6
	CALORIES: 91 per egg
	PREPARATION TIME: 10 minutes
	COOKING TIME: 40 minutes
	CHILLING TIME: 12 hours or overnight

Chinese tea eggs, ch'a yeh tan, resemble an antique porcelain masterpiece with their mottled shells and delicate appearance. These eggs were traditionally sold in Chinese markets and in theaters as snacks at intermission. Tea eggs differ from thousand-year-old eggs, which are duck eggs preserved in a coating of lime, salt, and ashes and cured for about 100 days. Thousand-year-old eggs, with their amber-colored whites and green yolks, have a cheeselike taste, and are a Chinese delicacy, served as an appetizer in very moderate amounts.

The marbled tea-steeped egg wedges make a pretty presentation as an appetizer or part of an appetizer platter.

6 eggs
3 tablespoons Chinese black tea wrapped in cheesecloth,
  or 2 tea bags
2–3 cloves star anise (see Notes)
1 tablespoon salt
1 tablespoon reduced-sodium soy sauce
1 teaspoon red pepper flakes
2 teaspoons liquid smoke

Garnish:
Chinese parsley (also called cilantro or coriander)

1. In a small saucepan place the eggs in cold water, bring to a boil, cover, reduce heat, and simmer slowly for 10 minutes. Run under cold water and then crack the shells by tapping lightly all over with the back of a spoon. Do not remove the shells.
2. Return the eggs to the pan, cover with water, add tea, salt, soy sauce, and red pepper, bring to a boil, cover, lower heat,

and simmer slowly for 30 minutes. Allow the eggs to cool in the liquid. Transfer to a container, add liquid smoke, cover, and refrigerate for 12 hours or overnight in the liquid.

3. The next day, carefully remove the shells, exposing a marbled appearance. Serve cut in halves and garnished with Chinese parsley.

COOK NOTES: Star anise is an herb with starlike clusters of light, elongated seeds whose flavor is similar to but more pungent than that of licorice. Although called anise, this Chinese herb is not actually related to the anise family but to the magnolia family. If star anise is unavailable, aniseseeds can be substituted.

The eggs will keep in a covered container in the refrigerator for 1 to 2 weeks.

VARIATION:
* Eggs can be served whole as a garnish for Asian salads.

BASICS AND SAUCES

Mexican Salsa

YIELD: 3 cups
CALORIES: 70 per cup
PREPARATION TIME: 15–20 minutes
CHILLING TIME: 1–2 hours

This spicy Mexican sauce is light on fat, light on calories, and light on sodium. Salt is listed to taste, but the chili peppers and garlic should give it enough flavor to eliminate the need for salt altogether. Serve salsa as a dipping sauce with Baked Corn Tortilla Chips (page 77) or chilled vegetable crudités, use as a topping for eggs or other dishes, or use in cooking such as in Grilled Mexican-Style Chicken with Salsa (page 133).

6 medium tomatoes, peeled, seeded, and chopped (see Tip)
½ cup finely chopped onions
¼ cup chopped fresh parsley
2 long green mild chile peppers, seeded, or to taste
1–2 tablespoons chopped fresh cilantro (coriander)
1 tablespoon red wine vinegar
1 clove garlic, minced
¼ teaspoon crumbled dried oregano
Salt and freshly ground pepper to taste

In a large bowl, combine all the ingredients and chill for 1 to 2 hours.

COOK NOTE: Salsa will keep for 1 to 2 weeks in a covered jar in the refrigerator.

VARIATION:
* For an easier version, substitute canned Italian tomatoes, peeled, drained, and chopped, although they will not have the texture of the fresh tomatoes.

MAKE-IT-EASY TIP
To peel tomatoes quickly, place in hot but not boiling water for 3 minutes and the skins will come off easily. If you drop in boiling water for too long the texture of the tomatoes often becomes mushy.

Light Red Sauce	YIELD: 4 cups
	CALORIES: 92 per cup
	PREPARATION TIME: 10–15 minutes
	COOKING TIME: 40 minutes

Use this versatile no-oil red sauce on pasta, pizza, fish, chicken, meats, or vegetables. Carrots are added for sweetness and to cut the acidity of the tomatoes.

¼ cup strong chicken broth
1 medium onion, finely chopped
2 cloves garlic, finely minced
1 carrot, peeled and finely chopped
1 28-ounce can crushed tomatoes (preferably packed in puree)
¼ cup chopped fresh parsley
¼ cup chopped fresh basil, or 1½ tablespoons crumbled dried
1 tablespoon apple cider vinegar
½ teaspoon red pepper flakes (optional)
Salt and freshly ground black pepper to taste

1. In a medium-sized nonstick skillet heat the chicken broth until boiling. Add the onion, garlic, and carrot, and simmer, uncovered, for 10 minutes, or until tender.
2. Add the remaining ingredients, bring to a boil, partially cover, and simmer slowly for 30 minutes, or until the sauce has reduced by one-third the amount, or until the desired thickness is achieved.
3. Allow to cool, place in containers, and refrigerate or freeze until ready to use.

VARIATIONS:
* If tomatoes packed in puree are unavailable, use regular whole juice-packed tomatoes; chop and drain off most of the

liquid. Return the tomatoes to the can, and fill to the top with canned tomato puree.

* For an easy pasta dish, add 1 cup sliced mushrooms; 2 medium zucchini, julienned; 1 red pepper, julienned; 1 green pepper, julienned; and other seasonal produce desired to the sauce and toss with hot pasta to taste.

MAKE-IT-EASY TIP:
* Freeze the sauce in 1-cup containers to have on hand for quick dinners.

Light White Sauce

YIELD: 4 cups
CALORIES: 96 per cup
PREPARATION TIME: 10–15 minutes
COOKING TIME: 15 minutes

This flavorful puree of leeks becomes a creamy sauce that can be used in pasta dishes, over vegetables, or in cooked casseroles.

4 cups (about 1½ pounds) chopped leeks (white part and pale green part of green stalks only), thoroughly washed
2 cups strong chicken broth
2 cloves garlic, finely minced
¼ cup nonfat dry milk
Salt and freshly ground white pepper to taste
2 tablespoons chopped fresh parsley

1. In a medium saucepan place the leeks, broth, garlic, milk, and salt and pepper. Bring to a boil, cover, reduce heat, and simmer until the leeks are tender, about 15 minutes, stirring occasionally.
2. Place the mixture in a food processor or blender and puree until smooth. Add the parsley, pulse to combine, and serve hot or use in cooked dishes.

VARIATION:

* Scallions can be substituted for the leeks.

MAKE-IT-EASY TIP:

* The sauce can be frozen successfully in small containers for future use.

Béchamel Sauce	YIELD: 1 cup CALORIES: 162 per cup PREPARATION TIME: 5 minutes COOKING TIME: 5 minutes

This is a slimmed-down version of the basic white sauce as prepared at Rancho La Puerta spa in Tecate, Mexico.

4 teaspoons arrowroot
1¼ cups nonfat milk
⅛ teaspoon grated nutmeg
Salt and freshly ground white pepper to taste

1. Stir the arrowroot into ¼ cup milk and stir until smooth.
2. In a small nonstick saucepan place the remaining 1 cup milk, nutmeg, and salt and pepper; scald until bubbles just form around the edges of the pan. Add the arrowroot, stir, and bring to a boil. Reduce heat and simmer slowly, uncovered, stirring often, until thickened, 3 to 4 minutes. Use the sauce as soon as possible after preparation. It tends to thicken up as it stands.

COOK NOTES: Arrowroot powder thickens better and faster than cornstarch. You only need 1 teaspoon arrowroot to every 1½ teaspoons cornstarch, and the arrowroot has a more neutral taste.

When removing cooked contents from a saucepan, avoid scraping the bottom of the pan, which may contain some scorched milk.

VARIATION:

* For a slightly richer result, use 1 cup low-fat milk and ¼ cup cold water to dissolve the arrowroot.

Orange-Lime Relish

YIELD: 3½ cups
CALORIES: 90 per cup; 6 per tablespoon
PREPARATION TIME: 15 minutes
CHILLING TIME: 6–8 hours or overnight

Serve this tart relish as an accompaniment to roast poultry. It will keep for a week in the refrigerator.

3 large navel oranges, peeled, thinly sliced, and slices cut into quarters
2 large limes, peeled, thinly sliced, and slices cut into quarters
1 tablespoon finely minced scallions (green and white part included)
1 tablespoon apple cider vinegar
2 teaspoons sugar
Salt and freshly ground white pepper to taste

1. Place the oranges and limes in a glass bowl and toss.
2. In a separate bowl combine remaining ingredients, stir to combine, pour over the fruits, and toss.
3. Chill in a covered container in the refrigerator for 6 to 8 hours or overnight.

COOK NOTE: Keep limes away from the light, which causes them to turn yellow and hastens their deterioration. Use limes that are turning yellow as quickly as possible. The juice will still be delicious although the yellow skin won't make as pretty a garnish.

VARIATION:

* Lemons can be substituted for limes.

Apricot Spread

YIELD: 1 cup
CALORIES: 281 per cup; 18 per tablespoon
PREPARATION TIME: 5 minutes
COOKING TIME: 45 minutes
CHILLING TIME: 4 – 6 hours or overnight

This apricot topping can be used as a natural low-sugar flavoring for plain yogurt as in Apricot-Yogurt Swirl (page 336), as a fruit spread on toast, or as a topping on pies or other desserts.

3 ounces dried apricots, roughly chopped
½ cup unsweetened apple juice

1. In a small saucepan bring the apricots and juice to a boil, cover, reduce heat, and simmer very slowly for 45 minutes, or until smooth and softened, stirring occasionally.
2. Allow the mixture to cool slightly, then process in a food processor or blender until smooth.
3. Place in a covered container and chill for 4 to 6 hours or overnight. Serve chilled.

VARIATION:
* Other dried fruits such as peaches or prunes can be substituted for the apricots.

Cranberry Chutney

YIELD: 2 cups
CALORIES: 222 per cup; 14 per tablespoon
PREPARATION TIME: 15–20 minutes
COOKING TIME: 1 hour 10 minutes

Chutney is a highly seasoned Indian relish made with fruits, vegetables, spices, sugar, and vinegar, or, for that matter, with any ingredient that excites the taste buds! Chutney is traditionally served with Indian curries but can be used as a flavorful accompaniment to roast meats or poultry, grilled fish, or even vegetable dishes.

This light version of chutney reduces the amount of sugar greatly, to only ¼ cup for the whole quantity.

½ cup chicken broth
1 small onion, finely chopped
½ teaspoon finely chopped garlic
1 navel orange, peeled and coarsely chopped
¾ cup finely chopped raw cranberries
½ cup orange juice
¼ cup firmly packed brown sugar
2 tablespoons cider vinegar
2 tablespoons raisins
1 teaspoon Worcestershire sauce
¼ teaspoon red pepper flakes
¼ teaspoon ground allspice
Pinch of salt

1. In a small nonstick saucepan boil the broth and cook the onion and garlic over medium heat until just softened and most of the liquid has been absorbed.
2. Add the remaining ingredients, stir well, bring to a boil, cover, reduce heat to very low, and simmer slowly for 1 hour, stirring occasionally.
3. Cool, then chill until ready to use. Serve at room temperature.

COOK NOTE: Chutney will keep in the refrigerator for several weeks or can be frozen for future use. To preserve in jars, pour hot chutney into sterilized jars, adjust caps according to manufacturer's directions; process in a hot water bath for 10 minutes, and store on the shelf or give as a thoughtful gift.

VARIATIONS:
* Chutney can also be used as a glaze for roasting poultry as in Rock Cornish Game Hens Glazed with Cranberry Chutney, or added to salads as a flavoring.
* Chopped apples, pineapple, mangoes, pears, peaches, and other fruits can be added to the chutney as desired.

MAKE-IT-EASY TIP:
* Purchase several packages of cranberries when in season and keep frozen for use year-round.
* Chop the cranberries and peeled oranges together by pulsating a few times in a food processor. Do not overprocess.

Papaya Salsa

YIELD: 1 cup
CALORIES: 216 per cup
PREPARATION TIME: 10–15 minutes
COOKING TIME: 7 minutes
CHILLING TIME: 3–4 hours or overnight

Green chile salsa is the popular all-purpose sauce found in Mexican restaurants. This papaya salsa is a unique variation that is wonderful with vegetables, cold seafood, or cooked fish such as Baked Fish with Papaya Salsa (page 163).

1 teaspoon oil
2 shallots, finely chopped
2 teaspoons finely grated ginger
½ teaspoon curry powder
1 medium papaya, finely chopped (see Note)
2 tablespoons lime juice
1 tablespoon finely chopped fresh cilantro (coriander)

1. In a small nonstick saucepan heat the oil and sauté the shallots and ginger over medium heat for 6 to 7 minutes, until softened, stirring often.
2. Remove the pan from heat and stir in the curry powder until well-blended. Add the remaining ingredients, place in a covered container, and chill for 3 to 4 hours or overnight. Serve chilled.

COOK NOTE: Select papayas that are more than half yellow and yield to gentle pressure between the palms of the hand, denoting ripeness. Fruit should be smooth, unshriveled, and free of bruises.

VARIATION:
* The white part of scallions can be substituted for the shallots.

SOUPS

Creamy Carrot Soup

SERVES: 4
CALORIES: 92 per serving
PREPARATION TIME: 10 minutes
COOKING TIME: 30 minutes

This creamy soup is naturally thickened by pureeing the cooked carrots with broth and a few tablespoons of cooked rice. Purchase carrots with their leafy greens still in tact—they are likely to be fresher than the packaged variety.

2 cups peeled, sliced carrots (5–6 carrots)
1½ cups strong chicken broth
1 medium onion, coarsely chopped
2 tablespoons raw white rice
Pinch of grated nutmeg
Salt and freshly ground pepper to taste

Garnish:
Grated lemon peel
Chopped fresh parsley

1. Place all the soup ingredients in a medium saucepan. Bring to a boil, cover, reduce heat, and simmer for 25 to 30 minutes, or until the vegetables and rice are tender.
2. Allow to cool slightly and then puree the mixture in a food processor or blender until smooth.
3. Just before serving, adjust the seasonings, reheat the soup, garnish with grated lemon peel and parsley, and serve hot.

VARIATION:
* The soup can also be served chilled.

Make-It-Easy Vegetable Soup	SERVES: 6 CALORIES: 127 per serving PREPARATION TIME: 15 minutes COOKING TIME: 40 minutes

This soup is so flavorful it's hard to believe that it is so low in calories. The zucchini is not added until during the last 10 minutes to preserve its crunchiness.

3 cups strong chicken broth
1 cup water
2 cups canned tomatoes, drained and coarsely chopped
1 onion, coarsely chopped
1 large or 2 small cloves garlic, finely chopped
2 stalks celery, finely chopped
2 carrots, peeled and sliced
½ teaspoon chili powder
Pinch of cayenne
Salt and freshly ground black pepper to taste
1½ cups fresh or thawed frozen corn kernels
3 medium zucchini, sliced into rounds
2 tablespoons chopped fresh parsley

Garnish:
Freshly grated Parmesan cheese (optional)

1. In a large pot combine the broth, water, tomatoes, onion, garlic, celery, carrots, and seasonings. Bring to a boil, cover, and simmer for 30 minutes.
2. Add the corn, zucchini, and parsley; continue to simmer for an additional 10 minutes.
3. Adjust the seasonings and serve hot with a light sprinkling of Parmesan cheese, if desired.

VARIATIONS:
* Sliced turnips, potatoes, broccoli, asparagus, or green peppers can be added with the zucchini in step 2.
* Poached chicken can be added to make the soup a one-dish dinner.

Curried Asparagus Soup

SERVES: 6
CALORIES: 53 per serving
PREPARATION TIME: 15 minutes
COOKING TIME: 12–15 minutes

This pungent soup is wonderful served either hot or chilled. The light soup is thickened by the pureed asparagus rather than rich cream.

1 pound asparagus, tough ends trimmed, cut into 2-inch pieces
4 cups strong chicken broth
4 scallions, coarsely chopped (green and white parts included)
3 tablespoons chopped fresh chives or scallion greens
2 teaspoons lemon juice
1–2 teaspoons curry powder or to taste
Salt and freshly ground pepper to taste

1. In a medium saucepan place the asparagus, broth, and greens, and bring to a boil. Cover, reduce heat, and simmer slowly for 12 to 15 minutes, or until the vegetables are very tender.
2. Place the mixture in a food processor or blender and add the lemon juice and seasonings. Puree until smooth.
3. Serve hot immediately, or chill.

COOK NOTE: To store asparagus, cut off an inch from the stem, wrap the bases in a damp paper towel, and store in a plastic bag in the refrigerator for 2 to 3 days. Use as soon as possible or the flavor will be lost.

VARIATIONS:
* To serve cold, add 1 cup buttermilk, and garnish with blanched asparagus tips.
* Broccoli, zucchini, pattypan squash, a yellow crookneck squash can be substituted for the asparagus.

Snow Pea Soup with Tofu and Enoki Mushrooms

SERVES: 6
CALORIES: 97 per serving
PREPARATION TIME: 10–15 minutes
COOKING TIME: 5 minutes

The following is an adaptation of a recipe from Freida's Finest, produce specialists in Los Angeles. The company's founder Freida Caplan has been a major force in developing and popularizing exotic vegetables and making them available nationwide.

6 cups chicken broth
1 tablespoon reduced-sodium soy sauce
⅛ teaspoon cayenne
2 ounces snow peas, washed and stringed
2 cups shredded, firmly packed spinach leaves
½ pound firm tofu (bean curd), drained and diced (1 cup)
½ cup enoki mushrooms (optional) (see Note)
2 scallions, finely chopped (green parts only)
2 eggs, lightly beaten

1. In a large saucepan bring the broth to a boil; add the soy sauce and cayenne and continue to cook over medium heat for 1 to 2 minutes.
2. Add the vegetables and simmer for 1 to 2 minutes, or until the vegetables are just tender.
3. While the soup is at a rolling boil (be careful to watch that it does not boil over), stir it with a fork with one hand and gradually pour the eggs into the soup in a stream with the other hand, scrambling with the fork.
4. Serve immediately.

COOK NOTE: Enoki mushrooms are slender snow-white Asian mushrooms with a bean sproutlike stem and a tiny white cap. Enoki mushrooms can be tossed fresh into salads, topped on steamed vegetables, or added to stir-fried dishes. To use, trim off half of the stems, rinse, and pat dry. Cook for no longer than 2 minutes.

VARIATION:

* 3 cups vegetable broth can be substituted for 3 cups chicken broth.

Bok Choy and Bean Curd Soup	SERVES: 4 CALORIES: 61 per serving PREPARATION TIME: 10–15 minutes COOKING TIME: about 8 minutes

This light soup is augmented with tofu, also called bean curd, an inexpensive and high-quality source of protein. The soup is cooked uncovered to preserve the bright green color of the bok choy.

4 cups chicken broth
2 tablespoons minced scallions
1slice ginger
1 teaspoon reduced-sodium soy sauce
Salt to taste
1 medium bok choy, washed and cut into 1" square pieces
  (4 cups chopped)
1 cake fresh bean curd (tofu), diced
1 teaspoon hot toasted sesame oil

1. In a medium saucepan bring the broth to a boil. Add the scallions, ginger, soy sauce, and salt and boil for 1 minute. Add the bok choy and continue to boil, uncovered, over medium heat, for 3 to 4 minutes, or until tender. Remove the ginger.
2. Reduce heat to low, add the bean curd, and gently stir to heat through.
3. Add the oil, stir gently, and serve piping hot.

VARIATION:

* Add minced cooked chicken.

Egg Drop Soup with Corn	SERVES: 8 CALORIES: 87 per serving PREPARATION TIME: 5 minutes COOKING TIME: 20 minutes

Egg drop soup is a clear broth with eggs scrambled into it just before serving.

8 cups chicken broth
2 scallions, green parts only
1 thin slice ginger, peeled
1 10-ounce package frozen whole kernel corn, thawed
2 tablespoons dry sherry
1 tablespoon reduced-sodium soy sauce
Freshly ground pepper to taste
2 eggs, lightly beaten

Garnish:
Minced scallion tops

1. In a deep saucepan heat the broth with the scallions and ginger. Bring to a boil, cover, reduce heat, and simmer for 15 minutes. Remove the scallions and ginger and discard.
2. Add the corn, sherry, soy sauce, and pepper; bring to a boil, cover, and cook for 2 to 3 minutes, or until the corn is just heated through.
3. While the soup is at a rolling boil (be careful that it does not boil over) stir it with a fork with one hand, while gradually pouring the eggs into the soup in a stream with the other hand, scrambling with the fork.
4. Serve hot, garnished with scallion tops.

COOK NOTE: Store fresh gingerroot in the refrigerator for 3 to 4 weeks. To avoid molding, do not cover with plastic wrap or aluminum foil or keep in a covered container.

VARIATION:
* Very thin pasta—cappellini or capelli d'angelo—can also be cooked in the broth until just al dente.

Polpette di Pollo in Brodo (Chicken Balls in Soup)	SERVES: 8 CALORIES: 134 per serving PREPARATION TIME: 15 minutes COOKING TIME: 6–7 minutes

Lean chicken is used to create low-fat meatballs for this light but filling soup that can easily be served as a one-dish supper.

Chicken Balls:

1 pound raw lean ground chicken
2 slices whole-grain bread, crumbled
3 tablespoons freshly grated Parmesan cheese
2 tablespoons chopped fresh parsley
1 egg, lightly beaten
1 teaspoon minced garlic
1 teaspoon grated lemon rind
¼ teaspoon grated nutmeg
Salt and freshly ground pepper

10 cups chicken broth
Garnish:
Freshly grated Parmesan cheese
Chopped fresh parsley

1. In a mixing bowl combine the chicken ball ingredients and mix together with your hands until well-combined. Form into balls the size of walnuts.
2. Bring the broth to a full boil, carefully drop in the balls, cover, reduce heat, and simmer for 6 to 7 minutes, or until just tender but not overcooked.
3. Serve the soup hot, garnished with a light sprinkling of Parmesan cheese and freshly chopped parsley.

VARIATION:
* Lean turkey can be substituted for the chicken.

MAKE-IT-EASY TIP:
* Ready-grated nutmeg is convenient but lacks the flavor of freshly grated. Keep a tiny grater in your nutmeg jar ready for fresh grating.

Spinach Ravioli in Brodo	SERVES: 6 CALORIES: 97 per serving PREPARATION TIME: 25–30 minutes COOKING TIME: 5 minutes

It is said that Marco Polo first brought pasta from the Orient to Europe. If this is so, the pattern is reversed here with Italian fillings in Chinese "pasta." The wrappers are slightly lower in calories than regular pasta dough, since they are considerably thinner than the pasta we can roll out, and the filling is prepared with part-skim ricotta cheese.

3 dozen won ton wrappers

Filling:
5 ounces frozen chopped spinach, thawed and totally squeezed dry
½ cup part-skim ricotta cheese
½ egg, lightly beaten
2 tablespoons chopped fresh basil, or 1½ teaspoons crumbled dried
2 tablespoons chopped fresh parsley
2 tablespoons grated Parmesan cheese
½ teaspoon finely minced garlic
¼ teaspoon grated nutmeg
Salt and freshly ground pepper to taste

1 egg yolk mixed with 2 tablespoons water
6 cups chicken broth
Salt and freshly ground white pepper to taste

Garnish:
3 tablespoons grated Parmesan cheese

1. Place the won tons under a moist towel while preparing the filling.
2. Place the filling ingredients in a food processor or blender and process until smooth.

3. Place 1 won ton wrapper on a board and place 1 to 2 teaspoons filling in its center. Form the filling into a neat ball and brush the edges of the wrapper with the egg wash. Cover with another wrapper. Seal the edges of the dough with your fingers, removing any air pockets. Trim the ravioli using a biscuit cutter, pastry ring, or pastry wheel. Remove and discard the trimmings and store the ravioli on waxed paper covered with plastic wrap.

4. Bring the broth to a boil, drop in the ravioli, bring to a second boil, reduce heat, and simmer for 2 minutes longer, or until just tender and not overcooked. Drain thoroughly.

5. In the meantime, reheat the broth until boiling and season. Place the broth in a tureen, add the cooked ravioli, garnish with cheese, and serve hot.

COOK NOTE: Always keep the unused portion of won tons or other skins covered with a moist towel or plastic wrap to prevent drying out and cracking.

VARIATIONS:
* Other fillings can be substituted for the spinach. Try leftover chicken or fish with minced vegetables and seasonings to taste.
* Beef broth can be substituted for the chicken broth.

MAKE-IT-EASY TIP:
* Place the finished pasta on baking sheets in a single layer; cover with plastic wrap. Chill up to 4 hours or freeze until solid; transfer to containers to store. Label and date. Add the frozen pasta to the broth (without thawing first) but add 2 minutes to the cooking time.

Spicy Wild Rice Soup

SERVES: 8
CALORIES: 73 per serving
PREPARATION TIME: 15 minutes
COOKING TIME: 55 minutes

Wild rice soup is a Minnesota specialty often prepared with ground beef or cream. In this light version, the wild rice is cooked with vegetables and broth.

1 tablespoon olive oil
3 medium carrots, peeled and thinly sliced
2 stalks celery, thinly sliced
1 large onion, finely chopped
¼ cup finely chopped long mild green chile peppers
1 tomato, peeled, seeded, and roughly chopped
4 cups chicken broth
Salt and freshly ground pepper
1 cup cooked wild rice

Garnish:
Chopped fresh parsley

1. In a large nonstick Dutch oven or kettle, heat the oil and sauté the carrots, celery, onion, and chilies over medium heat, until soft, about 8 minutes. Add the tomato and cook for another 2 minutes, stirring often.
2. Add the broth and salt and pepper, bring to a boil, cover, reduce heat, and simmer for 30 minutes. Add the rice and cook for an additional 15 minutes.
3. Serve the soup piping hot, garnished with chopped parsley.

COOK NOTE: Wild rice is low in moisture and therefore has a long shelf life. For best storage, place the unused portion of rice in a sealed container and keep in a cool place for several months. For longer storage refrigerate or even freeze.

VARIATION:
* For a one-dish meal, add cooked chicken or other cooked meats to the soup and heat through.

MAKE-IT-EASY TIP:

* The easiest way to obtain 1 cup cooked wild rice is to combine ⅓ cup raw wild rice with 1 cup water. Bring to a boil, cover, reduce heat, and simmer slowly for 40 to 45 minutes, or until the liquid is absorbed and the grains have puffed up. Remove the cover immediately, fluff the rice with a fork, and allow to cool. (If left covered, the wild rice will become gummy.)

Chunky Fish Chowder	SERVES: 8
	CALORIES: 207 per serving
	PREPARATION TIME: 20 minutes
	COOKING TIME: 25–35 minutes

This recipe is a light adaptation of a creamy fish chowder prepared by my chief recipe tester Anne Natwick. This chowder freezes well.

*2 pounds red snapper, sea bass, halibut, orange roughy, or
   other fleshy fish fillets*
8 cups chicken broth
3 medium red potatoes, cut into 8 pieces
2 carrots, peeled and cut into diagonal slices
½ pound green beans, cut into 1" lengths
1 yellow onion, finely chopped
2 cloves garlic, finely minced
½ cup nonfat dry milk
¼ cup chopped fresh parsley
¼ cup lemon juice
2 tablespoons grated lemon rind
Salt and freshly ground pepper to taste

Garnish:
Chopped fresh parsley

1. Preheat the oven to 375°F. Lightly coat a glass or ceramic dish with vegetable cooking spray or line a baking dish with aluminum foil.

2. Place the fish in the prepared dish and bake for 5 to 10 minutes, uncovered, or just until flaky. Cook, break into chunks, and set aside.

3. Bring the broth to a boil, add the potatoes, and cook for 10 minutes. Add carrots and green beans and cook for 10 to 15 minutes more or until the vegetables are tender.

4. In the meantime, cook the onions and garlic in two tablespoons of the broth, over medium heat, until tender, 5 to 10 minutes.

5. Add the onions to the broth along with the remaining chowder ingredients and stir gently to combine.

6. Add the fish just before serving and cook just to warm through; serve hot, garnished with parsley.

VARIATIONS:

* Soup may be served to 6 as a main dish accompanied by Whole-Wheat Popovers (page 323) and a tossed green salad.
* Clam juice can be substituted for the chicken broth, but omit the salt.
* For slightly thicker soup, ½ cup potatoes can be pureed with 2 to 3 tablespoons broth in a food processor, blender, or through a sieve and added.

Manhattan Clam Chowder

SERVES: 6
CALORIES: 129 per serving
PREPARATION TIME: 15–20 minutes
COOKING TIME: about 45 minutes

The origin of the word "chowder" has been said to come from the French word for cauldron, *chaudiere*, in which French sailors threw their catch to make a communal stew, a creamy white mixture of fish or clams. In Rhode Island, however, cooks often added tomatoes to their chowder, causing a major stir among traditional New England chowder fanciers in Massachusetts and Maine who, for no discernible reason, associated this concoction with New York. Hence, the dish became Manhattan clam chowder.

This light version is prepared with only 1 tablespoon olive oil to serve 6 people. Salt is added only *after* cooking the clams because of the high amount of salt in the canned clams.

1 tablespoon olive oil
2 large carrots, peeled and finely chopped
2 medium stalks celery, finely chopped
1 large onion, finely chopped
1 large potato, peeled and coarsely diced
2 tablespoons dry red wine
1 16-ounce can juice-packed tomatoes, coarsely chopped (including liquids)
2 cups chicken broth
1 tablespoon chopped fresh parsley
1 teaspoon finely minced garlic
¼ teaspoon crumbled dried thyme
Freshly ground pepper to taste
1 10-ounce can whole baby clams, including liquid
Salt

Garnish:
Chopped fresh parsley

1. In a large nonstick pot heat the oil, and sauté the carrots, celery, and onions over medium heat for 5 to 6 minutes, or until just softened. Add the potatoes and stir to combine.
2. Add the wine and allow to boil for 1 minute. Add the tomatoes, broth, and seasonings and bring to a boil. Cover, reduce heat, and simmer for 25 minutes.
3. Add the clams and continue to cook for an additional 10 minutes, or until heated through.
4. Season to taste with salt and serve the soup hot, garnished with freshly chopped parsley.

VARIATIONS:
* Additional vegetables such as mushrooms or zucchini can be sautéed with the carrots and added.
* Of course, if fresh clams are in season, they can be steamed and used in this recipe, along with their delicious broth.
* Minced or chopped clams can be substituted for whole baby clams.

COLD SOUPS

Gazpacho Blanca	SERVES: 4
	CALORIES: 105 per serving
	PREPARATION TIME: 15 minutes
	CHILLING TIME: 4–6 hours or overnight

Gazpacho Blanca is a chilled cucumber soup, spiced with scallions and garlic, and made creamy with low-fat yogurt. "European" hothouse cucumbers are a variety that need no peeling or seeding.

1 large "European" hothouse cucumber, split and coarsely chopped, or 2 medium cucumbers, peeled, seeded, and coarsely chopped
4 scallions, coarsely chopped (green and white parts included)
1¼ teaspoons minced garlic
1 cup plain low-fat yogurt
1 cup chicken broth
2 tablespoons lemon juice
Pinch of cayenne
Salt to taste
Generous sprinkling of freshly ground white pepper

Garnish:
Quartered cherry tomatoes
Chopped scallions
Chopped cucumbers
Toasted sesame seeds

1. In a food processor or blender process the cucumber, scallions and garlic until well-combined. Add the remaining soup ingredients and continue to puree until smooth.
2. Chill for 4 to 6 hours or overnight.
3. Adjust the seasonings and serve the soup with the accompanying garnishes of cherry tomatoes, scallions, cucumbers, and sesame seeds.

VARIATION:
* Vegetable broth may be substituted for the chicken broth.

Cold Dilled Borscht with Chopped Cucumber

SERVES: 6
CALORIES: 120 per serving
PREPARATION TIME: 15 minutes
CHILLING TIME: 4–6 hours or overnight

The traditional Russian creamy borscht is thickened with sour cream. Here a combination of buttermilk and low-fat yogurt are used as light replacements.

1 16-ounce can chopped beets including liquid
2 scallions, finely chopped (green and white parts included)
2½ tablespoons freshly snipped dill or 1 teaspoon crumbled dried
¼ cup lemon juice
1 tablespoon sugar
Salt and freshly ground white pepper to taste
2 cups buttermilk
1½ cups plain low-fat yogurt
¾ cup finely chopped cucumber (see Note)

Garnish:
Finely chopped hard-cooked egg

1. In a food processor or blender combine the beets with scallions, dill, lemon juice, sugar, and salt and pepper; process until smooth.
2. Place the mixture in a large bowl, stir in the remaining borscht ingredients, cover, and chill for 4 to 6 hours or overnight.
3. Serve the soup chilled, garnished with chopped egg.

COOK NOTE: Use "European" hothouse cucumbers, which need no peeling or seeding. If European cucumbers are unavailable, substitute regular cucumbers, peeled, seeded, and finely chopped.

VARIATION:
* For a chunkier-style soup, do not puree the ingredients in step 1 but add them in with the others.

Mexican Gazpacho	SERVES: 6
	CALORIES: 72 per serving
	PREPARATION TIME: 20–25 minutes
	CHILLING TIME: 4–6 hours or overnight

This Mexican gazpacho contains no fat and is a spicy and refreshing first course on a hot summer night.

½ large "European" hothouse cucumber, split and coarsely chopped, or 1 medium cucumber, peeled, seeded, and coarsely chopped
2 scallions, cut into large chunks (green and white parts included)
1 green bell pepper, seeded, and cut into large chunks (see Note)
½ clove garlic
2 tablespoons freshly snipped dill, or 1 teaspoon crumbled dried
2 tablespoons chopped fresh cilantro (coriander)
2 tablespoons chopped mild green chile peppers
2 cups crushed tomatoes packed in puree
1 cup vegetable juice
1 tablespoon red wine vinegar
1 teaspoon Worcestershire sauce
3 shakes of Tabasco or to taste
Salt and freshly ground pepper to taste

Garnish:
Minced Tomatoes
Minced chives
Minced cucumbers
Minced green bell peppers
Minced fresh cilantro (coriander)

1. In a food processor or blender place the cucumber, scallions, green pepper, garlic, dill, cilantro, and chilies. Process until finely chopped.

2. Add the remaining gazpacho ingredients, and continue to process until smooth. Chill for 4 to 6 hours or overnight.
3. Serve chilled, and pass bowls of minced tomatoes, chives, cucumbers, green bell peppers, and cilantro (coriander) at the table.

COOK NOTE: Select well-shaped, firm, unblemished green bell peppers that have a glossy green color. They can be stored for 3 to 4 days in plastic bags in the refrigerator.

VARIATIONS:
* Red onion can be substituted for the scallions.
* If tomatoes packed in puree are unavailable, use regular whole juice-packed tomatoes; chop, drain off most of the liquid. Return the tomatoes to the can, and fill to the top with canned tomato puree.

MAKE-IT-EASY TIP:
* Soup can be prepared 1 to 2 days in advance and chilled until ready to serve.

Parsnip and Spinach Soup with Mustard Flavor	SERVES: 6 CALORIES: 78 per serving PREPARATION TIME: 10–15 minutes COOKING TIME: 30 minutes CHILLING TIME: 6 hours or overnight

Parsnips are often much maligned vegetables but can be quite tasty, especially in soup. They are high in potassium and have iron, calcium, and some protein; ½ cup of cooked parsnips contains about 70 calories.

½ pound parsnips, peeled and sliced (see Note)
1 medium onion, sliced
1 stalk celery, sliced
3 cups chicken broth

1 10-ounce package frozen chopped spinach, thawed and
squeezed dry
Salt and freshly ground pepper to taste
1 cup buttermilk
2 teaspoons grainy-style Dijon mustard

Garnish:
Grated carrot

1. In a medium-sized saucepan place the parsnips, onion, and celery; cover with the chicken broth, bring to a boil, cover, reduce heat, and simmer slowly for 20 minutes.
2. Add the spinach and salt and pepper, stir, and continue to simmer for 5 minutes longer, or until the vegetables are tender. Allow to cool slightly, place in a covered container, and chill for 6 hours or overnight.
3. When ready to serve, process the mixture in a food processor or blender with the buttermilk and mustard. Season with salt and pepper and serve chilled, garnished with grated carrots.

COOK NOTE: Select firm, well-shaped small- to medium-sized parsnips without any discoloration marks, which are signs that the parsnips were frozen.

VARIATION:
* ½ cup plain low-fat yogurt can be substituted for ½ cup buttermilk to give a thicker consistency.

Chilled Summer Squash Soup with Fresh Herbs	SERVES: 6 CALORIES: 65 per serving PREPARATION TIME: 10–15 minutes COOKING TIME: 20–25 minutes CHILLING TIME: 6 hours or overnight

This soup can be prepared as below or varied by using all zucchini, all crookneck, or even all pattypan squash. Pattypan squash, also known as cymling or scallop squash, is a tiny saucer-shaped vegetable with a scalloped edge. It should be firm and without blemishes. It is best to use fresh herbs for this soup.

4 medium zucchini, washed and cut into 1" slices
1 large yellow crookneck squash, washed and cut into 1" slices
1 pattypan squash, quartered
1 large onion, thinly sliced
1 teaspoon finely minced garlic
3–3½ cups chicken broth
Salt and freshly ground white pepper to taste
2 tablespoons finely chopped fresh basil
2 tablespoons finely chopped fresh parsley
1 tablespoon lemon juice
1 cup buttermilk

Garnish:
Chopped fresh basil and parsley

1. In a large saucepan place all the squash. Add the onion, garlic, broth, and salt and pepper; bring to a boil, cover, reduce heat, and simmer for 20 to 25 minutes, or until the vegetables are very tender.
2. Allow to cool slightly; puree in a food processor or blender with the basil, parsley, and lemon juice until smooth. Place in a container, cover and refrigerate for 6 hours or overnight.
3. When ready to serve, add the buttermilk, whisk until smooth, and adjust the seasonings with salt and pepper. Serve chilled, garnished with chopped basil and parsley.

COOK NOTE: It is always important to taste food for seasoning after chilling since the flavor is more pronounced when the food is hot.

VARIATIONS:
* Plain low-fat yogurt can be substituted for the buttermilk.
* If fresh basil is unavailable, substitute ¼ cup parsley for the basil-parsley combination.

Iced Broccoli Soup with Dill Flavor	SERVES: 6 CALORIES: 52 per serving PREPARATION TIME: 10 minutes COOKING TIME: 20 minutes CHILLING TIME: 6 hours or overnight

Buttermilk is a wonderful substitute for heavy cream in cold soups. Buttermilk results from regular nonfat milk that has been treated with special bacteria. Thick and tangy, it is low in fat, cholesterol, and calories.

1 16-ounce package frozen chopped broccoli
2 cups chicken broth
1 small onion, finely chopped
2 tablespoons snipped fresh dill, or 2 teaspoons crumbled dried
1 cup buttermilk
2 tablespoons chopped fresh chives or scallion greens
1 tablespoon lemon juice
Salt and freshly ground pepper to taste

Garnish:
Snipped fresh dill

1. In a medium saucepan combine the broccoli with the broth, onion, and dill. Bring to a boil, cover, reduce heat, and cook slowly for 25 to 30 minutes, or until the vegetables are very tender. Allow to cool slightly and then chill for 6 hours or overnight.
2. Place the chilled mixture in a food processor or blender and puree until smooth. Add the remaining soup ingredients and serve garnished with dill.

COOK NOTE: Fresh herbs such as dill, basil, or parsley can be kept fresh stored in a tall glass jar in the refrigerator. Place the stems in a few inches of water, cover with the jar top, or put the jar in a plastic bag and seal with a twist tie.

VARIATION:
* Frozen chopped spinach can be substituted for the broccoli.

Cold French Pea Soup with Mint

SERVES: 6
CALORIES: 75 per serving
PREPARATION TIME: 10–15 minutes
COOKING TIME: 15 minutes
CHILLING TIME: 4–6 hours or overnight

The French technique of cooking peas with lettuce, *petit pois Française*, is used in this cold soup.

1 onion, coarsely chopped
2 large iceberg lettuce leaves, coarsely chopped
2 cups chicken broth
Salt and freshly ground white pepper to taste
1 10-ounce package frozen garden peas
1 tablespoon lemon juice
1 tablespoon finely chopped fresh chives or scallion greens
⅔ cup buttermilk
⅓ cup plain low-fat yogurt
1 tablespoon finely chopped fresh mint

Garnish:
Sprigs of mint

1. In a medium saucepan place the onion, lettuce, broth, and salt and pepper. Bring to a boil, cover, and cook over medium heat for 8 minutes; add the peas and continue to cook for 7 minutes, or until very soft.
2. Allow the mixture to cool slightly; puree in a food processor or blender with the lemon juice and chives or scallions. Place in a covered container and chill for 4 to 6 hours or overnight.
3. When ready to serve, add the buttermilk, yogurt, and chopped mint, stir to combine. Adjust the seasonings with salt and pepper and serve garnished with mint sprigs.

VARIATION:
* If fresh mint is unavailable, substitute chopped chives or scallion greens.

Chilled Tomato-Lime Soup	SERVES: 6
	CALORIES: 143 per serving
	PREPARATION TIME: 15–20 minutes
	COOKING TIME: 25 minutes
	CHILLING TIME: 4–6 hours or overnight

Low-fat yogurt adds a creamy taste and texture to this soup without adding fats. A pinch of sugar is added to cut the acidity of both the tomato and lime.

1 tablespoon olive oil
1 large onion, chopped
2 large carrots, peeled and chopped
2 16-ounce cans tomatoes, well-drained and coarsely chopped
   (2 cups)
1 cup chicken broth
Pinch of salt
Salt and freshly ground pepper to taste
1½ cups plain low-fat yogurt
3 tablespoons fresh lime juice
1 tablespoon chopped fresh parsley
1 tablespoon chopped fresh basil, or 1 teaspoon crumbled dried
Dash of Tabasco

Garnish:
Dollop of yogurt
Sprig of fresh basil or parsley

1. In a large, nonstick saucepan heat the oil and sauté the onions and carrots over medium heat, until just soft, but not browned.
2. Add the tomatoes, broth, sugar, and salt and pepper. Bring to a boil, cover, and simmer for 25 minutes, or until vegetables are soft. Cool.
3. Place the mixture in a food processor and add the yogurt, lime juice, parsley, basil, and Tabasco; puree until smooth.

Place in a covered container and chill for 4 to 6 hours or overnight.

4. Adjust the seasonings and serve each portion garnished with a dollop of yogurt and a sprig of fresh basil or parsley.

VARIATION:

* If desired, ¾ cup buttermilk and ⅓ cup low-fat yogurt can be substituted for the yogurt.

POULTRY

Chicken

Chinese Chicken Cooked in Clay	SERVES: 4
	PREPARATION TIME: 10 minutes
	CALORIES: 303 per serving
	MARINATING TIME: 2 hours
	COOKING TIME: 1½ hours

Food cooked in wet terra-cotta clay pots is self-basted and kept moist and juicy so that no additional fats or oils are necessary. And, no browning of meats in oil or butter is required; as a result, the food cooked in this manner is delicious, low in calories, and healthful.

We are all accustomed to the taste of chicken with crisp skin. But this light method of cooking allows you to roast the bird with the skin on (keeping it juicy), and then remove it, along with the excess fat and calories, before eating.

1 3½–4-pound whole roasting chicken, washed and dried

Marinade:
¼ cup reduced-sodium soy sauce
3 tablespoons dry sherry
2 teaspoons toasted sesame oil
2 scallions, finely minced (green and white parts included)
1 slice fresh ginger, peeled and finely minced
1 clove garlic, finely minced

1 unglazed terra-cotta pot large enough to hold a chicken

Garnish:
Scallion greens

1. Place the chicken in a deep, narrow bowl. Combine the marinade ingredients, stir, and pour over the chicken. Turn the chicken to coat, cover, and marinate in the refrigerator for 2 hours, turning once or twice.
2. Soak the clay pot and lid in cold water for 20 minutes.
3. Discard the water from the clay pot and lid. Remove the chicken from the marinade, pour half the marinade into the bottom of the clay pot, place the chicken on top, and pour the remaining marinade over the chicken.
4. Place the lid on the cooker and put in a cold oven. (Clay pots must be put in a cold oven or they will crack from the intense sudden heat of a preheated oven.) Set the oven to 450°F and roast undisturbed for 1½ hours.
5. Place the chicken on a bed of scallion greens. Remove and discard the skin from the chicken and the fat from the collected juices; serve the juices alongside in a gravy boat.

ACCOMPANIMENTS:
Plain white rice and Snow Pea Salad with Lemon-Ginger Dressing

VARIATIONS:
* Larger chickens may be used to serve 6; cook them for 15 minutes longer.
* Chicken may be marinated overnight in the refrigerator.
* Chicken may be cut into pieces, marinated, and cooked as above; cut cooking time by 15 minutes.
* For added flavor, stuff the chicken with peeled onions.

MAKE-IT-EASY TIP:
* The easiest way to remove excess fat from the gravy is with a gravy strainer. It is a pitcher with the spout based at the bottom. The gravy is poured in, the fat quickly rises to the top, the gravy is poured off from the bottom, and the fat remains in the pitcher.

Vertically Roasted Chicken with Dried Mushrooms and Leeks	SERVES: 4 CALORIES: 365 per serving PREPARATION TIME: 20–30 minutes COOKING TIME: 1 hour

Cooking on a vertical roaster enables easy cooking of any type of fowl without butter or fat added. The bird is placed on a steel tower frame which conducts heat to sear the inside of the poultry while allowing the juices to flow downward into the breast area. The results are perfectly browned birds with juicy and tender meat that can be carved neatly off the roaster. Paprika enhances the browned look on poultry, especially when cooking without butter.

1 4-pound roasting chicken
1 tablespoon fresh lemon juice
Paprika
Salt and freshly ground pepper to taste
2 ounces dried French or Italian mushrooms soaked in hot water
*   to cover for 20–30 minutes, or until soft (strain and reserve*
*   soaking liquid)*
1 large or 2 medium leeks, finely minced (white part only)
½ cup dry red wine
½ cup chicken broth

1 vertical roaster (I prefer Spanek)

Garnish:
Sprigs of watercress

1. Preheat the oven to 450°F.
2. Dry the chicken inside and out, rub with lemon juice, season with paprika, salt and pepper, and place on the vertical roaster.
3. Squeeze the excess water from the mushrooms and chop. Combine with the leeks and mix with 1 tablespoon of the mushroom liquid.

4. Gently pull the skin away from the neck down to the breast area and stuff the mixture between the skin and flesh.
5. Place the wine, broth, and reserved mushroom liquid in the bottom of the roasting pan, place the vertical roaster in the pan, and put on a lower rack of the oven. Cook for 15 minutes.
6. Reduce the heat to 350° and continue to cook for about 45 minutes (15 to 20 minutes per pound), or until tender and the juices run clear; baste occasionally with the pan juices.
7. Remove the bird from the oven, carve from the rack, and remove the skin. Top each portion with some of the mushroom-leek mixture.
8. Skim the fat from the pan juices and serve alongside the bird, garnished with sprigs of watercress.

COOK NOTE: To prevent food spoilage and contamination from bacteria, do not stuff the chicken until ready to pop in the oven.

ACCOMPANIMENTS:
Wild Rice Pilaf and Two-Lettuce Salad with Creamy Horse-radish Dressing

VARIATION:
* Scallions or shallots can be substituted for the leeks.

Yunnan Chicken	SERVES: 4 CALORIES: 284 per serving PREPARATION TIME: 20–30 minutes COOKING TIME: 1–2 hours

A Yunnan pot is a round earthenware pot with a cone in the center that tapers to a small hole at the top, used for steaming food. The same process can be achieved just as easily by using a deep bowl placed on a rack in a deep kettle. If possible, cook the broth with the scallion and ginger for 20 minutes before cooking the recipe. Strain the broth and proceed with the recipe.

*8 dried Chinese or Japanese shiitake mushrooms soaked in 1
  cup hot water for 20–30 minutes, or until soft*
1 3–3½-pound chicken, washed and cut into 8–10 pieces
2 scallions, cut into 2" lengths (green part only)
2 thin slices ginger, peeled
*2 cups Chinese cabbage (also called celery or lettuce cabbage),
  cut into 1" pieces*
1 cup chicken broth
1 tablespoon reduced-sodium soy sauce

1. Squeeze the mushrooms dry. Remove the stems and cut into
   quarters. Strain the liquid and set aside.
2. In a deep bowl arrange the chicken, mushrooms, scallions,
   ginger, and cabbage. Combine the chicken broth with the
   reserved mushroom liquid and soy sauce. Pour over the ingredients in the bowl.
3. Fit the bowl in a large pot filled with 2" to 3" of hot water
   with a rack supporting the bowl. Cover the pot and cook the
   chicken over medium-high heat for about 1½ hours, or until
   the chicken is tender and firm, but not falling apart. (The
   water level should be checked every 30 minutes to maintain
   constant steam, but if you remove the lid too often the
   escaping steam will slow the cooking process.)

   If cooking in a Yunnan pot, arrange the chicken around
   the cone, top with the remaining ingredients, cover the pot,
   and place over a large saucepan of boiling water. Cook
   over medium-high heat for 1 to 2 hours.
4. Remove the chicken from the pot, pull off the chicken skin,
   and discard along with the ginger. Skim fat from pan juices.
   Replace chicken in bowl and serve.

ACCOMPANIMENTS:
Plain white rice and Stir-Fried Kale with Garlic

VARIATIONS:
* Other vegetables such as broccoli or bok choy can be added.
* A Yunnan pot may be used to prepare lean stewing beef sub-
  stituting beef broth for the chicken broth.

MAKE-IT-EASY TIP:
* The butcher will cut the chicken into 2 legs, 2 thighs, 2 wings, 2 breasts, and the back and neck. You can include the back and neck in the pot or reserve it for making stock. Cut the larger breast pieces in half so the chicken will fit snugly in the pot.

Chinese Chicken Stew	SERVES: 4 CALORIES: 346 per serving PREPARATION TIME: 20–25 minutes MARINATING TIME: 30 minutes COOKING TIME: 30–35 minutes

This recipe is a light variation of a chicken casserole created by noted cooking authority Florence Lin. It is preferable to prepare the dish a day in advance, refrigerate, and allow the fat to congeal, and then remove the excess fat before reheating.

3 pounds chicken, cut into 8 pieces, washed and dried
6 dried Chinese or Japanese shiitake mushrooms soaked in hot
    water for 20–30 minutes, or until soft
3 tablespoons reduced-sodium soy sauce
2 tablespoons oyster sauce
2 tablespoons dry sherry
2 teaspoons finely minced garlic
2 teaspoons finely minced fresh ginger
1½ tablespoons arrowroot
1 teaspoon toasted sesame oil
½ teaspoon sugar
Salt to taste
2 tablespoons peanut oil
4 scallions, cut into 2″ lengths (green parts only)

Garnish:
Scallion greens

1. Place the chicken in a large mixing bowl. Squeeze the water from the mushrooms, remove the stems, and cut into julienne strips. Add the mushrooms to the chicken.
2. In a separate bowl combine the soy sauce, oyster sauce,

sherry, garlic, ginger, arrowroot, sesame oil, sugar, and salt. Pour the mixture over the chicken, toss well, cover, and allow to marinate for 30 minutes at room temperature.

3. In a large Dutch oven or heavy saucepan heat the peanut oil and stir-fry the scallions over high heat for 1 minute. Add the chicken and marinade, stir-fry for 1 to 2 minutes, stirring to brown on all sides, cover, reduce heat to medium low, and cook for 30 minutes, stirring occasionally.

4. Remove chicken from pan and discard skin. Serve hot, garnished with scallion greens.

ACCOMPANIMENTS:

Plain white rice and Snow Pea Salad with Lemon-Ginger Dressing

VARIATION:

* Blanched broccoli can be added with the mushrooms and chicken.

MAKE-IT-EASY TIP:

* Chinese oyster sauce, available in both jars and cans, is a thick brown Cantonese-style sauce prepared from ground oysters. This unique sauce adds a surprisingly "meaty" rather than fishy flavor to dishes and a richness, due in part to the small percentage of cornstarch in the sauce. Once opened, it will store indefinitely in a jar in the refrigerator.

Tandoori Chicken

SERVES: 4
CALORIES: 297 per serving
PREPARATION TIME: 10–15 minutes
MARINATING TIME: 1–2 hours or overnight
COOKING TIME: 25 minutes

This Indian dish is especially low in calories since the skin of the chicken, which contains most of the fat, is removed. The yogurt marinade keeps the chicken juicy.

1 2½–3-pound chicken, halved and skinned

Marinade:
1 medium onion, coarsely chopped
3 cloves garlic, crushed

1 thin slice ginger, crushed
2 cups plain low-fat yogurt
¼ cup lemon juice
4 teaspoons garam masala (see Note)
1 teaspoon paprika
Salt to taste

Garnish:
Sprigs of coriander (cilantro)

1. Place the chicken in a baking dish and slash in several places to allow the marinade to penetrate.
2. In a food processor or blender place the onion, garlic, and ginger and chop finely. Add the remaining marinade ingredients and continue to process until smooth.
3. Pour the mixture over the chicken, cover the pan, and allow to marinate in the refrigerator for 1 to 2 hours or overnight.
4. Preheat an outdoor grill or broiler. Remove the chicken from the marinade and grill until the chicken is tender and golden brown, about 25 minutes.
5. Serve hot, garnished with sprigs of coriander.

COOK NOTE: Garam masala is available at Indian groceries. If unavailable, the following recipe can be used:

Garam Masala:
1¼ teaspoon freshly ground black pepper, 1 teaspoon each ground cumin, coriander, and cinnamon; and ½ teaspoon each ground cloves and cardamom (if available).

ACCOMPANIMENTS:
Basmati Rice with Orange Flavor and Spinach Salad with Creamy Curry Dressing

VARIATION:
* Tandoori chicken can be served cold.

MAKE-IT-EASY TIP:
* If you have difficulty removing the skin while keeping the chicken halves intact, try securing the chicken by holding it with paper towels.

One-Pot Chicken

SERVES: 4
CALORIES: 391 per serving
PREPARATION TIME: 15 minutes
COOKING TIME: about 50 minutes

If possible, prepare this one-pot dinner a day in advance and refrigerate overnight. Just before serving, remove the congealed fat at the top, reheat, and serve.

2 teaspoons olive oil
1 large onion, thinly sliced
2 stalks celery, cut into 1" slices
1 3½-pound chicken, cut into 8 pieces, washed and dried
½ cup dry vermouth
¾ cup chicken broth
1 teaspoon finely minced garlic
½ teaspoon crumbled dried thyme
Salt and freshly ground white pepper to taste
16–20 tiny red potatoes, or 4 new potatoes, cut into 1½" cubes

Garnish:
Sprigs of parsley

1. In a large skillet heat the oil and sauté the onion and celery over medium heat for 3 to 4 minutes, or until just softened. Add the chicken, increase heat, and toss with the vegetables for 1 minute longer.
2. Add the vermouth and allow to boil for 1 minute. Add the broth, garlic, thyme, and salt and pepper; bring to a boil, cover, reduce heat to medium-low, and cook for 10 minutes.
3. Add the potatoes, stir, return to a boil, cover, reduce heat, and simmer for an additional 30 to 35 minutes, or until the chicken is tender.
4. Remove skin from chicken and discard. Place the chicken on a serving platter along with the vegetables; remove the fat from the pan juices, pour the juices over the chicken and vegetables, and serve hot, garnished with parsley.

COOK NOTE: Do not store potatoes with onions. Onions release a gas that hastens the spoilage of potatoes.

ACCOMPANIMENTS:
Watercress Salad with Orange and Red Onion and Fluffy Corn Muffins

VARIATION:
* 2 carrots, peeled and sliced, can be added with the onions and celery.

MAKE-IT-EASY TIP:
* The easiest way to remove excess fat from gravy is with a gravy strainer. (See the recipe for Chinese Chicken Cooked in Clay, page 114.)
* Use the chicken back and neck in the recipe. They will add extra flavor to the dish. Freeze the giblets for future use.

Apple-Baked Chicken	SERVES: 4 CALORIES: 380 per serving PREPARATION TIME: 15 minutes COOKING TIME: 25–30 minutes

Frozen apple juice concentrate is a wonderful way to sweeten foods without added sugars. Once thawed, the concentrate will keep in a jar in the refrigerator for 3 to 4 weeks.

4 whole chicken breasts
1 tablespoon lemon juice
2 teaspoons grated lemon rind
2 teaspoons freshly grated ginger (see Note), or ½ teaspoon ground
1 tart apple, cored, peeled, and sliced
Salt and freshly ground pepper to taste
½ cup frozen apple juice concentrate, thawed
½ cup dry red wine

Garnish:
Chopped fresh parsley

1. Preheat the oven to 375°F.
2. Place the chicken breasts on a board and flatten with the palm of your hand. Loosen the skin from the flesh.
3. In a small bowl mix the lemon juice, rind, and ginger. Dip the apple slices in the mixture and slide under the skin of each of the chicken breasts until all the sides are used up. Place the chicken skin side up in a roasting pan, and sprinkle with salt and pepper.
4. Combine the apple juice and wine, stir, and pour over the chicken. Bake for 15 minutes, baste, and continue to bake for another 10 to 15 minutes, or until lightly browned, basting occasionally.
5. Remove the chicken to a heated platter. Strain the juices, place in a small saucepan, bring to a boil, and cook over medium heat until reduced in half.
6. Serve the chicken hot, garnished with parsley, with sauce on the side.

COOK NOTE: Select fresh gingerroot that has an even-colored brown skin with a firm texture. Avoid ginger with withered or dry skin, a sure sign of aging often resulting in a bitter taste and stringy texture.

ACCOMPANIMENTS:
Brown Rice Pilaf with Asparagus and Mushrooms, Brussels Sprouts with Basil, and Cranberry Chutney

VARIATIONS:
* Orange slices and orange juice can be substituted for the apple.
* For a slightly thicker sauce, add 1 teaspoon arrowroot to the reduced pan juices, stir until thickened, and serve.

Glazed Orange Chicken

SERVES: 6
CALORIES: 343 per serving
PREPARATION TIME: 10 minutes
MARINATING TIME: 2 hours
COOKING TIME: 20–22 minutes

The use of skinless chicken breasts cuts down on added fats in this easy recipe.

6 whole skinless, boneless chicken breasts

Marinade:
½ cup fresh orange juice
2 tablespoons lemon juice
2 tablespoons honey
2 tablespoons Worcestershire sauce
2 tablespoons Dijon mustard (grainy-style preferred)
1 tablespoon grated orange rind
1 tablespoon chopped fresh tarragon, or 1 teaspoon crumbled dried

Garnish:
Orange slices
Sprigs of watercress

1. Place the chicken in a large glass or ceramic baking dish in a single layer.
2. In a bowl combine the marinade ingredients, stir well, pour over the chicken, cover, and marinate in the refrigerator for 2 hours.
3. Preheat the oven to 375°F.
4. Bake the chicken in the marinade for 16 to 18 minutes, increase heat to broil, and run under the broiler for 4 minutes, or until golden.
5. Remove the chicken to a heated platter; place the pan juices in a saucepan and heat, stirring often, until slightly thickened.
6. Serve the chicken hot, garnished with oranges and watercress.

<u>COOK NOTE:</u> Do not refrigerate honey, as this will hasten granulation. Store it in a dry place, since honey will absorb moisture. To reliquefy granulated honey, place it in a nonplastic container in a pan of warm—not hot—water, until clarified.

ACCOMPANIMENTS:
Curried Toasted Rice, Turnips au Gratin, and Orange-Lime Relish

VARIATION:
* One whole cut-up chicken can be substituted for the boneless chicken; cook for 40 minutes. The skin must be removed from the chicken and the fat must be removed from the sauce before serving.

Grilled Chicken with Chinese Ginger Sauce	SERVES: 4 CALORIES: 354 per serving PREPARATION TIME: 5 minutes MARINATING TIME: 30 minutes COOKING TIME: 6 minutes

Pounding the chicken will produce uniform thickness that will ensure even cooking.

4 6–7-ounce whole skinless, boneless chicken breasts

Marinade:
1 cup chicken broth
4 scallions, finely minced (green and white parts included)
3 tablespoons reduced-sodium soy sauce
2 tablespoons dry sherry
2 tablespoons grainy-style Dijon mustard
1 tablespoon hoisin sauce (available at Chinese grocery stores or at many supermarkets)
2 teaspoons finely minced ginger
2 teaspoons toasted sesame oil
1 teaspoon honey
Freshly ground pepper to taste

Garnish:

Sprigs of cilantro (coriander)

1. Pound the chicken to uniform thickness between sheets of waxed paper. Place the chicken in a single layer in a shallow dish.
2. In a large bowl combine the marinade ingredients and whisk. Pour 1⅓ cups marinade mixture over the chicken, coat both sides well, cover, and allow to marinate for 30 minutes at room temperature.
3. Preheat an outdoor grill or broiler.
4. Grill the chicken for about 3 minutes per side, or until just tender, basting with the marinade. (Do not overcook.)
5. Place the cooked chicken breasts on a platter, spoon the remaining ⅔ cup marinade over the top, and serve hot, garnished with cilantro sprigs.

COOK NOTE: Remove the supermarket wrapping from the chicken as soon as you arrive home. Rewrap loosely and store in the refrigerator.

ACCOMPANIMENTS:
Lemon Brown Rice and Broccoli with Sesame Flavor

VARIATION:
* The chicken can be marinated for up to 2 hours in a covered container in the refrigerator.

Chicken Packets with Dill Flavor	SERVES: 4 CALORIES: 410 per serving PREPARATION TIME: 20 minutes COOKING TIME: 33–38 minutes

The skinless chicken breasts in this recipe are sealed in packets with vegetables and liquid and then steamed in the oven to bring out the natural juices and flavors in the ingredients.

4 6–7-ounce whole skinless, boneless chicken breasts
Salt and freshly ground pepper to taste
1 tablespoon olive oil
1 medium onion, finely chopped
3 medium carrots, finely chopped
1 2"–3" piece parsnip, peeled and finely chopped (about ¼ cup)
1 large stalk celery, finely chopped
⅓ cup dry vermouth
1 teaspoon finely minced garlic
1½ tablespoons freshly snipped dill, or 1 teaspoon crumbled dried
½ cup strong chicken broth

Garnish:
Sprigs of dill

1. Preheat the oven to 350°F. Cut four 14" to 16" squares of aluminum foil or parchment paper.
2. Place a chicken breast on each of the pieces of foil. Season with salt and pepper.
3. In a medium skillet heat the olive oil and sauté the onion, carrots, parsnip, and celery over medium heat for 5 minutes, or until soft but not brown, stirring often.
4. Add the vermouth and allow to boil away. Remove the skillet from heat, add the garlic and dill, stir well, and set aside to cool slightly.
5. Cover each of the chicken breasts with the vegetable mixture; top each with 2 tablespoons chicken broth, fold over

the foil or paper envelope-style, and place on a large baking sheet. Bake for 25 minutes, or until just tender. (Do not overcook.)

6. Remove the packets from the oven, open, and carefully transfer the chicken to a heated platter, making sure to keep the vegetable mixture on top.

7. Pour all the juices collected on the baking sheet into a saucepan and reduce over high heat for 3 minutes. Pour the hot juices over the chicken and serve immediately, garnished with dill sprigs.

ACCOMPANIMENTS:
Carrot and Bulgur Pilaf and Mixed Green Salad with Light Vinaigrette

VARIATIONS:
* Firm fleshy fish fillets can be substituted for the chicken, but cook only for 10 to 15 minutes, depending on the thickness of the fish.
* 2 tablespoons tomato paste can be added to the vegetable mixture along with the garlic and dill in step 4.

MAKE-IT-EASY TIP:
* Serve any leftover chicken the next day, cool or at room temperature, topped with a sprinkling of balsamic or other flavored vinegars to taste.
* Buy fresh dill when it is available, remove the stems, chop, and freeze to use in cooked dishes. Frozen/fresh dill is far superior in flavor to the dried variety.

Poached Chicken Breasts with Basil-Lemon Sauce	SERVES: 8 CALORIES: 298 per serving PREPARATION TIME: 20 minutes COOKING TIME: 10–15 minutes

These boneless and skinless chicken breasts are poached in broth for a low-fat dish, and they are topped with an aromatic basil-lemon sauce that is similar in flavor to a pesto but is made with only 1 tablespoon of oil.

6 whole skinless, boneless chicken breasts
1 large onion, thinly sliced
2 tablespoons lemon juice
2 sprigs of parsley
1 bay leaf
6 peppercorns
Salt to taste
Chicken broth to cover

Basil-Lemon Sauce:
¾ cup firmly packed fresh basil leaves
¼ cup firmly packed parsley leaves
3 tablespoons chicken broth
2 tablespoons whole-grain bread crumbs
2 tablespoons lemon juice
2 tablespoons pine nuts
2 tablespoons olive oil
1 clove garlic, finely minced
2 teaspoons grated lemon rind
Salt and freshly ground white pepper to taste

Garnish:
Basil leaves
Cherry tomatoes

1. Place the chicken breasts in a single layer in a large skillet. Top with the onion, lemon juice, parsley, bay leaf, peppercorns, and salt. Pour over enough chicken broth to cover.

2. Bring to a boil, cover, reduce heat to medium-low, and cook for 10 to 15 minutes, or until the chicken is just tender and is no longer pink in the center. Remove from heat and allow the chicken to cool in the liquid.
3. In the meantime, add the sauce ingredients to a food processor or blender and pulsate until just combined.
4. With a slotted spoon remove the chicken from the broth and arrange on a platter. (Strain and reserve stock for another use.) Coat the chicken with sauce and serve garnished with basil leaves and cherry tomatoes.

COOK NOTE: Store fresh basil, as other fresh herbs, with stems down in a jar of water. Place the jar with herbs in it in a plastic bag, tie at the top, and refrigerate. The basil, or other herbs, will keep for a week or longer.

ACCOMPANIMENTS:
Toasted Barley and Dried Mushrooms Cooked in Broth, and Puree of Carrot with Lemon Accent

VARIATIONS:
* Fish fillets can be substituted for the chicken, but poach for 10 minutes per inch at the thickest point of the fish.
* The chicken can be topped with Mexican Salsa (page 82) instead of the basil-lemon sauce.
* 1 to 2 tablespoons grated Parmesan cheese can be added to the sauce, if desired.

Chicken Paillard

SERVES: 4
CALORIES: 303 per serving
PREPARATION TIME: 5 minutes
MARINATING TIME: 15 minutes
COOKING TIME: 8 minutes

A paillard is a thin piece of chicken, beef, or veal that is well-seasoned, cooked very rapidly, usually grilled, without fat. This recipe is a variation on one of my favorites from *Make It Easy in the Kitchen*, called Mustard Grilled Boneless Chicken Breasts. In this recipe, the paillard is pounded to a uniform thickness first to allow for even cooking. The marinade is enhanced with grainy-style Dijon mustard, hoisin sauce and extra Worcestershire sauce.

4 whole skinless, boneless chicken breasts

Marinade:
¼ cup grainy-style Dijon mustard
3 tablespoons lemon juice
1 tablespoon hoisin sauce (available at Chinese grocery stores or at many supermarkets)
2 teaspoons Worcestershire sauce
Salt and freshly ground pepper to taste

Garnish:
Sprigs of watercress

1. Pound the chicken to uniform thickness between sheets of waxed paper. Place the chicken in a shallow dish.
2. In a small bowl whisk the marinade ingredients together, pour over the chicken, toss to coat, and allow to marinate at room temperature for 15 minutes.
3. Preheat an outdoor grill or a broiler.
4. Grill the chicken for 3 to 4 minutes per side—no longer—until just tender, basting occasionally with the marinade. (Do not overcook.)
5. Serve hot, garnished with watercress sprigs.

COOK NOTE: For an attractive presentation place the chicken at a perpendicular angle to the grill rungs. After 2 minutes, turn 90 degrees to make a crisscross grill mark effect. This technique works particularly well when using a cast-iron skillet with grill ridges.

ACCOMPANIMENT:
Vegetable Pasta Primavera

VARIATIONS:
* The chicken can be covered and marinated in the refrigerator for several hours.
* The chicken can be grilled in a cast-iron skillet with grill ridges that has been lightly sprayed with vegetable cooking spray.

Grilled Mexican-Style Chicken with Salsa	SERVES: 4 CALORIES: 389 per serving PREPARATION TIME: 5 minutes MARINATING TIME: 2–3 hours COOKING TIME: 6 minutes

These boneless chicken breasts are low in fat and low in salt, but full of flavor since they are seasoned with a topping of spicy salsa.

4 whole skinless, boneless chicken breasts

Marinade:
½ cup lime juice
2 tablespoons olive oil
1 onion, thinly sliced
2 teaspoons finely minced garlic
½ teaspoon crumbled dried oregano
½ teaspoon chili powder
Salt and freshly ground pepper to taste

Garnish:
1 cup Mexican Salsa (page 82)
Sprigs of cilantro (coriander)

1. Pound the chicken to uniform thickness between sheets of waxed paper. Place the chicken in a single layer in a shallow dish.
2. In a large bowl combine the marinade ingredients and stir; pour the mixture over the chicken, coat both sides well, cover, and leave for 2 to 3 hours in the refrigerator. Turn occasionally.
3. Preheat an outdoor grill or broiler.
4. Grill the chicken for about 3 to 4 minutes per side, or until just tender, basting with the marinade. (Do not overcook.)
5. Place the chicken breasts on a platter, spoon ¼ cup salsa on each breast, and serve hot, garnished with cilantro sprigs.

ACCOMPANIMENTS:
Mexican Bulgur and Jicama Salad

VARIATION:

* Fish steaks or fillets can be substituted for the chicken breasts.

MAKE-IT-EASY TIP:

* An excellent way to select a fresh lime is to sniff it. If the smell is not fresh and strong, pass it by.

Grilled Chicken Patties	SERVES: 4 CALORIES: 264 per serving PREPARATION TIME: 5 minutes CHILLING TIME: 10–15 minutes COOKING TIME: 5–10 minutes

Lean ground chicken or turkey makes a delicious low-fat patty when seasoned and grilled or broiled until golden.

1½ pounds lean ground chicken or turkey
3 tablespoons grainy-style Dijon mustard
3 tablespoons minced scallions (white parts only)
1 tablespoon reduced-sodium soy sauce
2 teaspoons Worcestershire sauce
Salt and freshly ground white pepper to taste

Garnish:
Remoulade sauce (see Celery Root Remoulade, page 66)

1. Combine the chicken or turkey with the mustard, scallions, and seasonings, mixing with your hand until well-blended. Chill until the mixture is easy to handle, about 10 to 15 minutes. Form into four 6-ounce patties.
2. Preheat an outdoor grill or broiler. Since the ground chicken and turkey are so lean, the patties may not hold together. If grilling outdoors, use a hamburger grill basket to hold the patties together.
3. Grill the patties for 5 to 10 minutes, turning once, until cooked through but not overdone.
4. Serve the patties hot with the remoulade sauce on the side.

ACCOMPANIMENTS:
Stuffed Baked Potatoes and Tomatoes Baked with Spinach Pesto

VARIATIONS:
* For firmer patties add 2 to 3 tablespoons whole-grain bread-crumbs to the mixture.
* 2 tablespoons drained capers can be added to the mixture if desired.
* Patties can be prepared with lean ground veal.

MAKE-IT-EASY TIP:
* If the mixture is difficult to form into patties, shape between sheets of waxed paper.

Buttermilk-Baked Chicken	Serves: 6 CALORIES: 444 per serving PREPARATION TIME: 10–15 minutes COOKING TIME: 25–30 minutes

Instead of using a rich egg or cream batter, the chicken in this recipe is dipped in whole-wheat flour, buttermilk-egg batter, and then unsweetened cereal crumbs to make a wonderfully crispy hot baked chicken, or cold picnic chicken.

½ cup whole-wheat flour
2 eggs, lightly beaten
½ cup buttermilk
1 tablespoon grainy-style Dijon mustard
2 cups crushed unsweetened whole-grain cereal (I use
*   Nutri-Grain Wheat or Corn Flakes)*
1 teaspoon paprika
Salt and freshly ground pepper to taste
12 chicken thighs, washed and patted dry on paper towels
1–2 tablespoons diced unsalted butter or margarine

Garnish:
Sprigs of parsley

1. Preheat the oven to 425°F. Generously coat a roasting pan with vegetable cooking spray.
2. Measure the flour onto a plate. Mix the eggs with buttermilk and mustard and whisk until smooth. Place the crumbs on another plate and season with paprika and salt and pepper.
3. Dip the chicken in the flour; coat well and shake off the excess. Dip the chicken in the egg mixture and then into the cereal crumbs, pressing to make the crumbs adhere.
4. Place in a prepared pan. Dot with the butter or margarine, and bake for 25 to 30 minutes, or until crispy, without turning.
5. Serve hot or at room temperature, garnished with parsley sprigs.

ACCOMPANIMENTS:
Sweet Potato and Carrot Tzimmes and Coleslaw with Sweet and Sour Creamy Dressing

VARIATIONS:
* A whole chicken, cut-up, or even chicken breasts alone can be substituted for the chicken thighs.
* Whole-grain bread crumbs can be substituted for the cereal crumbs.

MAKE-IT-EASY TIP:
* Cereal crumbs can easily be prepared in a food processor or blender.

Turkey

Turkey Scaloppine with Raspberry Vinegar	SERVES: 6 CALORIES: 242 per serving PREPARATION TIME: 10 minutes COOKING TIME: 5 minutes

Breast of turkey, also called turkey scaloppine or turkey fillets, is a flavorful and inexpensive substitute for more costly veal or even chicken scaloppine. Turkey breast is an excellent low-fat source of protein.

2 pounds turkey scaloppine
2–3 tablespoons whole-wheat flour seasoned with salt and
   freshly ground white pepper to taste
2 tablespoons olive oil
¼ cup raspberry vinegar
½ cup chicken broth
1 tablespoon tomato paste
Salt and freshly ground white pepper to taste

Garnish:
Chopped fresh parsley

1. Flatten the turkey breasts and lightly dust with the seasoned flour, shaking off any excess. (A powdered sugar shaker makes an excellent flour shaker for dusting.)
2. In a large nonstick skillet heat the oil and sauté the turkey over high heat, about 1 minute on each side, or until lightly browned. Do not crowd the pan and do not overcook the turkey. As the scaloppine is browned, remove to a warm platter.
3. Add the vinegar and then broth, bring to a boil, and continue to stir until the sauce is smooth.
4. Season to taste with salt and pepper, pour over the turkey, and serve immediately garnished with the parsley.

ACCOMPANIMENTS:
Brown Risi e Bisi and Watercress Salad with Orange and Red Onion

VARIATIONS:
* Flattened chicken breasts or veal scaloppine can be substituted for turkey.
* Other types of flavored vinegars or lemon juice can be substituted for raspberry vinegar.

Stir-Fried Turkey Fillets with Broccoli Florets	SERVES: 4 CALORIES: 267 per serving PREPARATION TIME: 15–20 minutes COOKING TIME: about 7 minutes

Turkey scaloppine, also called turkey fillets or turkey cutlets, are used in this easy recipe. Turkey is very low in fat, particularly when it is cooked without its skin, as in this recipe.

1 pound turkey fillets, cut into 1"- × -2" strips
1 head broccoli (about 1½–2 pounds), broken into florets, stems saved for another use
3 scallions, finely chopped (green and white parts included)
1 teaspoon finely minced garlic

Sauce:
⅔ cup chicken broth
2 tablespoons oyster sauce
2 tablespoons reduced-sodium soy sauce
1 tablespoon dry sherry
1 tablespoon arrowroot
Tabasco sauce to taste
Salt to taste

2½ tablespoons peanut oil

1. Place the turkey strips, broccoli, scallions, and garlic near the cooking area. In a small bowl combine the sauce ingredients, whisk until smooth, and set near the other ingredients.
2. In a wok or large skillet heat 1½ tablespoons oil. Stir-fry the scallions and garlic for 30 seconds. Add the turkey and stir-fry for 2 minutes, or until the meat just loses its pinkness. Remove and set aside on a warm platter.
3. Place the remaining oil in the wok, add the broccoli, and stir-fry for 2 minutes. Add the sauce ingredients, bring to a boil, cover, and cook over medium heat for 1 to 2 minutes, or until the broccoli is just tender.
4. Return the turkey to the wok, stir until just heated through, and serve immediately.

ACCOMPANIMENTS:
Plain white rice and Chilled Chinese Bean Curd in Sauce

VARIATION:
* Asparagus can be substituted for the broccoli.

MAKE-IT-EASY TIP:
* It is easier to cut the turkey when it is semi-frozen.

Butterflied Turkey Breast on Apple-Flavored Stuffing	SERVES: 8 CALORIES: 363 per serving PREPARATION TIME: 20 minutes COOKING TIME: about 1 hour

Turkey is a very lean meat if all visible fat is removed before roasting.

Stuffing:
1 tablespoon vegetable oil
1 small onion, finely chopped
2 stalks celery, finely chopped
1 tart apple, peeled and finely chopped
About 4 cups dry whole-grain bread cubes (see Notes)
⅔ cup chicken broth
2 tablespoons raisins
2 teaspoons grated lemon rind
½ teaspoon crumbled dried sage
½ teaspoon crumbled dried thyme
¼ teaspoon grated nutmeg
¼ teaspoon ground mace
¼ teaspoon ground coriander
Salt and freshly ground pepper to taste

1 3½–4-pound skinned turkey breast, butterflied
⅓ cup frozen orange juice concentrate, thawed
⅓ cup dry vermouth

Garnish:
Sprigs of watercress

1. In a large nonstick skillet heat the oil, and sauté the onion and celery over medium heat for 3 minutes. Add the apple, and continue to cook until softened, about 5 minutes longer.
2. In a large bowl combine the remaining stuffing ingredients, top with the cooked vegetables, and stir to combine. (The

stuffing can be prepared a day or two in advance, covered, and refrigerated until ready to assemble the recipe.)

3. Preheat the oven to 350°F.
4. Place the stuffing in a mound in the center of a roasting pan and lay the turkey breast over, covering the stuffing. Combine the orange juice and vermouth together and baste the turkey all over.
5. Roast for 50 to 55 minutes, or until just tender, but not over-cooked, basting every 10 to 15 minutes. Slice the turkey and serve the slices with a dollop of stuffing on top garnished with watercress sprigs.

COOK NOTES: If stale bread is not available, place the slices in a 250°F oven for 15 minutes, or until dry.

Do not place the turkey on the stuffing until just before baking to avoid spoilage.

ACCOMPANIMENTS:
Butternut Squash with Ginger Flavor, Coleslaw with Sweet and Sour Creamy Dressing, and Cranberry Chutney

VARIATION:
* Turkey can be filled with stuffing, rolled and tied, and roasted on a rack for approximately 40 minutes, or until cooked through.

Ground Turkey Loaf with Creole Sauce	SERVES: 4 CALORIES: 261 per serving PREPARATION TIME: 20 minutes COOKING TIME: 40 minutes

Ground turkey is a good source of low-fat protein. Since it is quite lean, the loaf needs a topping of a tomato Creole sauce for added flavor and moisture.

Loaf:
1 pound lean ground turkey
½ cup whole-grain bread crumbs
1 small onion, finely chopped
¼ cup finely chopped carrot
2 eggs, lightly beaten
1 tablespoon finely chopped fresh parsley
1 clove garlic, finely minced
½ teaspoon crumbled dried rosemary
¼ teaspoon paprika
Pinch of cayenne pepper
Salt and freshly ground black pepper to taste

Sauce:
½ cup chicken broth
1 small onion, finely chopped
1 clove garlic, finely minced
½ cup crushed canned tomatoes in puree
8–10 basil leaves, finely chopped
2 tablespoons finely chopped fresh parsley
Salt and freshly ground pepper to taste

Garnish:
1–2 tablespoons grated Parmesan cheese

1. Preheat the oven to 375°F. Lightly coat a loaf pan with vegetable cooking spray.
2. In a large bowl combine the loaf ingredients and stir with your hands until well-mixed. Press gently into the prepared

pan and bake for 40 minutes, or until the center is firm to the touch. Allow the loaf to rest at room temperature for 10 to 15 minutes.

3. In the meantime, prepare the sauce in a nonstick saucepan. Bring the broth, onion, and garlic to a boil; cook over medium heat for 7 to 10 minutes, or until the vegetables are softened. Add the tomatoes, basil, parsley, and salt and pepper, bring to a boil, cover, and simmer slowly for 15 minutes.

4. Slice the loaf, arrange the slices attractively on a platter, top with sauce, garnish with Parmesan cheese, and serve hot or at room temperature.

ACCOMPANIMENTS:
Stuffed Baked Potatoes, Onions Baked in Their Skins, and Two-Lettuce Salad with Creamy Horseradish Dressing

VARIATIONS:
* Ground chicken can be substituted for the ground turkey.
* The meat loaf can be served cold the next day.
* If tomatoes packed in puree are unavailable, use regular whole juice-packed tomatoes; chop, drain off most of the liquid. Return the tomatoes to the can, and fill to the top with canned tomato puree.

MAKE-IT-EASY TIP:
* To quickly prepare whole-grain bread crumbs, toast the whole-grain bread slices in a 350°F oven for 10 to 15 minutes, until dry. Place in a food processor or blender and crumble.

Minced Turkey in Lettuce Leaves	SERVES: 6 CALORIES: 261 per serving PREPARATION TIME: 20 minutes COOKING TIME: 5 minutes

This recipe is a variation on a traditional Chinese dish prepared with pork or squab. Here lower-fat, lean ground turkey, is a flavorful and healthy substitute.

2 large heads iceberg lettuce
1 ounce (about 6–10) dried Chinese or Japanese shiitake
   mushrooms soaked in hot water for 20 minutes
10 water chestnuts, drained and finely chopped
4 large stalks celery, finely chopped
1 pound lean ground turkey
1 egg, lightly beaten
2 tablespoons reduced-sodium soy sauce
5 teaspoons arrowroot
½ cup chicken broth
2 tablespoons dry sherry
1 teaspoon sugar
Salt and freshly ground white pepper to taste
2½ tablespoons peanut oil

Garnish:

Hoisin sauce (available at Chinese grocery stores or at many
   supermarkets)

1. Bang the core ends of lettuce on a board and remove the core easily. Peel off 12 of the largest leaves and arrange on a serving dish. (Save the lettuce hearts for another use.)
2. Drain the mushrooms, squeeze dry, remove the stems, and chop finely. Combine with the water chestnuts and celery and set near the cooking area.
3. Combine the turkey with the egg, 1 tablespoon soy sauce, and 3 teaspoons arrowroot; mix with your hands until the mixture is well-combined and set near the cooking area with

the celery. (The turkey mixture may be soupy in texture.) In a small bowl whisk the remaining 2 teaspoons arrowroot with the chicken broth, sherry, remaining 1 tablespoon soy, the sugar, and salt and pepper and set alongside the other ingredients.

4. Heat a wok or large skillet and add the oil. When hot, stir-fry the turkey until the meat crumbles and loses its pink color, 2 to 3 minutes. When the turkey is cooked, add the mushroom mixture and continue to cook for 1 to 2 minutes. Add the remaining ingredients and stir until heated through.

5. Spoon the mixture into the prepared leaves, top each leaf with ½ teaspoon hoisin sauce, and serve immediately.

ACCOMPANIMENT:
Stir-Fried Tofu and Vegetables on Buckwheat Noodles

VARIATIONS:
* ⅓ cup chopped bamboo shoots can be added to the mushroom-vegetable mixture.
* Ground chicken may be substituted for the turkey.

MAKE-IT-EASY TIP:
* It is necessary to use 2 heads of lettuce to obtain enough of the largest leaves. The leaves can be prepared in advance by washing, drying, and storing wrapped in paper towels in a plastic bag in the refrigerator overnight.

Rock Cornish Game Hens

Roasted Rock Cornish Game Hens with Lemon Flavor	SERVES: 4 CALORIES: 300 per serving PREPARATION TIME: 20 minutes COOKING TIME: 40–50 minutes

Rock Cornish Game Hens were developed by crossing Cornish chickens with White Rocks. These small hens range from 1 to 2 pounds but average about 1¼ pounds. Like chicken and turkey, these lean birds are an excellent low-cholesterol source of protein.

1 large juicy lemon
4 scallions, cut into 1" lengths (green and white parts included)
2 Rock Cornish game hens, excess fat removed
Salt and freshly ground pepper to taste
1 clove garlic, finely minced
Paprika
½ cup dry white wine
½ cup chicken broth

Garnish:
Lemon wedges
Sprigs of parsley

1. Preheat the oven to 375° F.
2. Grate the rind from the lemons, squeeze the juice, and set both the rind and juice aside. Cut the lemons into small pieces and place in a bowl. Combine with the scallions.
3. Season the cavity of the hens with salt and pepper and stuff with the lemon-scallion mixture. Place the hens breast side up on a rack in a roasting pan.
4. In a small bowl combine the lemon rind, juice, and garlic. Rub the mixture over the outside of the hens, sprinkle with paprika, and additional salt and pepper, pour the wine and broth into the pan, and bake for 40 to 50 minutes, or until the juices run clear when the knife is inserted between the leg and thigh. Baste occasionally.

5. Remove the fat from the pan juices. Split the hens in half with a cleaver or heavy sharp knife. Divide the stuffing and serve each half garnished with lemon wedges and parsley sprigs, with the defatted pan juices on the side.

ACCOMPANIMENT:
Baked Pasta with Spinach-Ricotta Sauce

VARIATIONS:
* An orange can be substituted for the lemon.
* Shallots can be substituted for the scallions.

MAKE-IT-EASY TIPS:
* Select thin-skinned lemons which will be the juiciest; juice them at room temperature.
* Scallions, also called spring onions, are straight-sided shoots that are pulled before the bulbs have had a chance to fully develop. Green onions, on the other hand, are shoots that are pulled once a firm white bulb has developed, but before a papery skin has formed. Green onions have a firmer texture while scallions have a finer and more delicate one.
* If desired, the hens can be trussed, but it is not necessary if time is a factor.

Rock Cornish Game Hens Glazed with Cranberry Chutney	SERVES: 4 CALORIES: 535 per serving PREPARATION TIME: 10 minutes COOKING TIME: 45–50 minutes

Rock Cornish game hens are lean poultry but often contain a deposit of fat near the cavity that should be removed before cooking.

2 Rock Cornish game hens, washed, dried, and halved (see Notes)
Salt and freshly ground pepper to taste
1 large onion, quartered
1 cup Cranberry Chutney (page 88)
¼ cup frozen orange juice concentrate, thawed

Garnish:
Orange slices
Sprigs of parsley

1. Preheat the oven to 375° F.
2. Sprinkle the hens on both sides with salt and pepper. Place 4 onion quarters in a roasting pan, place the hen halves, cut side down, atop each onion quarter, and bake for 15 minutes.
3. In a bowl combine the chutney and juice, stir, spoon over the hens, and continue to cook for 30 to 35 minutes longer, or until golden, basting occasionally.
4. Remove the hens from the oven, place them with the onion quarters on a platter, spoon the sauce over all, and serve hot, garnished with orange slices and parsley sprigs.

COOK NOTES: Rock Cornish game hens are now available fresh or frozen in supermarkets. Select the smallest and lightest ones, which are generally more tender.

If the hens are not golden after cooking time, place under the broiler for 2 to 3 minutes to brown.

ACCOMPANIMENTS:
Oven-Fried Potatoes, and Romaine Lettuce and Grapefruit Salad with Red Onion

VARIATION:
* Chicken breasts can be substituted for the hens.

Belgian Rock Cornish Hens Waterzooi	SERVES: 4 CALORIES: 402 per serving PREPARATION TIME: 20 minutes COOKING TIME: about 50 minutes

This is a Flemish dish, usually prepared with chicken, called Waterzooi van Kip. It is served in deep soup bowls to catch all the wonderful broth. If possible, prepare a day in advance and refrigerate overnight. Just before serving, remove the congealed fat at the top, reheat, and serve.

2 Rock Cornish game hens, washed, dried, and quartered
Salt and freshly ground white pepper to taste
1 tablespoon unsalted butter or margarine
3 carrots, peeled and finely chopped
2 leeks, finely chopped
2 stalks celery, finely chopped
1 large onion, finely chopped
3 cups strong chicken broth, plus a little extra
2 tablespoons lemon juice
2 teaspoons grated lemon rind
3 egg yolks, lightly beaten, at room temperature
3 tablespoons finely chopped fresh parsley

Garnish:
Thin slices of lemon

1. Season the hens with salt and pepper and set aside.
2. In a large nonstick pan heat the butter or margarine and sauté the carrots, leeks, celery, and onion over medium heat until just softened, about 8 minutes. Add the hens, stirring to toss.
3. When the hens are hot, add the broth, lemon juice, and lemon rind. Bring to a boil, cover, reduce heat, and simmer for 40 minutes. Remove the game hens and keep warm. Remove as much accumulated fat as possible and return the pan to very, very low heat.
4. Add a little of the hot broth to the egg yolks and stir well (this will help avoid curdling the sauce). Add the egg yolks to the pan and, stirring constantly, incorporate the yolks into the sauce. Immediately remove from heat, add the parsley, season to taste with salt and pepper, and stir to combine.
5. Serve hot garnished with lemon slices.

ACCOMPANIMENTS:
Mixed Vegetables Cooked in Lettuce Packages and Whole-Wheat Popovers

VARIATION:
* Chicken can be substituted for the game hens.

FISH AND SEAFOOD

Grilled Swordfish with Spinach Pesto	SERVES: 4 CALORIES: 342 per serving PREPARATION TIME: 15 minutes MARINATING TIME: 1 hour COOKING TIME: 12–16 minutes

Unlike the traditional basil pesto which is prepared with a cup of oil, this spinach pesto contains only 2 tablespoons of oil. The uses for spinach pesto are not limited to swordfish. Use it on grilled chicken, pasta, as a topping for steamed vegetables, or as a flavoring for tomatoes, as in Tomatoes Baked with Spinach Pesto (page 281).

4 swordfish steaks (about 2 pounds), cut 1" thick

Spinach Pesto:
1 cup firmly packed young and tender spinach, washed, dried, with stems removed (see Notes)
2 tablespoons olive oil
2 tablespoons grated Parmesan cheese
1 tablespoon pine nuts
1 clove garlic, finely minced
Salt and freshly ground pepper to taste

Garnish:
Lemon wedges
2 tablespoons lemon juice

1. Preheat an outdoor grill or broiler. Place the fish in a shallow dish.
2. In a food processor or blender combine the spinach pesto ingredients and process until smooth. Slather on both sides of the fish, cover, and refrigerate for 1 hour.
3. Grill or broil the fish for 6 to 8 minutes per side, or until just flaky, basting occasionally. (Do not overcook or the fish will dry out.)

4. Place the fish on a platter, sprinkle with lemon juice, and serve hot, garnished with lemon wedges.

COOK NOTES: Since the water content of spinach is as high as 80 to 90 percent, it will wilt easily upon standing and is therefore highly perishable. Avoid washing the greens before storing, for even if it is well dried, some water still adhere to the leaves, causing them to rot. Better to store, grit and all, in plastic bags.

Thoroughly wash the spinach in a basin full of lukewarm water, which stimulates the dirt to float off the leaves. Run under tap water and dry well before using.

ACCOMPANIMENTS:
Pasta with Light Red Sauce and Greek Salad with Lemon-Herb Dressing

VARIATION:
* Other firm fleshy fish or fish steaks such as halibut or salmon can be substituted.

Grilled Fish Escabeche	SERVES: 4 CALORIES: 252 per serving PREPARATION TIME: 15 minutes COOKING TIME: 10–15 minutes MARINATING TIME: 6–8 hours or overnight

Escabeche is a spicy dish of Spanish origin, usually prepared with fish or chicken, cooked lightly, and then pickled or soused in a marinade. According to Craig Claiborne in *Craig Claiborne's New York Times Food Encyclopedia*, "Escabeche is Spanish, derived from the Arabic sakbay, which means a mixture or stew of meat with vinegar. As near as I can trace the history of escabeche, they are, like many dishes popular in Spain, of Arab origin."

The difference between escabeche and seviche is that in escabeche the food is cooked before pickling, while seviche is "cured" with lime juice and eaten raw.

2 pounds thick fish fillets (snapper, sea bass, orange roughy, or others)
2 tablespoons olive oil

Pickling Sauce:
2 tablespoons finely chopped green pepper
2 tablespoons finely chopped shallots
2 tablespoons olive oil
2 tablespoons orange juice
1 tablespoon white wine vinegar
1 tablespoon lime juice
1 teaspoon grated orange rind
Pinch of cayenne
Salt and freshly ground pepper to taste

Garnish:
Orange slices
Sprigs of parsley

1. Preheat an outdoor grill or broiler.
2. Brush the fish with the olive oil and grill until just flaky. (Remember the rule of thumb for cooking fish is 10 minutes per inch at the thickest point.) Do not overcook.
3. In the meantime, in a bowl combine the ingredients for pickling sauce and stir to combine.
4. Place the cooked fish on a platter, pour the sauce over, cover, and refrigerate for 6 to 8 hours or overnight, basting once or twice.
5. Serve the fish garnished with orange slices and parsley sprigs.

ACCOMPANIMENTS:
Wild Rice Pilaf and Braised Artichokes with Vegetables

VARIATIONS:
* Grilled chicken breasts can be substituted for the fish.
* The white part of scallions can be substituted for the shallots.

MAKE-IT-EASY TIP:
* The fish must be firm and fleshy to hold up on the grill. If necessary, use a wire hamburger grill basket to keep the fish intact.

Japanese Grilled Fish Steaks

SERVES: 4
CALORIES: 158 per serving
PREPARATION TIME: 10 minutes
MARINATING TIME: 1 hour
COOKING TIME: about 10 minutes

Grilling or broiling are perfect low-fat techniques for cooking. All the fats drip off and the results are juicy and flavorful.

4" fish steaks (tuna, swordfish, halibut, shark, salmon, or sable-
fish), cut 1" thick

Marinade:
¼ cup reduced-sodium soy sauce
3 tablespoons dry sherry
1 teaspoon toasted sesame oil
1 teaspoon sugar
1 teaspoon minced fresh ginger

Garnish:
Trimmed scallions
Radishes

1. Place the fish in a single layer in a glass or ceramic baking dish.
2. In a bowl combine the marinade ingredients, stir well, and pour over the fish. Cover and refrigerate for 1 hour, turning once.
3. Preheat an outdoor grill or broiler. (If cooking in a broiler, spray the rack with vegetable cooking spray before setting the steaks on top.)
4. Drain and reserve the marinade from the fish, place on the grill or 4" to 6" from direct heat under the broiler, and cook for 5 minutes per side, or until the fish is flaky, basting occasionally.
5. Serve immediately, garnished with scallions and radishes.

ACCOMPANIMENT:
Salad of Buckwheat Noodles with Crunchy Vegetables

VARIATION:

* Very firm fish fillets may be substituted for the fish steaks. Cook them in a fish or hamburger-style grill basket for only 3 to 4 minutes per side, or until just flaky.

MAKE-IT-EASY TIPS:

* The rule of thumb for cooking fish is 10 minutes per 1″ of thickness, at the thickest point of the fish.
* When cooking fresh Hawaiian tuna, try undercooking it so that it is browned on the outside and rare on the inside, creating a grilled sushi flavor.

Grilled Packets of Fish, Rice, and Vegetables	SERVES: 6 CALORIES: 321 per serving PREPARATION TIME: 20 minutes COOKING TIME: 15–20 minutes

This complete dinner of fish, rice, and vegetables is sealed in a foil packet and cooked on the grill or broiler until the fish is tender and the vegetables are cooked. Allow room for the foil to expand during cooking. It is best to use 1 packet for each pound of fish and cup of rice.

2 cups cooked brown rice
2 pounds fish fillets (any seasonal type preferred)
4 cups crushed tomatoes packed in puree
2 tablespoons lemon juice
1 large onion, thinly sliced
1 green pepper, seeded and cut into julienne strips
1 red pepper, seeded and cut into julienne strips
4 large mushrooms, wiped clean, thinly sliced
1 clove garlic, finely minced
2 tablespoons finely chopped fresh basil, or ½ teaspoon crumbled dried
2 tablespoons finely chopped fresh parsley
½ teaspoon crumbled dried oregano

Salt and freshly ground pepper to taste
1 tablespoon diced unsalted butter or margarine
¼ cup grated Parmesan cheese

Garnish:
Lemon wedges
Sprigs of parsley

1. Preheat an outdoor grill or broiler. Cut two 20″ square pieces of aluminum foil and spray with vegetable cooking spray.
2. Place 1 cup rice in the center of each piece of foil, top with 1 pound fish and 2 cups tomatoes. Distribute the remaining ingredients between the pieces of foil, ending with the Parmesan cheese.
3. Fold over the foil, seal the ends and edges, allowing room for expansion. Place on the grill or under the broiler and cook for 15 to 20 minutes over medium heat, or until the fish is flaky and the vegetables are cooked.
4. Serve the fish hot over rice, garnished with lemon wedges and parsley.

COOK NOTE: High-fat fish, such as bluefish, trout, and pompano are particularly tasty cooked this way. Recently a group of substances found in fish oil, called Omega-3 long chain fatty acids, have been discovered. These fatty acids are known to protect against heart disease.

ACCOMPANIMENT:
Spinach Salad with Creamy Curry Dressing

VARIATIONS:
* If tomatoes packed in puree are unavailable, use regular whole juice-packed tomatoes. Chop the tomatoes, drain off most of the liquid, return the tomatoes to the can, and fill to the top with canned tomato puree.
* Almost any seasonal vegetables desired may be added to the packet.

Herb-Broiled Fish Fillets	SERVES: 4 CALORIES: 314 per serving PREPARATION TIME: 20 minutes COOKING TIME: about 15 minutes

The eggplant is brushed lightly with oil and broiled as a base layer to add flavor and moisture to the fish fillets as they cook. Any type of fresh fish fillets will work in this recipe.

1 medium eggplant, washed and dried (see Note)
2½ tablespoons olive oil
1¾ pounds fish fillets
2 medium tomatoes, seeded, chopped, and drained
⅓ cup minced scallions
2 tablespoons lemon juice
2 tablespoons chopped fresh parsley
1 tablespoon chopped fresh basil, or 1 teaspoon dried
1 tablespoon chopped fresh oregano, or 1 teaspoon dried
2 teaspoons finely minced garlic
1 teaspoon grainy-style Dijon mustard
Pinch of cayenne
Salt and freshly ground black pepper to taste

Garnish:
Sprigs of fresh herbs

1. Preheat the broiler.
2. Slice the eggplant horizontally ¼" thick, place in a single layer in a broiling pan, brush lightly with ½ tablespoon oil, and broil for 2 minutes, or until just lightly golden. Turn, brush with an additional tablespoon oil and broil as before.
3. Place the eggplant in a single layer in an ovenproof serving dish. Top with a layer of fish. It may be necessary to cook the fish and the eggplant in 2 separate pans in order to keep the fish in a single layer.
4. In a small bowl combine the remaining ingredients together, stir, and spread over the fish.
5. Broil for 8 to 10 minutes, without turning, or until the fish flakes easily.

6. Serve hot, garnished with sprigs of fresh herbs.

COOK NOTE: Select eggplants with clear, dark, satiny color that covers the entire surface evenly. The eggplants should feel firm all over and should not yield to gentle pressure.

ACCOMPANIMENTS:
Asparagus Flan with Pasta, and Mushroom Salad

Baked Fish with Dill Flavor	SERVES: 4 CALORIES: 191 per serving PREPARATION TIME: 10–15 minutes COOKING TIME: 10–15 minutes

The general rule of thumb in cooking fish is to cook for 10 minutes per inch at the thickest point of the fish. Here the fish is baked without any added oils, just vegetables, fresh herbs, and seasonings.

1½ pounds thick, firm, fleshy fish fillets (sea bass, snapper, halibut, orange roughy)
2 ripe tomatoes, peeled, seeded, and cut into chunks, or 1 16-ounce can Italian tomatoes, well-drained
1 small onion, finely chopped
2 tablespoons freshly snipped dill
Salt and freshly ground pepper to taste

Garnish:
Sprigs of dill
Tomato wedges

1. Preheat the oven to 350°F.
2. Place the fish in a baking dish and sprinkle with tomatoes, onion, dill, and salt and pepper.
3. Cover with foil and bake for 10 to 15 minutes, or until the fish is tender and flaky.
4. Serve hot, garnished with dill sprigs and tomato wedges.

ACCOMPANIMENT:
Brown Rice Baked with Vegetables and Tofu

VARIATIONS:

* Finely chopped green or red peppers can be placed over the fillets with the tomatoes.
* If fresh dill is not available, substitute parsley and avoid the dried variety.

MAKE-IT-EASY TIPS:

* To keep fish fresh on the journey from market to home, take along an insulated tote bag with a freezer cold pack inside.
* To keep fish fresh in the refrigerator, place in a shallow pan, unwrapped, and cover with a dampened towel until ready to bake.

Cold Salmon Baked in Foil with Tangy Sorrel Sauce	SERVES: 6 CALORIES: 327 per serving PREPARATION TIME: 15 minutes COOKING TIME: about 15 minutes CHILLING TIME: 6 hours or overnight

In this recipe the salmon is easily poached by baking in foil packets. The traditional sorrel sauce which is laden with cream is replaced by a light one prepared with low-fat yogurt. Sorrel, also called sour dock, are crisp bitter green leaves often used in soups or sauces.

4 6-ounce salmon steaks
¼ cup chopped fresh parsley
¼ pound mushrooms, wiped clean, sliced
8 teaspoons lemon juice
Salt and freshly ground pepper to taste

Tangy Sorrel Sauce:
⅔ cup strong chicken or vegetable broth
¼ cup finely minced shallots
3 tablespoons shredded fresh sorrel
2 tablespoons white wine vinegar
¾ cup plain low-fat yogurt
2 tablespoons mayonnaise
Salt and freshly ground white pepper to taste

Garnish:
Lemon wedges
Sorrel leaves

1. Preheat the oven to 450°F. Cut four pieces of aluminum foil into 16″ squares.
2. Place each salmon steak on the prepared foil. Top each with 1 tablespoon parsley. Distribute the mushrooms over each, top with 2 teaspoons lemon juice, and finally a sprinkling of salt and pepper.
3. Seal the packages of foil shut tightly, place on a baking sheet, and bake for 12 minutes, or until the fish flakes. Cool and chill for 6 hours or overnight.
4. To prepare the sauce, in a medium skillet heat the broth with the shallots, sorrel, and vinegar. Cook over medium heat until the vegetables are soft and the liquid is absorbed. Cool slightly. Mix together the yogurt and mayonnaise, stir in the vegetable mixture, season with salt and pepper, cover, and chill for 2 to 3 hours or overnight.
5. Serve the salmon on a platter surrounded by lemon wedges and sorrel leaves, with sauce on the side.

ACCOMPANIMENT:
Brown Rice Salad with Crunchy Vegetables

VARIATION:
* Halibut steaks may be substituted for the salmon.

MAKE-IT-EASY TIP:
* To easily clean mushrooms, lightly dip a paper towel in lemon juice and wipe the mushrooms clean.

Food Processor Fish Quenelles with Lemon Sauce	SERVES: 6 CALORIES: 312 per serving PREPARATION TIME: 25 minutes COOKING TIME: 10–15 minutes CHILLING TIME: 1–2 hours

Quenelles are soufflé-light dumplings prepared with fish, chicken, or even veal that are poached, drained, and served with a sauce. They are traditionally made with cream, but here evaporated skimmed milk is used as a low-fat substitute.

1 pound monkfish or other white fish fillets, cut into 1" pieces
½ pound bay shrimp
1 tablespoon finely minced fresh chives
Pinch of grated nutmeg
Salt and freshly ground white pepper to taste
⅓ cup evaporated skimmed milk
2 tablespoons fine bread crumbs
3 egg whites
1 quart water
½ teaspoon vinegar

Lemon Sauce:
1 tablespoon vegetable oil
1 tablespoon arrowroot
1 cup chicken or fish broth
2 egg yolks, lightly beaten
2 tablespoons lemon juice
2 tablespoons chopped fresh parsley

1. Place the fish, shrimp, chives, nutmeg, and salt and pepper in a work bowl of a food processor and pulsate for 30 seconds. Turn the machine on and add the milk and bread crumbs and blend for 2 seconds. Scrape the sides of the bowl down and add the egg whites; pulsate 3 to 4 times until just combined but not overmixed. Place in a bowl and chill for 1 to 2 hours, or until firm enough to shape.

2. In a large deep skillet heat the water and vinegar. Dip 2 soup spoons in ice water and shape the chilled fish mixture into ovals between the spoons. When the water in the skillet is just simmering slowly, gently drop the ovals into the water, and poach in an uncovered pan for 4 to 5 minutes, or until just firm, turning once. It may be necessary to cook the quenelles in several batches to avoid overcrowding. Do not allow the poaching water to boil or the quenelles may fall apart.

3. Remove the quenelles with a slotted spoon to a heated platter.

4. In the meantime, prepare the sauce in a small nonstick pan. Whisk the oil and arrowroot together until smooth. Add the broth, whisk again, and cook over medium heat, for 2 to 3 minutes, until slightly thickened, stirring constantly.

5. Off heat, add 1 tablespoon of the hot mixture to the egg yolks; whisk, and then add the egg yolks to the hot arrowroot mixture, whisking constantly. Return the pan to low heat, and cook, continuing to whisk for 1 to 2 minutes, or until thick and smooth.

6. Add the lemon juice and parsley to the sauce, stir well, and pour over the finished quenelles. Serve hot.

COOK NOTE: Do not poach quenelles in an iron or aluminum skillet or they may become discolored.

ACCOMPANIMENTS:
Lemon Brown Rice, and Mixed Vegetables Cooked in Lettuce Packages

VARIATION:
* Quenelles can be served cold topped with sorrel sauce (see Cold Salmon Baked in Foil with Tangy Sorrel Sauce, page 158).

Poached Monkfish with Lemon Sauce	SERVES: 4 CALORIES: 342 per serving PREPARATION TIME: 15–20 minutes COOKING TIME: 15–20 minutes

Monkfish, also called lotte, angler, allmouth, bellyfish, and goosefish, has a mild flavor and a texture similar to lobster. Only the tail section with its bone-free white flesh is edible. Since monkfish is unknown in the United States, it is often sold at a very low price, making it a wonderful, inexpensive source of protein.

Poaching and steaming the fish keeps it moist and tender without added fats.

2 pounds monkfish or other firm fleshy fish

Poaching Liquid:
Chicken broth to cover
1 large onion, sliced
1 lemon, sliced
2 sprigs of parsley
2 sprigs of fresh dill
6 peppercorns
Salt to taste

1 recipe Lemon Sauce (see Food Processor Fish Quenelles with
*   Lemon Sauce, page 160)*

1. Place the fish in a large shallow pot and measure out enough broth to cover. Remove the fish and set aside.
2. Add the remaining poaching liquid ingredients to the broth in the pan, bring to a boil, cover, reduce heat, and simmer for 10 minutes.
3. Add the fish, cover, and continue to simmer for 5 to 10 minutes, depending on the thickness of the fish.
4. In the meantime, prepare the Lemon Sauce.
5. Drain the fish, reserve the liquid for another use, and serve hot with the lemon sauce.

ACCOMPANIMENTS:
New Potatoes with Dill and Puree of Carrot with Lemon Accent

VARIATION:
* To serve cold, place the cooked fish on a platter, cover, and chill for 3 to 4 hours. Serve with Mustard Coating (see Terrine of Chicken with Mustard Coating, page 70).

MAKE-IT-EASY TIP:
* The poaching liquid can be strained, chilled, frozen, and reused.

Baked Fish with Papaya Salsa	SERVES: 4 CALORIES: 283 per serving PREPARATION TIME: 5 minutes COOKING TIME: 15–20 minutes

Papaya salsa makes a low-fat flavorful topping for baked or poached fish, chicken, or vegetables.

1½–2 pounds thick, firm, fleshy fish fillets (sea bass, snapper, halibut, orange roughy)
1 cup Papaya Salsa (page 90)

Garnish:
Sprigs of cilantro (coriander)

1. Preheat the oven to 350°F.
2. Place the fish in a baking dish, spread the salsa on top, cover with foil, and bake for 10 minutes. Remove the foil and continue to bake for 5 to 10 minutes longer, or until the fish is tender and flaky.
3. Serve hot, garnished with cilantro sprigs.

ACCOMPANIMENTS:
Saffron-Flavored Rice and Mixed Vegetables Cooked in Lettuce Packages

VARIATION:

* The fish may be served cold the next day.

MAKE-IT-EASY TIP:

* To easily transfer a baked fish dish to a platter, before baking, lay the fillets on a piece of parchment paper or aluminum foil that has been sprayed with vegetable cooking spray. Once cooked, lift the fish by the paper and ease it off onto the platter.

Chinese Steamed Shrimp with Black Bean Sauce	SERVES: 4 CALORIES: 187 per serving PREPARATION TIME: 15–20 minutes COOKING TIME: 10 minutes

In steaming, food is cooked with moist heat and the flavor is locked in and not boiled out. Nutrients are maintained rather than lost in the water and the flavor is juicy and succulent.

1 pound raw shrimp, cleaned and deveined
2 tablespoons fermented black beans (available at Chinese groceries or at many supermarkets)
2 cloves garlic
2 teaspoons finely shredded fresh ginger
2 scallions, split and cut into 2" lengths (green part only)
3 tablespoons reduced-sodium soy sauce
2 tablespoons dry sherry
1 tablespoon toasted sesame oil
½ teaspoon sugar

Garnish:
Chinese parsley (coriander)

1. Pat the shrimp dry with paper towels. Lightly spray a heat-proof platter or shallow dish that will fit into a steamer with vegetable cooking spray.
2. On waxed paper mash the black beans with the side of a cleaver or chef's knife with the garlic and ginger; sprinkle over the shrimp along with the scallions.

3. In a small bowl combine the soy sauce, sherry, oil, and sugar and stir well. Pour over the shrimp.
4. Place the shrimp in the steamer and steam over boiling water for 10 minutes, or until they turn pink.
5. Remove the shrimp to a platter, garnish with Chinese parsley, and serve immediately.

ACCOMPANIMENT:
Stir-Fried Tofu and Vegetables on Buckwheat Noodles

VARIATION:
* For a French version of steamed shrimp, try lemon, capers, tarragon, and when cooked, top with a bit of melted butter or margarine.

MAKE-IT-EASY TIP:
* If a steamer is unavailable use a wok or deep saucepan with a rack. Make sure to keep the bottom of the food container just above the surface of the water.

Greek Baked Shrimp with Feta Cheese	SERVES: 4 CALORIES: 251 per serving PREPARATION TIME: 10 minutes COOKING TIME: about 50 minutes

Although shrimp is considered higher in cholesterol than most other seafood, it is still low in fat and low in calories.

1 tablespoon olive oil
1 large onion, finely minced
1 28-ounce can crushed tomatoes packed in puree
1 tablespoon finely chopped fresh parsley,
1½ teaspoons freshly snipped dill
1 teaspoon finely minced garlic
Pinch of sugar
Salt and freshly ground pepper to taste
1 pound peeled and deveined large shrimp (see Note)
2 ounces feta cheese

1. In a large nonstick saucepan heat the oil and sauté the onion over medium heat for 7 to 8 minutes, or until soft and lightly golden, stirring often.
2. Add the tomatoes, parsley, dill, garlic, sugar, and salt and pepper; bring to a boil, cover, reduce heat, and simmer slowly for 30 minutes, stirring occasionally.
3. Preheat the oven to 375°F. Generously spray a shallow ovenproof dish with vegetable cooking spray.
4. Place the shrimp in the bottom of the prepared dish, pour the cooked sauce over, and crumble the feta cheese on top. Bake for 10 to 12 minutes, or until the shrimp are tender and the feta cheese begins to melt slightly.
5. Serve the shrimp hot.

COOK NOTE: If peeling the shrimp yourself, remember to account for ¼ pound of weight for the shells, so you would need about 1¼ pounds shrimp in their shells for this recipe.

ACCOMPANIMENTS:
Plain brown or white rice and Greek Salad with Lemon-Herb Dressing

VARIATIONS:
* Remember to adjust the cooking times according to the size of the shrimp. Medium shrimp will take just under 10 minutes, while the larger shrimp will take from 10 to 12 minutes.
* If tomatoes packed in puree are unavailable, use regular whole juice-packed tomatoes; chop, drain off most of the liquid, return the tomatoes to the can, and fill to the top with canned tomato puree.
* Serve the baked shrimp over 8 ounces of cooked linguine.

MAKE-IT-EASY TIP:
* The recipe calls for large shrimp because fish markets generally will only peel larger shrimp. If using medium shrimp, peel them yourself with the aid of a shrimp deveiner or sharp paring knife.

Spanish Shrimp and Rice

SERVES: 4
CALORIES: 324 per serving
PREPARATION TIME: 15–20 minutes
COOKING TIME: about 30 minutes

This combination of shrimp and rice is an easy version of Spanish paella. It makes a wonderful one-pot dinner served in soup plates.

1 tablespoon olive oil
4 shallots, finely chopped
6 mushrooms, wiped clean, thinly sliced
1 red pepper, seeded and finely chopped
1 cup uncooked white rice
⅓ cup dry vermouth
1⅔ cups chicken broth
2 tablespoons lemon juice
1 teaspoon finely minced garlic
½ teaspoon crumbled dried oregano
⅛ teaspoon powdered saffron, or ¼ teaspoon saffron threads
*   dissolved in 2 tablespoons hot chicken broth*
Pinch of red pepper flakes
Salt and freshly ground black pepper to taste
¾ cup cleaned and deveined medium shrimp, cut into small
*   pieces*
1 cup frozen tiny peas, thawed
Garnish:
2 tablespoons grated Parmesan cheese
1 tablespoon chopped fresh parsley

1. In a medium nonstick saucepan heat the oil and sauté the shallots, mushrooms, and red pepper over medium heat for 7 to 8 minutes, or until softened.
2. Add the rice and stir to coat; add the vermouth and allow to boil and then add the broth, lemon juice, garlic, oregano, saffron, red pepper flakes, and salt and pepper. Bring to a boil, cover, reduce heat, and simmer slowly for 20 minutes. (Do not open the saucepan until 20 minutes have passed or

the steam will escape and the rice will not absorb the liquid properly.)

3. Add the shrimp and peas, stir to combine, cover, and continue to cook for 3 to 5 minutes, or until the shrimp are cooked through and the rice is fluffy.

4. Add the cheese and parsley, stir, and serve immediately.

ACCOMPANIMENTS:
Braised Scallions, and Gazpacho Salad

VARIATIONS:
* The white parts of scallions can be substituted for the shallots.
* Other seafood such as crabmeat, lobster, scallops, or even chunks of thick fleshy fish can be substituted for the shrimp.

Cold Poached Shrimp in Creamy Watercress Sauce	SERVES: 4 CALORIES: 239 per serving PREPARATION TIME: 15 minutes COOKING TIME: 3–5 minutes CHILLING TIME: 2–3 hours or overnight

The chilled shrimp make a wonderful cold supper entrée on a hot night or can be served as an appetizer or first course on small plates. The creamy sauce is prepared with a base of low-fat yogurt.

1½ cups chicken broth
1 cup dry vermouth
1 small onion, finely sliced
2 slices of lemon
2 sprigs of parsley
1 clove garlic, smashed and peeled but still intact
1 bay leaf
6 peppercorns
Salt to taste
2 pounds cleaned and deveined medium or large shrimp

Creamy Sauce:
½ *cup firmly packed watercress leaves (see Note)*
¼ *cup firmly packed parsley leaves*
¼ *cup finely chopped fresh chives or scallion greens*
1 *tablespoon freshly snipped dill*
1 *cup plain low-fat yogurt*
2 *tablespoons mayonnaise*
1½ *tablespoons lemon juice*
Salt and freshly ground white pepper to taste

Garnish:
Lettuce leaves
Sprigs of watercress

1. In a medium saucepan place the broth, vermouth, onion, lemon, parsley, garlic, bay leaf, peppercorns, and salt and bring to a boil; add the shrimp, bring to a second boil, cover, reduce heat, and simmer slowly for 3 to 5 minutes, or until the shrimp are pink and just tender. (Do not overcook.)
2. Drain the shrimp and reserve the liquid for another use, such as fish soup. Place the shrimp in a bowl and allow to cool. Chill for 2 to 3 hours or overnight.
3. In the meantime, prepare the sauce by chopping the watercress, parsley, chives, and dill in a food processor or blender. Place in a bowl, add the remaining ingredients, and stir together until well-mixed. Place in a covered container and chill until ready to use.
4. When ready to serve, place the chilled shrimp on a lettuce-lined platter, top with sauce and garnish with watercress sprigs.

COOK NOTE: Select fresh, bright green bunches of watercress with unblemished leaves. Wrap in a paper towel and store in a plastic bag in the refrigerator.

ACCOMPANIMENTS:
Tabbouleh and Whole-Wheat Popovers

VARIATIONS:
* The cooled shrimp can also be combined with the sauce and allowed to marinate for several hours.
* The sauce can be served as a dip with raw vegetable crudités.

Shrimp and Scallop Curry	SERVES: 4 CALORIES: 257 per serving PREPARATION TIME: 20 minutes COOKING TIME: about 35 minutes

The sauce for this curry is thickened naturally with finely chopped vegetables rather than the traditional butter and flour curry. Curry powder is actually a blend of spices usually containing cardamom, cloves, coriander, cumin, dill, fenugreek, ginger, mace, pepper, and turmeric. The taste varies with each different brand so try out several to find the one you prefer.

1 tablespoon olive oil
1 large onion, finely chopped
1 green pepper, finely chopped
1 red pepper, finely chopped
1 large zucchini, scrubbed and finely chopped
1 tart apple, peeled and finely chopped
½ cup dry white wine
1 cup strong chicken broth
2 tablespoons finely chopped fresh parsley
2 tablespoons raisins
2 tablespoons lemon juice
2 teaspoons finely minced garlic
1–2 teaspoons curry powder or to taste
Salt and freshly ground pepper to taste
½ pound cleaned and deveined medium shrimp, halved
½ pound sea scallops

Garnish:
Plain low-fat yogurt

1. In a large nonstick skillet heat the olive oil and sauté the onion, green and red peppers, zucchini, and apple over medium heat until just softened, about 7 minutes, stirring often.
2. Add the wine and allow to boil for 1 to 2 minutes. Add the broth, parsley, raisins, lemon juice, garlic, curry powder, and salt and pepper; bring to a boil, cover, reduce heat, and simmer slowly for 20 to 25 minutes, or until the vegetables are just soft.
3. Add the shrimp and scallops to the sauce, cover, and cook for 3 to 5 minutes, or until just cooked. (Do not overcook.)
4. Serve the curry hot with a dollop of yogurt on each portion.

ACCOMPANIMENTS:
Saffron-Flavored Rice and Mushroom Salad

VARIATIONS:
* The sauce can be pureed, if desired, after step 2.
* For thicker sauce, add a small sweet potato, peeled and diced, along with the vegetables.
* Cooked chicken or leftover meat can be added to the finished sauce.

MAKE-IT-EASY-TIP:
* If cleaned and deveined shrimp are unavailable, purchase a few additional ounces of shrimp in shells and quickly and easily remove the shells with a shrimp deveining tool that slides under the shell, removing both the shell and the vein in one motion.

Stir-Fry of Scallop and Swiss Chard	SERVES: 4 CALORIES: 164 per serving PREPARATION TIME: 20 minutes COOKING TIME: 5–6 minutes

This light stir-fry combines scallops with greens in a light sauce. The recipe calls for only 1 tablespoon peanut oil for the stir-frying and includes 1 teaspoon toasted sesame oil to give the dish a bright glaze and added flavor.

½ cup strong chicken broth
1 pound bay scallops or sea scallops, quartered
1 tablespoon peanut oil
3 scallions, finely chopped (green and white parts included)
1 teaspoon finely minced garlic
½ teaspoon finely minced fresh ginger
1 bunch (½ pound) red or white Swiss chard, washed and
    dried, with ribs and leaves cut into thin strips (see Note)
2 teaspoons arrowroot mixed with 1½ tablespoon water
Salt and freshly ground pepper to taste
1 teaspoon toasted sesame oil (optional)

1. In a small saucepan heat the broth, and when boiling, add the scallops. Reduce heat and cook slowly for 2 to 3 minutes, or until just tender. Avoid overcooking the scallops or they will surely toughen. Drain, set aside, and reserve the broth.
2. Heat a wok or large skillet and add the peanut oil; add the scallions, garlic, and ginger, and stir-fry for 30 seconds. Add the chard, and continue to stir-fry until the vegetables are limp.
3. Add the reserved broth, arrowroot mixture, and salt and pepper and cook until the sauce is slightly thickened. Add the scallops and sesame oil, toss to just warm through, and serve hot.

COOK NOTE: Swiss chard is a variety of beet with large edible leaves and thick stalks. Select only young, fresh, and crisp bunches, avoiding any that are rubbery and wilted.

ACCOMPANIMENTS:
Plain white rice and Sweet and Sour Chinese Cabbage

VARIATIONS:
* Peeled medium shrimp can be substituted for the scallops.
* Kale or spinach can be substituted for the Swiss chard.

Scallops en Papillote	SERVES: 4
	CALORIES: 224 per serving
	PREPARATION TIME: 20 minutes
	COOKING TIME: 10–12 minutes

In this recipe the scallops are flavored with spicy salsa, laid on a spinach leaf, wrapped in a parchment-paper package, and steamed in the oven to release natural juices and flavors without adding fat.

1 tablespoon olive oil
8 large spinach leaves, washed and well-dried, stems removed
20 sea scallops (about 1¾ pounds, quartered (see Notes)
Salt and freshly ground pepper to taste
1 cup Mexican Salsa (page 82)
¼ cup chopped pimiento
¼ teaspoon chili powder

Garnish:
Sprigs of cilantro or parsley

1. Preheat the oven to 400°F. Cut 4 sheets of parchment paper or foil into 15″- × -20″ rectangles. Fold each in half crosswise and cut the 15″- × -10″ rectangles into heart shapes with the fold running down the center. Open the hearts.
2. Very lightly brush each heart with oil. Place 2 spinach leaves in the center of half of each heart. Top each with 5 scallops. Sprinkle with salt and pepper.
3. In a small bowl combine the salsa with the pimiento and chili powder. Distribute evenly among the hearts.
4. Fold the heart over the scallops and, beginning at top of the heart, seal the edges by folding over and crimping them all the way around (see illustration). If the edges aren't tightly sealed, the paper won't puff up.
5. Place the packets on 2 cookie sheets and bake for 10 to 12 minutes, or until the papillotes are puffed and lightly

browned. The scallops should not be overcooked; heat toughens them quickly.

6. Place the papillotes on plates, open and serve immediately, garnished with sprigs of coriander or parsley.

<u>COOK NOTES:</u> In selecting scallops, look for fresh white ones with no odor.

Parchment paper, rather than aluminum foil or waxed paper, is incredibly moistureproof and heat-resistant and is treated with oil or silicone. Waxed paper often crumples and the wax can melt off while aluminum foil may react with acids such as the vinegar in the salsa.

ACCOMPANIMENTS:
Mushroom-Flavored Barley, and Jicama Salad

VARIATION:
* Tiny bay scallops can be substituted for the sea scallops.

Cajun Crab Cakes

YIELD: 4 crab cakes
CALORIES: 306 per crab cake
PREPARATION TIME: 10 minutes
COOKING TIME: 14–16 minutes

Crab cakes are traditionally prepared with white bread crumbs and cooked in fat of some sort. Here they are mixed with whole-grain bread crumbs and baked in a hot oven. The spiciness comes from the cayenne, which can be varied to taste. Serve the crab cakes as a light supper or lunch dish.

1 cup whole-grain bread crumbs
2 tablespoons finely chopped fresh chives or scallion greens
2 tablespoons finely chopped fresh parsley
2 tablespoons mayonnaise
1 egg, lightly beaten
1 tablespoon grainy-style Dijon mustard
1 teaspoon dry mustard
1 teaspoon Worcestershire sauce
½ teaspoon cayenne pepper or to taste
⅛ teaspoon crumbled dried dill
⅛ teaspoon ground coriander
⅛ teaspoon ground allspice
Salt and freshly ground black pepper to taste
½ pound crabmeat, flaked

Garnish:
Slices of lemon
Sprigs of parsley
Remoulade sauce (see Celery Root Remoulade, page 66)

1. Preheat the oven to 450°F. Spray a roasting pan generously with vegetable cooking spray.
2. In a large mixing bowl combine all the ingredients except the crabmeat and garnish; stir until well-mixed.
3. Fold in the crab, shape into balls, and flatten into cakes with the palm of your hand.

4. Place on the prepared pan and bake for 7 to 8 minutes per side, or until crisp and golden.
5. Serve hot with slices of lemon, parsley sprigs, and Remoulade Sauce.

ACCOMPANIMENTS:
Creole Black-Eyed Peas, and Coleslaw with Sweet and Sour Creamy Dressing

VARIATIONS:
* Chopped cornichons (French sour pickles) and minced capers can be added to taste.
* Since the cost of crab has skyrocketed, there is an inexpensive alternative called surimi, sea legs, or imitation crab that works well in this dish and many others. The imitation crab legs consist of fish and often some crab plus a sprinkling of crab juice that is pressed together and shaped into crab legs. The type of fish used differs regionally.

MAKE-IT-EASY TIP:
* To easily prepare fresh bread crumbs, place a few slices of whole-grain bread in a 350°F oven and bake for 10 to 15 minutes, or until dry. Allow to cool slightly and crush in a food processor.

MEATS

Veal

Make-It Easy Ossobuco	SERVES: 8 CALORIES: 382 per serving PREPARATION TIME: 25–30 minutes COOKING TIME: 2 hours

This traditional Milanese Italian specialty combines tender braised shanks of veal with a crunchy garnish of "gremolata," a combination of chopped fresh parsley, lemon peel, and garlic. This lighter version browns the veal shanks in the oven rather than sautéing them in butter and oil.

It is best to prepare ossobuco a day or two in advance and chill it so that the fat can congeal and easily be removed from the sauce before reheating—and the flavor improves as well.

1½ tablespoons olive oil
2 medium carrots, finely chopped
2 medium onions, finely chopped
2 stalks celery, finely chopped
2 cloves garlic, finely chopped
6 6½-pound veal shanks, sawed into 2"–2½" pieces (from the
*   shin of veal), about 10 pieces (see Note)*
2 tablespoons lemon juice
1 cup white wine
1 cup chicken broth
1 28-ounce can crushed tomatoes packed in puree, well-drained
1½ tablespoons potato starch dissolved in 3 tablespoons of
*   the broth*
1 tablespoon freshly grated lemon rind
1 tablespoon chopped fresh parsley
1 tablespoon chopped fresh basil, or 1 teaspoon crumbled dried
½ teaspoon crumbled dried thyme
1 bay leaf
Salt and freshly ground pepper to taste

Gremolata Garnish:
3 tablespoons finely chopped fresh parsley
1 tablespoon finely chopped lemon rind
1 teaspoon finely chopped garlic

1. Preheat the broiler. Brush the bottom of a large deep roasting pan with oil.
2. Place the chopped carrots, onions, celery, and garlic on the bottom of the pan. Top with veal shanks in a single layer. Squeeze the lemon juice over and sprinkle with ¼ cup wine.
3. Broil for 10 to 12 minutes, or until golden. Turn, baste with another ¼ cup wine, and continue to broil for an additional 10 to 12 minutes, or until the shanks are golden.
4. Reduce the oven to 325°F.
5. Remove the pan from the oven and transfer the veal and vegetables to a large Dutch oven. Place the pan on the range over medium heat, add the remaining ½ cup wine, and bring to a boil, incorporating the browned bits from the bottom of the pan.
6. Add the remaining ingredients to the pan, bring to a boil, and pour over veal. Cover and return to the oven for 1½ hours, or until the veal is very tender, stirring once or twice.
7. Remove the bay leaf and serve the ossobuco with the gremolata garnish.

COOK NOTE: The butcher may call this cut of meat shin of veal or shank, but they are one and the same. Make sure there is enough meat on the bones for sufficient portions.

ACCOMPANIMENTS:
Saffron-Flavored Rice, and Watercress Salad with Orange and Red Onion

VARIATIONS:
* If tomatoes packed in puree are unavailable, use regular whole juice-packed tomatoes; chop, drain off most of the liquid. Return the tomatoes to the can, and fill to the top with canned tomato puree.

* Finely chopped orange peel can be added to the gremolata.
* For thicker sauce without adding additional starch or flour, remove the shanks and puree the sauce in a food processor or blender until smooth.

MAKE-IT-EASY TIP:
* Ossobuco can be frozen and reheated successfully. Prepare the gremolata garnish just before serving.

Veal Chops Grilled with Herbes de Provence	SERVES: 4 CALORIES: 328 per serving PREPARATION TIME: 10 minutes MARINATING TIME: 15–20 minutes COOKING TIME: about 12 minutes

The veal chops will be most flavorful when cooked rare to medium-rare, or pink on the inside. If overcooked, veal tends to dry out, since it has little internal fat to keep it moist.

4 veal chops, cut 1" thick, well-trimmed
Salt and freshly ground pepper
1½ tablespoons olive oil
1 teaspoon crumbled herbes de Provence (see Note)

Garnish:
Sprigs of parsley or other fresh herbs

1. Preheat an outdoor grill or a broiler.
2. Place the veal chops in a shallow dish and season with salt and pepper.
3. Combine the oil with herbes de Provence and brush lightly over both sides of the chops. Allow to sit for 15 to 20 minutes at room temperature.

4. Grill the chops for 5 to 6 minutes per side, or until the desired degree of doneness.
5. Serve hot, garnished with parsley or other fresh herbs.

COOK NOTE: Herbes de Provence is a blend of herbs available in gourmet food shops and some supermarkets that is traditionally used in the south of France. If this blend is unavailable, substitute the following blend: 1 tablespoon each crumbled dried basil, oregano, and thyme; ½ teaspoon each crumbled dried sage and ground rosemary; and a pinch of dried lavender (optional).

ACCOMPANIMENTS:
Vegetable Pasta Primavera and Mixed Green Salad with Light Vinaigrette

VARIATION:
* Lamb chops can be substituted for the veal chops.

Cold Roast Veal with Creamy Sauce	SERVES: 8 CALORIES: 346 per serving PREPARATION TIME: 25–30 minutes COOKING TIME: 2–2½ hours CHILLING TIME: 6–8 hours or overnight

This lightened version of vitello tonnato is the perfect entrée to serve on a hot summer night. Instead of the traditional rich mayonnaise sauce, low-fat yogurt enriched with a small amount of mayonnaise is substituted. A single anchovy fillet is used as a more light and subtle flavoring instead of a combination of anchovy and tuna fish in the classic preparation.

3 pounds lean boneless roast of veal
2 carrots, peeled and cut into 2" lengths
1 small onion, sliced
1 stalk celery, cut into 2" lengths
1 clove garlic, sliced
2 sprigs of parsley
1 sprig of fresh thyme, or ½ teaspoon crumbled dried
1 bay leaf
Salt and freshly ground pepper to taste
5–6 cups chicken broth, or enough to cover

Sauce:
1 egg yolk, hard-cooked
1 scallion, coarsely chopped (green and white parts included)
1 anchovy fillet, patted dry on paper towel
2 teaspoons capers
½ cup plain low-fat yogurt
3 tablespoons mayonnaise
2 teaspoons lemon juice
1 teaspoon Dijon mustard (grainy-style preferred)
Salt and freshly ground pepper to taste

Garnish:
Lemon wedges
Parsley
Capers

1. Place the veal in a deep saucepan. Surround with the vegetables and seasonings. Add the chicken broth to cover. Bring to a boil, skim off the foam that accumulates on top, reduce heat, cover, and simmer slowly for 1½ to 2 hours, or until the meat is tender. Turn once or twice during cooking. Remove the lid and allow to cool for 30 minutes.

2. Remove the veal from the pan, wrap tightly in plastic wrap, and chill for 6 to 8 hours or overnight. Strain the vegetables from the broth, discard the bay leaf, and remove and discard any accumulated fat from the top of the liquid. Place the strained vegetables and ½ cup of the broth in a food processor or blender and puree until smooth. Remove from the food processor bowl and allow to cool.

3. Prepare the sauce by combining the egg yolk, scallion, anchovy, and capers in the food processor or blender and pulsating until just combined. Add the remaining ingredients and continue to process until smooth. Add the cooled vegetable puree, blend, place in a covered container, and refrigerate for 6 to 8 hours or overnight.

4. Slice the veal ¼" thick. Prettily arrange overlapping slices on a platter. Spoon the sauce over and chill until ready to serve.

5. Serve the veal chilled, garnished with lemon wedges, parsley, and capers.

VARIATIONS:

* Turkey breast may be substituted for the veal.
* Use less expensive cuts of veal such as the shoulder, boned and rolled rump roast, or leg (only if available reasonably priced), since this is a potted or braised dish and does not require the finer cuts of veal. Avoid the breast, however, which will be too fatty.

MAKE-IT-EASY TIP:

* Leftover strained broth can be frozen in 1- or 2-cup containers for future use.

Terrine de Veau
(Veal Loaf)

SERVES: 4
CALORIES: 316 per serving
PREPARATION TIME: 15 minutes
COOKING TIME: 45–50 minutes

An old-fashioned meat loaf generally combines ground beef and ground pork, both fatty meats, with bread crumbs and seasonings. Here the leaner ground veal is used as a substitute.

1¼ pound lean ground veal
1 10-ounce package frozen chopped spinach, thawed and totally squeezed dry
2 slices of whole-grain bread, crumbled
¼ cup finely chopped onion
3 tablespoons grated Parmesan cheese
1 egg, lightly beaten
1 teaspoon grated lemon rind
1 teaspoon Worcestershire sauce
½ teaspoon minced garlic
⅛ teaspoon grated fresh nutmeg
Salt and freshly ground pepper to taste

Garnish:
1 pint cherry tomatoes

1. Preheat the oven to 350°F.
2. In a mixing bowl combine the ingredients and mix well with your hands until well-combined. Form into a loaf, place in a loaf pan, and bake for 45 to 50 minutes.
3. Turn out onto a platter, garnish with the tomatoes, and serve warm.

ACCOMPANIMENTS:
Fettuccine with Creamy Mushroom Sauce, and Arugula and Persimmon Salad

VARIATION:
* Ground turkey or chicken can be substituted for the veal.

MAKE-IT-EASY TIP:
* A new gadget called a fat-free meat loaf pan is currently available. It consists of two pans, one fitting inside the other. The inner pan has holes in it to allow the fat to drip off into the other pan during cooking.

Veal Chop with Sauce of Sun-Dried Tomatoes and Vegetables	SERVES: 6 CALORIES: 393 per serving PREPARATION TIME: 15 minutes COOKING TIME: 35 to 40 minutes

Sun-dried tomatoes are naturally dried Roma tomatoes that are unsweetened and without preservatives. The variety used in this recipe are the dried ones that have not been packed in oil.

The chops can be cooked on an outdoor grill, under a broiler, or in a cast-iron pan with grill ridges that has been lightly sprayed with vegetable cooking spray.

15 sun-dried tomatoes soaked in hot water for 15 minutes
1 tablespoon olive oil
1 large onion, thinly sliced
6 large mushrooms, thinly sliced
2 tablespoons Madeira or Marsala wine (see Note)
½ cup chicken broth
1 teaspoon finely minced garlic
Salt and freshly ground pepper to taste
6 veal chops, cut 1" thick, well-trimmed
2 teaspoons arrowroot dissolved in 2 tablespoons chicken broth
1 tablespoon chopped fresh parsley

Garnish:
Sprigs of parsley

1. Squeeze the moisture from the tomatoes, cut into 2 or 3 pieces, and set aside.
2. In a large nonstick skillet heat the oil and sauté the onions over medium heat for 7 minutes; add the mushrooms and continue to sauté for 8 minutes, or until lightly golden, stirring occasionally.
3. Add the wine, allow to boil away, and add the tomatoes, broth, garlic, and salt and pepper; bring to a boil, reduce heat, and simmer slowly for 15 minutes.

4. In the meantime, preheat an outdoor grill, broiler, or skillet with grill ridges.
5. Grill the chops for 5 to 6 minutes per side, or until the desired degree of doneness. (Do not overcook.)
6. Add the arrowroot mixture and parsley to the sauce, stir until smooth and slightly thickened and serve over the finished chops garnished with parsley sprigs.

COOK NOTE: Madeira wines are fortified wines, usually sweet, although some, such as Sercial, are dry and pale, produced from a grape that came originally from the Rhine Valley of Germany. Marsala is a fortified dessert wine. There are several types of Marsala: the dry, which is the best to use in this recipe, the sweet, the medium, the aromatic, which has the addition of usually herbal flavorings.

ACCOMPANIMENTS:
Lemon Brown Rice and Fennel, Pepper, and Radish Salad with Lime Dressing

VARIATION:
* Lamb chops can be substituted for the veal chops.

Lamb

<table>
<tr><td>

Rack of Lamb with Mustard Coating

</td><td>

SERVES: 6
CALORIES PER SERVING: 309
PREPARATION TIME: 5–10 minutes
COOKING TIME: 30–35 minutes

</td></tr>
</table>

The mustard coating for the lamb is a variation on a recipe from Julia Child called Gigot à la Moutarde. The rack of lamb must be well-trimmed of all fat before painting with the coating mixture. For optimum flavor and juiciness, serve the lamb medium-rare.

2 1¾–2-pound racks of lamb, rib or loin section, well-trimmed

Mustard Coating:
1 cup grainy-style Dijon mustard
3 tablespoons reduced-sodium soy sauce
4 teaspoons olive oil
2 teaspoons finely minced garlic
1½ teaspoons finely minced fresh ginger
½ teaspoon ground rosemary
Salt and freshly ground pepper

Garnish:
Sprigs of mint

1. Preheat the oven to 425°F. Place the lamb fat side up in a roasting pan.
2. Combine the coating ingredients in a food processor, blender, or by hand and process until smooth. Generously paint the mixture over the lamb, covering the top and the sides.
3. Roast the lamb for 30 to 35 minutes, or until a meat thermometer registers 135° for medium-rare. Place the racks on a platter and allow to stand for 10 minutes.
4. Carve into chops and serve hot, garnished with mint sprigs.

ACCOMPANIMENTS:
Oven-Fried Potatoes and Spaghetti Squash Salad

VARIATIONS:
* Regular smooth-style Dijon mustard may be substituted for the grainy variety.
* 1 teaspoon ground ginger can be substituted for fresh.

MAKE-IT-EASY TIP:
* The lamb can be coated and kept in the refrigerator for several hours before cooking. Bring to room temperature for 1 hour before roasting.

Lancashire Hot Pot

SERVES: 6
CALORIES: 299 per serving
PREPARATION TIME: 15 minutes
COOKING TIME: 2½ hours

Every town in Lancashire, England, has its version of hot pot. This version of the flavorful lamb stew is cooked in a terra-cotta clay pot and is easy to prepare and more healthful since the vitamins and nutrients are retained. It is leaner, too, thanks to the porous clay pot, which is submerged in water for 20 minutes before using to soak up water like a sponge and then breathe while baking. With high oven temperatures, the water turns to steam, introducing a self-basting action, which eliminates the need for added fats or oils.

1½ pounds boiling potatoes, unpeeled, sliced ¾" thick
2 pounds lean lamb (preferably from the leg), cut into 1½" cubes
2 large onions, thinly sliced
4 carrots, peeled and sliced
1 teaspoon finely minced garlic
½ teaspoon crumbled dried thyme
Salt and lots of freshly ground pepper to taste
¾ cup dry red wine
½ cup beef broth

Garnish:

Chopped fresh parsley

1. Soak the clay pot and lid in cold water for 20 minutes.
2. Discard the water from the clay pot and lid and arrange the potatoes, lamb, onions, and carrots in layers in the pot.
3. Season lightly with garlic, thyme, and salt and pepper after each layer ending with the potatoes on top. Pour in the wine and broth.
4. Place the lid on the pot and put in a cold oven. (Clay pots must be put in a cold oven or they will crack from the intense sudden heat of a preheated oven.) Set the oven to 400°F and bake undisturbed for 2½ hours.
5. Serve stew hot garnished with chopped parsley.

ACCOMPANIMENTS:
Plain noodles and Two-Lettuce Salad with Creamy Horseradish Dressing

VARIATIONS:
* Lean beef can be substituted for the lamb.
* Turnips and parsnips can be added if desired.

MAKE-IT-EASY TIPS:
* If possible, remove any fat from the pan liquids before serving. The easiest way to remove excess fat from the gravy is with a gravy strainer.
* Never use scouring powder or detergent on a clay cooker since they block the pores and hinder its natural cooking methods. Clean pots with a stiff brush and lots of hot water.

Stir-Fried Lamb with Leeks

SERVES: 4
CALORIES: 382 per serving
PREPARATION TIME: 15 minutes
COOKING TIME: about 5 minutes

The meat from the leg of lamb is lean, particularly when trimmed well before cooking.

Marinade:
2 tablespoons reduced-sodium soy sauce
2 tablespoons cold water
4 teaspoons cornstarch
1 teaspoon sugar

1½ pounds boneless lean lamb, cut into 2"- × -2"- × -⅛" slices
3 large leeks, washed, cleaned, and cut into julienne strips
(mostly white and pale green parts included) (see Notes)
1 clove garlic, finely minced

Sauce:
2 tablespoons reduced-sodium soy sauce
2 tablespoons dry sherry
2 teaspoons rice or white wine vinegar
2 teaspoons toasted sesame oil

2 tablespoons peanut oil

1. In a medium bowl combine the marinade ingredients; add the lamb and set near the cooking area to marinate for 10 to 15 minutes while preparing the rest of the ingredients.
2. Place the leeks and garlic near the cooking area; mix the sauce ingredients together and set near the range.
3. Heat a wok or large heavy skillet, add the peanut oil, and when hot, stir-fry the leeks for 1 minute; add the garlic and continue to stir-fry for an additional 30 seconds.
4. Add the lamb and stir-fry just until the lamb loses its pink color, 1 to 2 minutes.
5. Add the sauce and stir until smooth.
6. Serve the lamb hot.

COOK NOTES: Select leeks with medium-sized necks and fresh green tops. They should give a little to the touch to indicate they are not tough and woody inside.

Wash leeks very carefully under cold running water to remove sand which lodges between the flat leaves.

ACCOMPANIMENTS:
Plain white rice and Sunomono

VARIATION:
* Lean beef can be substituted for the lamb.

MAKE-IT-EASY TIP:
* It is easier to cut the lamb when it's in a semi-frozen state.

Beef

Flank Steak Grilled with Grainy Mustard Marinade	SERVES: 8 CALORIES: 313 per serving PREPARATION TIME: 5 minutes MARINATING TIME: 1–3 hours COOKING TIME: 10 minutes

4 pounds lean flank steak, well-trimmed

Marinade:
¼ cup grainy-style Dijon mustard
2 tablespoons lime juice
1½ tablespoons reduced-sodium soy sauce
1 tablespoon hoisin sauce (see Note)
1 teaspoon Worcestershire sauce
1 teaspoon finely minced garlic
1 teaspoon finely minced fresh ginger
Freshly ground pepper to taste

1. Place the steak in a large glass or ceramic dish.
2. In a medium bowl whisk the marinade ingredients together,

pour over the meat, coat both sides, cover, and allow to marinate at room temperature for 1 hour, or in the refrigerator for 2 to 3 hours.

3. Preheat an outdoor grill or a broiler.
4. Remove the steak from the marinade and grill for 5 minutes on each side or until cooked to the desired doneness, basting occasionally with the marinade.
5. Serve immediately, sliced on the bias.

COOK NOTE: Hoisin sauce, also called haisein sauce or Peking sauce, is a thick, sweet sauce prepared from soybeans, flour, chili, red beans, and red color and sold in Chinese groceries, gourmet shops, and some supermarkets. Refrigerate after opening.

ACCOMPANIMENTS:
Stuffed Baked Potatoes, Crispy Onions, and Mixed Green Salad with Light Vinaigrette

VARIATIONS:
* Lemon juice can be substituted for the lime juice.
* The steak can be served cold if desired.

Marinated Chinese Hamburgers	SERVES: 4 CALORIES: 216 per serving PREPARATION TIME: 15 minutes COOKING TIME: 4–6 minutes

It is surprising how few calories are in one of these tasty hamburger patties.

16 ounces lean ground beef
2 egg whites
2 scallions, finely chopped (green and white parts included)
4 teaspoons reduced-sodium soy sauce
1 tablespoon cornstarch
2 teaspoons finely minced garlic
2 teaspoons finely minced fresh ginger
Freshly ground pepper to taste

1. Preheat an outdoor grill or a broiler until hot.
2. Combine the ingredients in a large mixing bowl, mix with your hands, and form into 4 patties.
3. Broil for 2 to 3 minutes per side, or until cooked to the desired degree of doneness.
4. Serve hot.

ACCOMPANIMENTS:
Oven-Fried Potatoes, Onions Baked in Their Skins, and Two-Lettuce Salad with Creamy Horseradish Dressing.

VARIATIONS:
* Lean ground veal can be substituted for the beef.
* Elephant garlic, also called Oriental garlic or great-headed garlic, can be substituted in this recipe, with its mild and delicate flavor, reminiscent of a leek. Elephant garlic differs from regular garlic in that it produces a number of small, thick-shelled cloves around the base of the bulb. It also has none of the aftereffects of regular garlic.

MAKE-IT-EASY TIP:
* Store garlic in a cool, dry place with good ventilation. If sprouts develop, the garlic is still useful although may not be quite as flavorful as when the garlic is fresher.

Beef Borscht

SERVES: 8
CALORIES: 383 per serving
PREPARATION TIME: 20 minutes
COOKING TIME: 2 hours

This recipe is more than just soup—it is substantial enough to qualify as a one-pot dinner.

2 beef shanks, well-trimmed
4 peppercorns
2 sprigs of dill
2 bay leaves

2 cups beef broth
2 cups crushed tomatoes packed in puree
1 16-ounce can diced beets, including liquid
2 large leeks, finely chopped (white part only)
2 carrots, peeled and finely chopped
2 onions, finely chopped
2 cloves garlic, finely minced
2–3 cups roughly chopped green cabbage (see Note)
Salt and freshly ground pepper to taste

Garnish:
1 cup plain low-fat yogurt
2 tablespoons freshly snipped dill
2 tablespoons chopped fresh parsley

1. In a small deep saucepan place the beef, peppercorns, dill sprigs, and bay leaves. Pour over the beef broth and enough water to cover. Bring to a boil, cover, reduce heat, and simmer for 1½ hours. Remove the meat from the liquid, cool slightly, discard the bones, and cut into small pieces.
2. Strain the liquid into a large pot, add the remaining ingredients and the beef pieces, bring to a boil, cover, reduce heat, and simmer for 30 minutes.
3. Stir the garnish ingredients together until smooth. Serve the soup hot with a dollop of yogurt garnish on top.

COOK NOTE: Select cabbage with solid heads that are heavy in relation to their size.

ACCOMPANIMENTS:
Two-Lettuce Salad with Creamy Horseradish Dressing and Whole-Wheat Popovers

VARIATIONS:
* A vegetarian version of this soup can be prepared by eliminating the beef but cooking the vegetables with the dill sprigs for flavor.
* The soup can be prepared several days in advance or frozen.
* Red cabbage can be substituted for green cabbage.

Stir-Fried Beef and Green Beans with Sun-Dried Tomatoes	SERVES: 4 CALORIES: 371 per serving PREPARATION TIME: 15–20 minutes MARINATING TIME: 1–3 hours COOKING TIME: about 8 minutes

Sun-dried tomatoes are naturally dried Roma tomatoes that are unsweetened and without preservatives. Select the dried variety rather than the oil-packed for use in this and other light recipes.

According to the late Nathan Pritikin, author of *The Pritikin Permanent Weight Loss Manual,* flank steak is one of the leanest cuts of meats available. In this dish, the proportion of vegetables is quite high, so each diner eats only 4 ounces or less of the meat.

1 pound green beans, tips removed, sliced diagonally into 2"
*   pieces*
1 pound lean flank steak, thinly sliced across the grain into 2"
*   square pieces*
1 egg white
2 tablespoons arrowroot
1 tablespoon reduced-sodium soy sauce
12–15 sun-dried tomatoes soaked in hot water for 15 minutes
1 teaspoon garlic, finely minced
3 scallions, cut into 2" sections (green parts only)

Sauce:
⅓ cup beef broth
2 tablespoons reduced-sodium soy sauce
2 tablespoons oyster sauce (available at Chinese groceries or at
*   most supermarkets)*
1 tablespoon dry sherry
1 teaspoon arrowroot
Freshly ground pepper to taste

2 tablespoons peanut oil
1 teaspoon hot chili oil

1. Bring a pot of water to a boil, drop in the green beans, and allow to cook for 1 to 2 minutes. Drain, run under cold water, and drain again.
2. Place the beef in a bowl, add the egg white, arrowroot, and soy sauce; stir until smooth and allow the beef to marinate until ready to cook—at least 1 hour at room temperature, or for 2 to 3 hours in the refrigerator.
3. Squeeze the moisture from the tomatoes, cut each into 2 or 3 pieces, and set near the cooking area along with the garlic and scallions.
4. Combine the sauce ingredients together and place alongside the other ingredients.
5. Heat a wok or large heavy nonstick skillet, add the peanut oil, and when hot, stir-fry the garlic and scallions for 30 seconds. Add the beef and continue to stir-fry for 2 minutes, or until it just loses its pink color.
6. Add the beans and tomatoes and continue to stir-fry for an additional 1 to 2 minutes. Add the sauce, stir to combine, cover, and allow to cook over medium heat for an additional minute.
7. Add the chili oil at the last moment, stir, and serve immediately.

ACCOMPANIMENTS:
Plain brown rice and Chilled Chinese Bean Curd in Sauce

VARIATIONS:
* Dried Chinese or Japanese mushrooms can be soaked, cut into quarters, and substituted for the sun-dried tomatoes.
* Asparagus can be substituted for the green beans.

MAKE-IT-EASY TIP:
* It is easier to cut beef when it's in a semi-frozen state.

Pork

Stir-Fried Pork with Sugar Snap Peas	SERVES: 4 CALORIES: 303 per serving PREPARATION TIME: 20 minutes COOKING TIME: 5–6 minutes

The pork found in the market today is much leaner than it used to be, and pound for pound it has almost the identical fat content and calorie count as beef.

1 pound pork tenderloins, well-trimmed, cut into julienne strips
½ pound sugar snap peas or Chinese snow peas, stringed (see Note)
1 4-ounce can whole peeled Chinese straw mushrooms, rinsed and drained
2 scallions, finely minced (both green and white parts included)
1 teaspoon finely minced fresh ginger

Sauce:
¼ cup chicken broth
2 tablespoons hoisin sauce (available at Chinese groceries or at many supermarkets)
1 tablespoon reduced-sodium soy sauce
1 tablespoon dry sherry
2 teaspoons arrowroot

2½ tablespoons peanut oil

1. Place the sliced pork strips, peas, mushrooms, scallions, and ginger in containers near the cooking area.
2. In a bowl combine the sauce ingredients, whisk, and place alongside the other ingredients.
3. Heat a wok or large skillet and add 1 tablespoon oil. Stir-fry the sugar snap peas for 1 minute; add the mushrooms, remove from the pan, and set aside on a warm platter.
4. Add the remaining 1½ tablespoons oil to the wok and stir-fry the scallion and ginger for 30 seconds. Add the pork and

continue to stir-fry for 2 to 3 minutes, or until the pork loses its pinkness. (Do not overcook.)

5. Add the sauce and stir to combine; return the snow peas to the pan, stir to coat with sauce, cover, and cook over medium heat for 1 minute.
6. Serve hot.

COOK NOTE: Sugar snap peas are a cross between a garden pea and Chinese snow pea that was introduced to produce markets in 1979. Select sugar snap peas that are round and fat like green beans with an even dark green color. Avoid flattish or yellowish pods, which will not have the sweet taste of the younger fresh ones. The whole pod is cooked and eaten.

ACCOMPANIMENTS:
Plain white or brown rice and Three-Pepper Salad with Oranges and Cumin-Flavored Dressing

VARIATIONS:
* Asparagus or broccoli florets can be substituted for the sugar snap peas.
* Four large dried Chinese or Japanese mushrooms soaked for 20 minutes in hot water then cut into quarters can be substituted for the straw mushrooms.

MAKE-IT-EASY TIPS:
* It is easier to cut the pork when it is semi-frozen.
* Straw mushrooms, sometimes called umbrella mushrooms, are available in cans. It is best to rinse off these slippery-textured mushrooms before cooking.

Grilled Marinated Pork with Sweet Mustard Sauce	SERVES: 4 CALORIES: 352 per serving PREPARATION TIME: 10–15 minutes MARINATING TIME: 5–6 hours or overnight COOKING TIME: 18 minutes

The pork tenderloin is a long cut of boneless meat from the underside of the loin. It is usually 12″ long and weighs about 1 pound. In this recipe, the cooked pork can be served with or without the sauce.

1 pound pork tenderloins

Marinade:
3 tablespoons frozen orange juice concentrate, thawed
2 tablespoons grainy-style Dijon mustard
2 tablespoons vegetable oil
2 tablespoons honey
1½ tablespoons reduced-sodium soy sauce
1 teaspoon finely minced garlic
1 teaspoon finely minced fresh ginger
Freshly ground pepper to taste

Sauce:
3 tablespoons frozen orange juice concentrate, thawed
2 tablespoons unsweetened apricot or peach marmalade or other preserves
2 tablespoons grainy-style Dijon mustard
1 tablespoon lemon juice
1 teaspoon grated lemon rind
1 teaspoon dry mustard

Garnish:
Thin slices of orange
Sprigs of watercress

1. Place the tenderloins in a small shallow dish. In a small bowl combine the marinade ingredients, mix well, and pour over

the pork tenderloin. Toss to coat, cover, and refrigerate for 5 to 6 hours or overnight, turning once. Bring the meat back to room temperature for 20 to 30 minutes before grilling.

2. Preheat an outdoor grill or a broiler.
3. Grill the pork over medium heat for about 18 minutes, or just until barely pink at the center, turning often and basting with the marinade.
4. In a small saucepan combine the sauce ingredients, bring to a boil, and cook, whisking until smooth.
5. Slice the tenderloin and serve hot, topped with sauce and garnished with orange slices and watercress sprigs.

ACCOMPANIMENTS:
Basmati Rice with Orange Flavor, Puree of Carrot with Lemon Accent, and Mixed Green Salad with Light Vinaigrette

MAKE-IT-EASY TIP:
* It is best to cut the long tenderloin in half so that the thinner tapered end can be removed from the heat first and the thicker piece can cook slightly longer.

CASSEROLES

Light Moussaka	SERVES: 6 CALORIES: 267 per serving PREPARATION TIME: 25 minutes COOKING TIME: about 1 hour

Moussaka is a classic Greek or Turkish dish consisting of layers of eggplant slices, chopped lamb or beef, and a rich layer of Béchamel, a white sauce prepared with cream. This light moussaka is prepared with grilled eggplant and potatoes that need only a light brushing of oil—rather than the usual cup or so needed to sauté the vegetables. The béchamel, too, has been lightened and prepared with nonfat milk.

6 medium red potatoes, sliced ¼" thick
2 tablespoons olive oil
1 large eggplant, sliced ¼" thick
1 cup part-skim ricotta cheese
1 10-ounce package frozen chopped spinach, thawed and totally squeezed dry of all moisture
1 egg
¼ cup plus 2 tablespoons chopped fresh parsley
2 tablespoons chopped fresh basil, or 1½ teaspoons crumbled dried
1 clove garlic, minced
1 teaspoon crumbled dried oregano
Salt and freshly ground pepper to taste
4 large tomatoes, sliced ½" thick
1 cup Béchamel Sauce (page 85)
1 tablespoon freshly grated Parmesan cheese

1. Preheat the broiler. Spray 2 cookie sheets with vegetable cooking spray.
2. Place a layer of potatoes on a cookie sheet, brush lightly

with 1 tablespoon oil, and broil for 3 to 4 minutes a side, or until golden. Repeat the process with the eggplant and remaining oil and set aside. Reduce the heat to 375° and coat a shallow 7"-×-11" or similar size baking dish with vegetable cooking spray.

3. In a food processor, blender, or by hand, combine the ricotta, spinach, egg, ¼ cup parsley, basil, garlic, oregano, and salt and pepper. Mix until smooth.

4. Place a layer of half the potatoes in the bottom of the prepared casserole followed by half the eggplant. Shake the seeds from tomato slices and place half the tomatoes over the eggplant layer. Top with the ricotta mixture then another set of layers of the remaining potatoes, eggplant, and tomatoes. Sprinkle with salt and pepper, top with béchamel sauce, and sprinkle with the 2 tablespoons parsley mixed with Parmesan cheese.

5. Bake for 40 minutes, or until hot, bubbling, and golden brown on top.

<u>COOK NOTE:</u> Select medium-sized eggplants that feel lightweight for their size. Large, heavy eggplants tend to taste bitter and contain more seeds.

ACCOMPANIMENTS:
Greek Salad with Lemon-Herb Dressing and Fluffy Corn Muffins

VARIATION:
* Well-drained canned tomatoes can be substituted for the fresh tomatoes.

MAKE-IT-EASY TIPS:
* Sliced eggplant absorbs fat easily, particularly if sautéed. By broiling the eggplant with a light brushing of oil, we can achieve the same results and a nice brown color without excess fat.
* An easy way to seed tomatoes is to cut them in half and gently squeeze the seeds out.

Polenta Lasagna

SERVES: 8
CALORIES: 246 per serving
PREPARATION TIME: 20–25 minutes
COOKING TIME: about 45 minutes

Polenta lasagna is a combination of cooked cornmeal layered into a wonderful baked casserole with tomato sauce and lean ground turkey.

Cornmeal Mixture:
1½ cups chicken broth
¾ cup yellow cornmeal (see Note)

Turkey Mixture:
1½ pounds lean ground turkey
1 medium onion, finely chopped
1 clove garlic, finely minced

Herb-Ricotta Mixture:
1 cup part-skim ricotta cheese
1 egg
2 tablespoons chopped fresh parsley
1 tablespoon chopped fresh basil, or 1 teaspoon crumbled dried
1 clove garlic, finely minced

2 cups Light Red Sauce (page 83)
¼ cup freshly grated Parmesan cheese

1. In a medium-sized heavy saucepan combine the broth and cornmeal. Stir until a paste is formed. Cook over medium heat for 10 minutes or less, until thickened, stirring often.
2. Preheat the oven to 350°F. Lightly spray a 9″ square or round baking dish with vegetable cooking spray.
3. In the meantime, in a skillet sauté the turkey with the onion and garlic over medium-high heat until the turkey crumbles. Drain off the fat and set aside.
4. In a food processor or by hand combine the herb-ricotta mixture and set aside.

5. Place one-third of the cornmeal mixture evenly across the bottom of the prepared casserole. Place half the turkey mixture over topped by 1 cup red sauce. Top this layer with one-third of the cornmeal mixture dropped in dollops all over, followed by half of the Parmesan cheese. Next, place the ricotta mixture, the remaining cornmeal, the remaining turkey, the remaining red sauce, and finally the rest of the Parmesan cheese.
6. Bake for 30 minutes, or until hot, bubbling, and warmed through.

COOK NOTE: Stone- or water-ground cornmeal is prepared from the whole corn, including the skin and the germ, and is therefore more nutritious than the granular kind. The stone- or water-ground is more perishable, so purchase this grain in smaller quantities.

ACCOMPANIMENTS:
Watercress Salad with Orange and Red Onion, and Whole-Wheat French Bread

VARIATION:
* Drained frozen chopped or quickly cooked fresh spinach can be added to herb mixture if desired.

Mexican Corn Pie with Chicken	SERVES: 6 CALORIES: 201 per serving PREPARATION TIME: 25–30 minutes COOKING TIME: 40–55 minutes

This tasty casserole uses cooked cornmeal layered with fresh vegetables and lean chicken for a flavorful one-dish meal.

1 cup cold water
½ cup plus 2 tablespoons yellow cornmeal
1 teaspoon chili powder
Salt
2 cups boiling chicken broth
2 whole skinless, boneless chicken breasts, cut into strips
½ cup chopped red onion
2 medium tomatoes, chopped
1 medium green pepper, seeded and chopped
1 medium red pepper, seeded and chopped
2 teaspoons finely minced garlic
Freshly ground pepper to taste
¼ cup chopped scallions (green and white parts included)
3 tablespoons grated sharp Cheddar cheese

Garnish:
Mexican Salsa (page 82)

1. In a medium-sized heavy saucepan combine the cold water, cornmeal, chili powder, and ½ teaspoon salt and stir until a paste is formed. Gradually add the boiling broth, place over low heat, and cook until thickened, 10 to 15 minutes, stirring occasionally.
2. Preheat the oven to 350°F. Spray a 9″ or 10″ square or round baking dish (or similar size dish) with vegetable cooking spray.
3. In the meantime, mix the chicken with the red onion, tomatoes, peppers, garlic, and salt and pepper and stir to combine.

4. Place a layer of half the cornmeal mixture on the bottom of the prepared baking dish. Cover with half of the chicken mixture. Repeat a second layer topping the pie with a mixture of the scallions and cheese.
5. Bake for 30 to 40 minutes, or until hot, bubbly, and thoroughly heated through.
6. Serve the pie hot, accompanied by the salsa.

ACCOMPANIMENTS:
Steamed corn tortillas (wrapped in foil and heated in a 325°F oven for 10 minutes or until hot) and Gazpacho Salad

VARIATION:
* Additional vegetables, such as julienned zucchini or hot green chilies, can be substituted or added to the chicken mixture as desired.

MAKE-IT-EASY TIP:
* The cooked cornmeal is easier to handle with wet hands.

PASTA, PIZZA, CREPES, RICE AND THEIR MORE EXOTIC RELATIVES

PASTA

Pasta with Light Red Sauce

SERVES: 6
CALORIES: 377 per serving
PREPARATION TIME: 5–10 minutes
COOKING TIME: 23 minutes

Lightly sautéed mushrooms are combined with the basic no-oil Light Red Sauce to create a flavorful topping for any type of pasta.

1 tablespoon olive oil
8 large mushrooms, wiped clean, thinly sliced (see Note)
4 cups Light Red Sauce (page 83)
1 pound spaghetti

Garnish:
2 tablespoons chopped fresh parsley
2 tablespoons grated Parmesan cheese

1. In a large nonstick skillet heat the oil and sauté the mushrooms over medium heat for 7 to 8 minutes, or until lightly golden.
2. Add the red sauce, stir to combine, bring to a boil, cover, reduce heat, and simmer slowly for 15 minutes, stirring occasionally.
3. In the meantime, cook the pasta in a pot of boiling water until just tender. Drain.
4. Top the hot pasta with sauce, toss well, and serve immediately garnished with parsley and cheese.

COOK NOTE: Mushrooms must never be washed but simply wiped clean with a damp cloth. If mushrooms are moist when sautéed, they will release so much moisture that they will steam instead of brown.

ACCOMPANIMENTS:
Watercress Salad with Orange and Red Onion, and Whole-Wheat French Bread

VARIATION:
* Mushrooms can be omitted and the pasta can simply be tossed with heated Light Red Sauce.

Fettuccine with Creamy Mushroom Sauce	SERVES: 4 CALORIES: 450 per serving PREPARATION TIME: 15–20 minutes COOKING TIME: 20 minutes

This cream sauce tastes rich but actually is prepared with low-fat milk that is reduced until thickened.

1 tablespoon olive oil
1 medium onion, finely minced
1 pound mushrooms, wiped clean, thinly sliced
12 ounces fettuccine
¼ cup dry red wine
1½ cups scalded low-fat milk
1 tablespoon finely chopped fresh chives
2 teaspoons arrowroot dissolved in 2 tablespoons chicken broth
2 tablespoons grated Parmesan cheese

Garnish:
2 tablespoons chopped fresh parsley

1. In a large nonstick skillet heat the oil and sauté the onion and mushrooms over medium heat for 8 to 10 minutes, or until golden, stirring often.

2. In the meantime, cook the fettuccine in a pot of boiling water until tender. Drain.

3. Add the wine to the onion mixture, increase heat, and cook until the liquid has been absorbed. Reduce heat to medium, add the scalded milk, and cook until the sauce thickens, about 3 minutes, stirring often.

4. Add the chives and arrowroot mixture, stir until smooth and thickened; add the cheese, stir, and place in a serving bowl.

5. Add the fettuccine to the serving bowl, toss well, garnish with parsley, and serve immediately.

ACCOMPANIMENTS:

Romaine Lettuce and Grapefruit Salad with Red Onion, and Whole-Wheat French Bread

VARIATION:

* For a sweeter taste, Marsala or Madeira wine can be substituted for the dry red wine.

MAKE-IT-EASY TIP:

* To scald milk easily, place in a nonstick saucepan and heat to a temperature just below its boiling point, when steam rises and bubbles begin to form around the edges.

California Pasta

SERVES: 6
CALORIES: 376 per serving
PREPARATION TIME: 15 minutes
COOKING TIME: 10–12 minutes

This recipe is a variation of my August Pasta from *Make It Easy in the Kitchen*. It should be prepared in the summer months when tomatoes are at their ripest and juiciest and basil is at its most plentiful. This variation increases the basil and adds some part-skim mozzarella cheese to create a delicious and healthful light dinner.

1 pound spaghetti
6 large very ripe, juicy tomatoes, cut into small chunks (see Note)
10 basil leaves, roughly chopped
2–3 ounces part-skim mozzarella, diced
2 tablespoons finely chopped fresh parsley
2 tablespoons olive oil
2 teaspoons finely minced garlic
Salt and freshly ground white pepper to taste

Garnish:
2 tablespoons grated Parmesan cheese

1. Cook the pasta in a pot of boiling water until just tender; drain.
2. In the meantime, place the remaining ingredients in a large serving bowl.
3. Toss the hot pasta with tomato-basil mixture, garnish with Parmesan cheese, and serve immediately.

COOK NOTE: This is a good time to use up overripe tomatoes, which will enhance the recipe.

ACCOMPANIMENTS:
Mushroom Salad and Whole-Wheat Popovers

VARIATIONS:
* Fusilli or similar size pasta twists can be substituted for the spaghetti.
* Serve leftovers as a cold pasta salad the next day by adding a few teaspoons of balsamic or red wine vinegar plus salt and pepper to taste.

Vegetarian Chili on Angel Hair Pasta	SERVES: 4 CALORIES: 369 per serving PREPARATION TIME: 25–30 minutes COOKING TIME: about 1 hour

This low-fat, low-calorie chili comes from a friend, Millie Loeb, who finds it one of the most satisfying and healthful dishes for those watching their calorie intake. The vegetables, which can be varied seasonally or to taste, are roughly chopped by hand but can also be sliced in a food processor if desired. Since chili powders vary in strength, it is advisable to add the spice to taste, a little at a time, tasting constantly, until the desired amount is achieved.

1 tablespoon olive oil
1 small red onion, roughly chopped
1 large carrot, peeled and roughly chopped
1 large stalk celery, roughly chopped
1 large zucchini, washed and roughly chopped
1 large yellow crookneck squash, washed and roughly chopped
1 large red, green, or yellow pepper, seeded and roughly chopped
3 large mushrooms, wiped dry, roughly chopped
½ cup dry vermouth
1 8-ounce can juice-packed tomatoes, roughly chopped, including liquid
¾ cup chicken broth
3 tablespoons tomato paste
2 tablespoons finely chopped fresh basil, or ½ teaspoon crumbled dried
2 tablespoons finely chopped fresh parsley
1 clove garlic, finely minced
2 teaspoons chili powder or to taste
1½ teaspoons ground cumin or to taste
½ teaspoon paprika
Salt and freshly ground pepper to taste
8 ounces capelli d'angelo (angel hair pasta) or capellini

Garnish:
2–3 tablespoons grated sharp Cheddar cheese

1. In a large nonstick skillet or Dutch oven heat the oil and sauté the fresh vegetables over medium heat for 7 to 8 minutes, or until softened, stirring often.
2. Add the vermouth and allow to boil for 1 to 2 minutes; add the tomatoes, chicken broth, tomato paste, and seasonings. Bring to a boil, cover, reduce heat, and simmer slowly for 40 to 45 minutes.
3. In the meantime, cook the pasta in a pot of boiling water until just tender; drain.
4. Pour the chili mixture over the hot pasta, toss, and serve immediately, garnished with the grated Cheddar.

ACCOMPANIMENT:
Fluffy Corn Muffins

VARIATIONS:
* The chili can be served without pasta as a vegetarian entrée thickened slightly by the addition of 2 tablespoons bulgur (cracked wheat) presoaked in ¼ cup boiling broth for 20 minutes. Add the soaked bulgur, stir well, and serve hot. Or else chill and serve cold, or serve at room temperature, the next day.
* Other vegetables and herbs can be added as desired.

MAKE-IT-EASY TIP:
* Always add wine, such as vermouth, before other liquid ingredients, to allow the alcohol to boil away.

Vegetable Pasta Primavera

SERVES: 6
CALORIES: 361 per serving
PREPARATION TIME: 25–30 minutes
COOKING TIME: 12–15 minutes

A classic pasta primavera, from which this recipe is derived, uses cream to bind the sauce. In this light version, a béchamel sauce prepared with nonfat milk is substituted. This pasta is best in summer when fresh basil is readily available; if it is not, substitute parsley and avoid the dried herb.

1 cup broccoli florets or diagonally cut asparagus
½ cup julienned zucchini
½ cup sliced mushrooms, wiped clean
½ pound dried spinach pasta
½ pound dried whole-wheat pasta
2 cups Béchamel Sauce (page 85)
1 sweet red pepper, seeded and julienned
1 green pepper, seeded and julienned
6 scallions, cut into ½" pieces (green and white parts included)
1 cup halved cherry tomatoes
½ cup chopped fresh basil (optional)
2 tablespoons grated lemon rind
2 tablespoons grated Parmesan cheese

1. In a pot with a steamer insert, heat water to a boil and steam the broccoli or asparagus for 1 to 2 minutes, and the zucchini and mushrooms for 30 seconds to 1 minute, or until barely tender.
2. In the meantime, cook the pasta in a pot of boiling water until just tender. Drain.
3. Drain the steamed vegetables and toss with the béchamel sauce. Add the remaining ingredients and toss again.
4. Pour the sauce over the hot drained pasta, toss, and serve immediately.

ACCOMPANIMENTS:
Romaine Lettuce and Grapefruit Salad with Red Onion, and Whole-Wheat Popovers

VARIATIONS:
* Substitute or add any seasonal vegetables desired: yellow squash, spinach leaves, carrots, baby peas, turnips, beets, celery, thawed, drained frozen artichoke hearts, etc. Steam all the vegetables until just tender.
* Light White Sauce (page 84) can be substituted for the Béchamel Sauce.
* Cook fresh pasta only 2 to 3 minutes and immediately drain and toss with the sauce.
* Fresh spinach or egg pasta, or any variety of dried pasta, may be used.
* Add lemon juice or vinegar to taste to cold leftovers for an easy pasta salad.
* For a heartier dish, add 1 cup sliced cooked chicken breast.

MAKE-IT-EASY TIPS:
* If you do not own a steamer basket, place a footed strainer in a saucepan. If not high enough, place on a small rack. The important thing about steaming is that the water should not touch the vegetables.
* Save nutritious leftover steaming water, or any vegetable cooking water, for use in cooked rice dishes and soups and stews.

Fusilli with Eggplant and Garlic Sauce	SERVES: 6 CALORIES: 373 per serving PREPARATION TIME: 20–25 minutes COOKING TIME: 30–35 minutes

The eggplant in the sauce is grilled with a light brushing of oil to reduce the fat content in the sauce.

1 medium eggplant, cut horizontally into ¼"-thick slices (see Note)
5 teaspoons olive oil
1 medium onion, finely chopped
2 medium carrots, peeled and finely chopped
1½ cups canned crushed tomatoes packed in puree
2 tablespoons finely chopped fresh basil, or ½ teaspoon crumbled dried
2 teaspoons finely minced garlic
¼ teaspoon red pepper flakes or to taste
Salt and freshly ground black pepper to taste
1 pound dried fusilli

Garnish:
2 tablespoons grated Parmesan cheese
2 tablespoons chopped fresh parsley

1. Preheat the broiler. Coat a broiling pan with vegetable cooking spray.
2. Place the eggplant in a single layer in the broiling pan, brush lightly with 2 teaspoons oil on one side and broil for 3 to 4 minutes, or until golden. Turn, brush with 2 more teaspoons oil and broil as before. Remove, slice into strips, and set aside.
3. In a nonstick skillet heat the remaining 1 tablespoon oil and sauté the onion and carrots over medium heat for 5 to 7 minutes, or until softened. Add the tomatoes, basil, garlic, red pepper, and salt and pepper, bring to a boil, cover, reduce heat, and simmer for 10 minutes. Add the eggplant strips and continue to cook for an additional 10 minutes.

4. In the meantime, cook the pasta in a pot of boiling water until just tender. Drain.
5. Toss the hot pasta with the sauce, top with Parmesan cheese and parsley, and serve hot.

COOK NOTE: It is unnecessary to peel eggplant. It has more texture and is more nutritious with the peel on.

ACCOMPANIMENTS:
Greek Salad with Lemon-Herb Dressing and Whole-Wheat French Bread

VARIATIONS:
* If tomatoes packed in puree are unavailable, use regular whole juice-packed tomatoes; chop, drain off most of the liquid. Return the tomatoes to the can, and fill to the top with canned tomato puree.
* Broiled zucchini can be added to the sauce along with the eggplant.
* You can use fresh rather than dried pasta: Cook only 2 minutes, or until just cooked. Do not overcook.

Hot and Spicy Chinese Noodles	SERVES: 4 CALORIES: 488 per serving PREPARATION TIME: 20 minutes COOKING TIME: 10 minutes

These spicy noodles have texture from lots of crunchy vegetables and have spiciness from chili paste with garlic. There is very little oil in the sauce, making it low in fat and low in calories.

2 scallions, finely minced (green and white parts included)
1½ teaspoons finely minced ginger
1½ teaspoons finely minced garlic
1 large zucchini, cut into julienne strips
2 crookneck yellow squash, cut into julienne strips
1 cup mung bean sprouts
¼ pound bay shrimp

Sauce:

3 tablespoons reduced-sodium soy sauce

1 tablespoon dry sherry

2 teaspoons toasted sesame oil

2 teaspoons Chinese Chenkung vinegar or red wine vinegar (see Notes)

½ teaspoon chili paste with garlic (available at Chinese grocery stores or at many supermarkets)

½ teaspoon sugar

12 ounces dried Chinese noodles or Italian spaghetti (see Notes)

2 tablespoons peanut oil

2 tablespoons roasted sesame seeds

Garnish:

Chopped fresh cilantro (coriander) or parsley

1. Place the scallions, ginger, and garlic on a plate near the cooking area. Organize the zucchini, yellow squash, sprouts, and shrimp and place alongside the scallions.
2. In a cup combine sauce ingredients, stir, and place near the cooking area.
3. Cook the pasta in a pot of boiling water until just tender. Drain.
4. In the meantime, heat a wok or large skillet, add the peanut oil, and stir-fry the scallions, ginger, and garlic for 30 seconds. Add the zucchini, squash, sprouts, and shrimp and continue to stir-fry for 2 minutes. Add the sauce and stir well.
5. Add the drained noodles, stir until coated with the sauce and vegetables, stir in the sesame seeds, and serve hot, garnished with cilantro.

COOK NOTES: Chenkung rice vinegar, also known as Chinkiang, Chekiang or Chen-jung, is a well-aged black Chinese vinegar that is distinctively mellow in flavor. A mild red wine vinegar, or even a raspberry vinegar, will be an adequate substitute.

Dried Chinese egg noodles need only 5 minutes to cook while the fresh Chinese egg noodles only 2 to 3 minutes. Do not substitute very fine noodles such as capellini or capelli d'angelo (angel hair), which tend to become gummy with the sauce.

ACCOMPANIMENT:
Snow Pea Salad with Lemon-Ginger Dressing

VARIATIONS:
* Shredded cooked chicken or lean beef can be substituted for the bay shrimp.
* Blanched broccoli florets, diagonally cut string beans or aspar-agus, julienned peppers, or other seasonal vegetables can be substituted for the zucchini and yellow squash.

Baked Pasta with Spinach-Ricotta Sauce	SERVES: 6 CALORIES: 340 per serving PREPARATION TIME: 20 minutes COOKING TIME: 6–8 minutes

This is an old-fashioned noodle bake but without the fatty butter or sour cream.

8 ounces broad noodles

Sauce:
1 10-ounce package frozen spinach, thawed
2 cups part-skim ricotta cheese
2 eggs, lightly beaten
¼ cup grated Parmesan cheese
2 tablespoons finely chopped fresh basil
2 tablespoons finely chopped fresh parsley
1 teaspoon finely minced garlic
¼ teaspoon grated nutmeg
Salt and freshly ground white pepper to taste

Garnish:
2 tablespoons grated Parmesan cheese

1. Preheat the oven to 350°F. (If baking in glass, preheat the oven to 325°F.) Spray an 8″ to 9″ square baking dish with vegetable cooking spray.
2. Cook the pasta in a pot of boiling water until just tender. Drain.
3. In the meantime, combine the sauce ingredients in a large bowl and stir until smooth.
4. Toss the hot pasta with the sauce, making sure to coat the noodles well. Pour into the prepared dish, top with the Par-

mesan cheese, and bake for 25 to 30 minutes, or until very hot.

5.   Serve immediately.

ACCOMPANIMENTS:
Gazpacho Salad and Whole-Wheat French Bread

VARIATION:
* Bow-tie pasta can be substituted for the broad noodles.

Chicken with Tomatoes and Fresh Herbs on Linguine	SERVES: 8 CALORIES: 343 per serving PREPARATION TIME: 20−25 minutes COOKING TIME: about 55 minutes

This recipe is a variation of an Italian dish called chicken cacciatore, which means "in the style of the hunter," usually in a sauce of tomatoes, wine, and garlic. Here the sauce is served on a bed of linguine. Chicken breasts are poached in the finished sauce without added fats.

1 tablespoon olive oil
1 medium onion, finely chopped
1 red or green pepper, seeded and finely chopped
6 large mushrooms, wiped clean, thinly sliced
⅓ cup dry red wine
1 28-ounce can crushed tomatoes packed in puree
1 clove garlic, finely minced
1 teaspoon sugar
Salt and freshly ground pepper to taste
2 whole skinless, boneless chicken breasts (about 1 pound), cut into 1½" cubes
2 tablespoons chopped fresh basil, or 1 teaspoon crumbled dried
1 tablespoon chopped fresh parsley
1 tablespoon chopped fresh sage leaves, or ½ teaspoon crumbled dried
1 pound linguine

Garnish:
2–3 tablespoons grated Parmesan cheese
1–2 tablespoons chopped fresh parsley

1. In a large nonstick saucepan or skillet heat the oil and sauté the onion, pepper, and mushrooms over medium heat for 6 to 7 minutes, until softened, stirring occasionally.
2. Add the wine, bring to a boil, and allow to boil for 2 minutes. Add the tomatoes, garlic, sugar, and salt and pepper, and stir to combine; bring to a second boil, cover, reduce heat, and simmer for 25 minutes. Add the chicken, stir, cover, and continue to cook for 15 minutes, or until the chicken is tender.
3. When the sauce is nearly finished, cook the pasta in a pot of boiling water until just tender. Drain.
4. In the meantime, add the basil, parsley, and sage to the sauce and continue to simmer for 5 minutes.
5. Toss the hot pasta with the sauce, garnish with cheese and parsley, and serve immediately.

ACCOMPANIMENTS:
Mixed Green Salad with Light Vinaigrette and Whole-Wheat French Bread

VARIATIONS:
* If tomatoes packed in puree are unavailable, use regular whole juice-packed tomatoes; chop, drain off most of the liquid. Return the tomatoes to the can, and fill to the top with canned tomato puree.
* Fusilli or other pasta twists can be substituted for the linguine.

MAKE-IT-EASY TIPS:
* Fresh sage is difficult to locate in supermarkets but can be grown outdoors or on a windowsill in full sunlight.
* Prepare the chicken and sauce a day in advance through step 2, cool, and refrigerate. The next day remove any congealed fat which has risen to the top, reheat, and proceed with the recipe.

Stir-Fried Tofu with Vegetables on Buckwheat Noodles	SERVES: 6 CALORIES: 272 per serving PREPARATION TIME: 25 minutes COOKING TIME: about 10 minutes

Chinese-style tofu, which is firmer than the Japanese or health food store variety of tofu, is the best tofu for use in stir-frying. The others will fall apart during cooking and will not readily absorb the flavor of the dish. Japanese buckwheat noodles—soba—are actually a combination of wheat and buckwheat flours available in many east Asian markets as well as health food stores.

8 Chinese or Japanese shiitake dried mushrooms soaked in
*   warm water for 30 minutes*
1 bunch watercress, tough stems trimmed, washed, dried
1 red bell pepper, seeded and julienned
1 mild green chile pepper, seeded and julienned
1 tablespoon chopped Chinese parsley (cilantro or coriander)

Sauce:
½ cup chicken broth
2–3 tablespoons reduced-sodium soy sauce or to taste
2 tablespoons dry sherry
1½ teaspoons arrowroot
1 teaspoon hot chili oil

½ pound buckwheat noodles (soba)
2 tablespoons peanut oil
1 scallion, cut into 1" lengths (green and white parts included)
1 teaspoon finely minced garlic
1 1-pound package Chinese-style tofu (either 1 large or 4 small
*   cakes), cut into 1" cubes (see Notes)*

Garnish:
Chinese parsley (cilantro or coriander)

1. Squeeze the mushrooms dry, remove the stems, and cut into julienne strips. Cut the watercress into 2″ lengths. Combine the red pepper, chile pepper, and Chinese parsley with the other vegetables and set aside. In a small bowl, combine the sauce ingredients together and whisk until smooth.
2. Cook the soba in a pot of boiling water, stir, allow the water to reach a second boil, and cook over medium heat for 3 to 5 minutes, or until just tender. Drain.
3. Heat a wok or large skillet, add the oil, and stir-fry the scallion and garlic for 30 seconds. Add the vegetables and stir-fry for 2 to 3 minutes, or until just cooked.
4. Add the tofu and shake the pan, without stirring, to combine. Whisk in the soy sauce mixture, pour over the tofu, bring to a boil, and stir until smooth and slightly thickened.
5. Gently toss the tofu and vegetables with the soba and serve hot, garnished with Chinese parsley.

COOK NOTES: Tofu is available in 1 pound or occasionally 14.2-ounce packages. Either size will work in this recipe. The fragile tofu is shaken, not stirred into the mixture, to avoid breaking it apart.

If only Japanese or soft-variety of bean curd is available, you can press the water from the curds to make them firmer. Wrap each bean curd cake (or slice a whole cake into 2″ horizontal lengths) in cheesecloth and place in a large dish; place a 2- to 3-pound weight on top. A large book or several cans will do. After 1 hour, unwrap the bean curd and proceed with the recipe.

ACCOMPANIMENT:
Sunomono

VARIATION:
*   Bay shrimp, crab, fish, or even chicken can be added to turn this vegetable dish into a substantial entrée.

Linguine with Sweet Red Pepper Sauce

SERVES: 6
CALORIES: 364 per serving
PREPARATION TIME: 15–20 minutes
COOKING TIME: about 55 minutes

This wonderful red pepper sauce is prepared with only 1 tablespoon olive oil. A pear cooked in the sauce adds natural sweetness.

1 tablespoon olive oil
4 sweet red peppers, seeded and julienned (see Note)
2 carrots, finely chopped
2 cups canned crushed tomatoes, packed in puree
½ ripe Anjou, Bartlett, or Comice pear, peeled and thinly sliced
1 tablespoon chopped fresh basil, or ½ teaspoon crumbled dried
1 teaspoon finely minced garlic
Salt and freshly ground pepper to taste
1 pound linguine

Garnish:
2 tablespoons grated Parmesan cheese
2 tablespoons chopped fresh parsley

1. In a large nonstick saucepan heat the oil and sauté the peppers and carrots over medium heat, for 5 to 7 minutes, or until softened.
2. Add the remaining ingredients, bring to a boil, cover, reduce heat, and simmer for 45 minutes, or until very tender.
3. In the meantime, cook the pasta in a pot of boiling water until just tender. Drain.
4. Puree the vegetables in a food processor or blender, adjust the seasonings, and toss with the cooked pasta.
5. Serve hot, garnished with cheese and parsley.

COOK NOTE: Sweet red peppers should be well-shaped, firm, and have a glossy red color. These peppers do not keep well, so purchase just before using.

ACCOMPANIMENTS:
Watercress Salad with Orange and Red Onion, and Whole-Wheat Popovers

VARIATIONS:
* If tomatoes packed in puree are unavailable, use regular whole juice-packed tomatoes; chop, drain off most of the liquid. Return the tomatoes to the can, and fill to the top with canned tomato puree.
* Two yellow peppers and 2 sweet red peppers can be substituted for the 4 red peppers.

Asparagus Flan with Pasta	SERVES: 6 CALORIES: 175 per serving PREPARATION TIME: 20 minutes COOKING TIME: about 45 minutes

This vegetable flan is a light version of a quiche with pasta and vegetables. It is prepared with nonfat and low-fat milk instead of half and half. The eggs, milk, and cheese are pureed to smooth out the texture of the ricotta.

1 cup small dried pasta shells
1 pound asparagus, stalks trimmed, cut on the bias into 1½"
  lengths (2 cups)
3 eggs
½ cup nonfat milk
½ cup low-fat milk
½ cup part-skim ricotta cheese
2 tablespoons grated Parmesan cheese
1 scallion, finely minced
1 teaspoon Worcestershire sauce
Salt and freshly ground white pepper to taste

1. Preheat the oven to 375°F. Spray an 8" square ovenproof dish with vegetable cooking spray.
2. Drop the pasta into a pot of boiling water and cook until just tender. Drain, run under cold water. Drain again.

3. Drop the asparagus into a pot of boiling water, allow the water to return to a full boil, drain, run under cold water. Drain again.

4. In a food processor or blender combine the remaining ingredients and puree for just a few seconds until smooth.

5. Place the drained pasta and asparagus in the prepared dish and stir to distribute evenly. Pour the remaining ingredients over and bake for 40 minutes, or until lightly golden and a knife inserted in the center comes out clean.

6. Cut into squares and serve hot.

ACCOMPANIMENTS:
Mushroom Salad and Fluffy Corn Muffins

VARIATIONS:
* Tricolor pastas make a pretty presentation in this recipe.
* Substitute any seasonal vegetables desired or use any leftover steamed or cooked vegetables.

Chinese Stir-Fried Fish and Three Squashes on Noodles	SERVES: 4 CALORIES: 474 per serving PREPARATION TIME: 20 minutes COOKING TIME: about 10 minutes

Stir-frying requires complete organization beforehand since the cooking is done at the last minute. All ingredients should be assembled near the cooking area ready to be added. The pasta should be started at the same time as the stir-frying so that both are completed at the same time.

Monkfish, also called lotte, angler, allmouth, bellyfish, and goosefish, has a mild flavor and a texture similar to lobster. Because monkfish is so firm, it is excellent for stir-frying.

2 pattypan squash, cut in julienned strips
2 crookneck yellow squash, cut in julienned strips
2 medium zucchini, cut in julienned strips
2 teaspoons finely minced ginger

1 teaspoon finely minced garlic
1¼ pounds monkfish or other fleshy fish, cut into 1½" pieces
½ pound Chinese noodles or spaghetti
2 tablespoons peanut oil

Sauce:
½ cup chicken broth
3 tablespoons reduced-sodium soy sauce
2 tablespoons dry sherry
1 tablespoon arrowroot
1 teaspoon Chinese chili paste with garlic

Garnish:
Chinese parsley (cilantro or coriander)

1. Place the squashes and zucchini on a plate near the cooking area. Combine the ginger and garlic and place near the cooking area along with the fish.
2. Cook the pasta in a pot of boiling water until just tender. Drain.
3. In the meantime, heat a wok or large skillet, add the oil, and stir-fry the ginger and garlic for 30 seconds. Add the vegetables and continue to stir-fry for an additional 1 to 2 minutes. Add the fish and stir-fry for 2 to 3 minutes, or until the fish is no longer opaque.
4. Combine the sauce ingredients, add to the wok, stir, cover, reduce heat to medium, and simmer for 2 minutes.
5. Toss the drained pasta with the fish mixture and serve hot, garnished with Chinese parsley.

ACCOMPANIMENT:
Snow Pea Salad with Lemon-Ginger Dressing

VARIATION:
* 1 large head broccoli broken into florets, or 1 pound asparagus, trimmed, and sliced into 1" pieces can be substituted for the squash.

Pasta with Clams in Red Sauce

SERVES: 6
CALORIES: 441 per serving
PREPARATION TIME: 25 minutes
SOAKING TIME: 20 to 30 minutes
COOKING TIME: about 35 minutes

Hard-shell clams such as littlenecks or cherrystones are best for this dish but, if necessary, the soft-shell variety steamer clams can be used.

2½–3 dozen (5 pounds) littleneck or cherrystone clams (see Notes)
2 tablespoons cornmeal
1½ tablespoons olive oil
1 medium onion, finely chopped
2 leeks, finely chopped (white part only)
2 carrots, peeled and finely chopped
2 tablespoons dry white wine
1 28-ounce can crushed tomatoes packed in puree, well-drained
2 teaspoons finely minced garlic
1 teaspoon lemon juice
½ teaspoon sugar
⅛ teaspoon powdered saffron, or ¼ teaspoon saffron threads dissolved in 2 tablespoons hot water
⅛ teaspoon red pepper flakes or to taste
Salt and freshly ground black pepper to taste
12 ounces spaghetti or linguine

Garnish:
Grated Parmesan cheese
Chopped fresh parsley

1. Place the clams in a large bowl, fill with cold water, and sprinkle with cornmeal. Allow to soak for 20 to 30 minutes. Rinse, place in a covered container, and chill until ready to cook.
2. In a large nonstick skillet heat the olive oil, and sauté the onion, leeks, and carrots over medium heat, for 5 to 7 min-

utes, or until just soft. Add the white wine, allow to boil, then add the tomatoes, garlic, lemon juice, sugar, saffron, red pepper, and salt and pepper. Stir, bring to a boil, cover, and simmer very slowly for 25 minutes.

3. In the meantime, cook the pasta in a pot of boiling water until just tender. Drain.
4. Add the clams to the sauce, cover, and cook over medium heat for 3 to 5 minutes, or until the clams open.
5. Top the cooked pasta with the sauce, toss to combine, and serve immediately, garnished with cheese and parsley.

COOK NOTES: A tightly closed shell is the best indication of a fresh clam. Discard all clams that are not tightly shut before cooking.

Cornmeal is added to the clams' soaking water to help clean them. The clams take it in and spit it out along with any sand that is in the shell.

ACCOMPANIMENTS:
Mixed Green Salad with Light Vinaigrette and Whole-Wheat French Bread

VARIATIONS:
* If tomatoes packed in puree are unavailable, use regular whole juice-packed tomatoes; chop, drain off most of the liquid. Return tomatoes to the can, and fill to the top with canned tomato puree.
* Mussels, shrimp, lobster, or any other seafood or even fleshy fish can be substituted for the clams.

MAKE-IT-EASY-TIP:
* The sauce can be prepared in advance up through step 2 and refrigerated or even frozen until ready to add seafood. Reheat and continue with the recipe.

Pasta with Moules Marinière (Pasta with Marine-Style Mussels)

SERVES: 6
CALORIES: 359 per serving
PREPARATION TIME: 15–20 minutes
COOKING TIME: 15–20 minutes

There is an old French saying: "Fish must swim three times. Once in water, then in butter, and finally in wine." The following recipe adheres to this old adage but gives the fish only 1 tablespoon butter for the second swim.

3½ pounds mussels
1 tablespoon unsalted butter or margarine
1 teaspoon olive oil
4 shallots, finely minced
1 large leek, thoroughly cleaned, finely minced (white part only)
1 stalk celery, finely minced
1 cup dry white wine or vermouth
½ cup chicken broth
1 bay leaf
Salt and freshly ground pepper to taste
12 ounces linguine

Garnish:
2 tablespoons finely chopped fresh parsley
2 tablespoons finely chopped fresh chives or scallion greens

1. Discard any open and broken mussels or any not firmly closed. Place them in cold water immediately and scrub the shells with a stiff brush, removing all dirt. Cut off the "beard," the hairy material attached to the shell. Wash the mussels in several changes of cold water until the water is free of sand.
2. In a large nonstick pot heat the butter or margarine and oil

and sauté the shallots, leek, and celery over medium heat for 7 minutes, or until just softened, stirring often.

3. Add the white wine and allow to boil; add the broth, bay leaf, salt and pepper, bring to a boil, reduce heat, and simmer for 3 minutes. Add the mussels, cover, and cook for 5 to 10 minutes, or until the shells open, shaking the pan occasionally.
4. In the meantime, cook the pasta in a pot of boiling water until just tender. Drain.
5. Toss the hot pasta with the mussels and liquid, top with parsley and chives, and serve immediately.

ACCOMPANIMENTS:
Fennel, Pepper, and Radish Salad with Lime Dressing, and Whole-Wheat French Bread

VARIATION:
*   The white parts of scallions can be substituted for the shallots.

MAKE-IT-EASY TIP:
*   If a large nonstick pot is unavailable, sauté the shallots, leek, and celery in a nonstick skillet until softened, add wine, allow to boil, and transfer to a large pot.

PIZZA

Calzone Filled with Chicken, Spinach, and Ricotta	YIELD: 6 calzone CALORIES: 434 per calzone PREPARATION TIME: 20 minutes COOKING TIME: 15–20 minutes

Calzone are turnovers made with pizza dough that is rolled, filled, and baked. Here, again, we use the no-oil or fat whole-wheat French bread dough, which is easily prepared and easily rolled. There is no need to let the bread dough rise for calzone —and the freshly made unleavened dough is easier to work with.

½ recipe Whole-Wheat French Bread, not risen (page 326)
1 egg white, lightly beaten
3 whole skinless, boneless chicken breasts, each halved and then each half sliced into 4 pieces

Filling (1½ cups):
1 10-ounce package frozen chopped spinach, thawed and totally squeezed dry of moisture
8 ounces part-skim ricotta cheese
1 teaspoon minced garlic
1 egg white
4 teaspoons grated Parmesan cheese
1 tablespoon chopped fresh parsley
Pinch of grated nutmeg
Salt and freshly ground white pepper to taste

Sprig of fresh herbs (thyme, parsley, oregano) for decoration (optional)

1. Preheat oven to 400°F.
2. With kitchen shears cut the dough into 6 pieces. On a floured board press each piece into a circle. Roll each circle into an oval 8″ long by about 6″ wide. Brush a 1″ border of the edges with egg white.

3. Place half of a chicken breast (cut into 4 strips) just above the center of the dough.
4. Combine the filling ingredients together in a food processor or by hand and mix until smooth. Place ¼ cup of the filling on top of the chicken and fold over, pressing the edges together.
5. Crimp with a fork, top with a sprig of fresh herbs, and paint with egg white. Finish the remaining dough and fillings and place the calzone on a nonstick baking sheet.
6. Bake for 15 to 20 minutes, or until golden and crisp on top.
7. Serve immediately.

VARIATION:
* Any variety of light fillings can be substituted. Try shrimp with scallions, low-fat cheese, and tomatoes; or wild mushrooms, garlic, and peppers. By all means be creative and invent your own fillings with seasonal ingredients!

MAKE-IT-EASY TIP:
* Calzone can be filled and frozen, uncooked, for future use. Thaw and bake as above.

Light Pizza with Red Sauce, Mushrooms, Onions, and Cheese	SERVES: 8 CALORIES: 197 per one-slice serving PREPARATION TIME: 15 minutes COOKING TIME: 20 minutes

This recipe makes enough for two pizzas using the no-oil or fat whole-wheat French bread which is easily prepared in a food processor and can be frozen in advance. There is no need to let the bread rise for pizza. It is easier to work with the freshly made unleavened dough.

Try this Italian-style topping or invent a topping of your own such as wild mushrooms, low-fat cheese, and garlic or shrimp, scallions and tomatoes.

½ recipe Whole-Wheat French Bread, not risen (page 326)
1 egg white, lightly beaten
¾ cup Light Red Sauce (page 83)
10 medium mushrooms, wiped clean, sliced (see Note)
1 small red onion, thinly sliced
½ cup low-fat, low-sodium Muenster cheese (or similar part-skim cheese such as mozzarella)
2 tablespoons grated Parmesan cheese

1. Preheat the oven to 400°F.
2. With kitchen shears, cut the dough into 2 pieces. On a floured board press each piece into a circle. Roll each circle into a 12" round. Brush a 1" border of the edges with egg white. Transfer the dough to a nonstick baking pan.
3. Divide the red sauce between the two pizzas, top with mushrooms, onions, Muenster cheese, and finally a sprinkling of Parmesan cheese.
4. Bake the pizzas for 20 minutes, or until the edges are crisp and the cheese is hot and bubbly.
5. Serve immediately.

COOK NOTE: Don't peel mushrooms or you will lose valuable flavor, nutrients, and texture. Just cut off a thin slice from the bottom of the stem, wipe with lemon-soaked paper towel to clean, and slice.

VARIATION:
* Choose any variety of light toppings that you desire: shrimp, leek, and feta cheese; or shrimp, scallion, tomato, with Parmesan; or tomato puree, three kinds of peppers, fresh basil, and garlic.

Ricotta Cheese Whole-Wheat Blintzes	YIELD: 10 blintzes CALORIES: 165 per blintz PREPARATION TIME: 20 minutes COOKING TIME: 25–30 minutes

These unsweetened blintzes, formed from whole-wheat crepes, are designed to be served with a topping of naturally sweetened apple butter or apple sauce. If you prefer the filling sweetened, 1 to 2 tablespoons honey can be added to taste.

Filling:
1¾ cups skim-milk ricotta cheese
2 tablespoons golden raisins
1 egg, lightly beaten
1 teaspoon vanilla
¼ teaspoon ground cinnamon

Crepe Batter:
2 eggs, lightly beaten
1¾ cups skim milk
1 cup whole-wheat flour
Pinch of salt

1 tablespoon unsalted butter or margarine, softened

Topping:
Unsweetened apple butter or unsweetened apple sauce

1. In a bowl combine the filling ingredients, cover, and chill until ready to use.
2. In a separate mixing bowl beat the eggs and milk until smooth. Add the flour and salt and continue to beat until well-combined.
3. Preheat a 10″ omelet skillet over medium-high heat. Coat the surface with vegetable cooking spray. Using a ¼-cup ladle or similar measuring tool, pour the batter into a pan and quickly turn the pan to distribute evenly over the bot-

tom. Cook the crepe for about 1 minute, or until dry on top and lightly browned on bottom. Turn the pan over and flip the crepe out onto a towel to cool. (The crepe should be brown side up.) Continue to cook the crepes, spraying the pan every other time.

4. Preheat the oven to 400°F. Coat a large shallow baking dish with the vegetable cooking spray.
5. To form a blintz from a crepe, spoon 2 heaping tablespoons of the filling in the center of the browned side of each crepe. Fold 2 sides over the filling and then fold in the remaining ends, envelope style, enclosing the filling completely.
6. Place the blintzes in the prepared pan, fold side down; brush lightly with butter or margarine and bake for 25 minutes, or until puffed and beginning to crisp.
7. Serve hot with apple butter or apple sauce.

VARIATIONS:
* Pot or farmer cheese can be substituted for the ricotta.
* For a savory crepe, prepare the filling with chives and freshly ground pepper and omit the apple sauce or apple butter.
* For smaller crepes, use a 7″ skillet.

MAKE-IT-EASY TIP:
* An ice cream scoop makes an excellent ladle for dispensing batter.

Blue Cornmeal Crepes	YIELD: 14 crepes CALORIES: 82 per crepe PREPARATION TIME: 5 minutes COOKING TIME: 15–20 minutes

These crepes are a light version of ones created by noted cooking experts Craig Claiborne and Pierre Franey. The crepes can be topped with yogurt and caviar or Baked Ratatouille and served as a luncheon dish or appetizer course.

Blue cornmeal comes from blue corn, a strain cultivated around the pueblos in New Mexico. It has a distinctive blue color, which is of great religious importance to many American

Indian tribes. Before cooking, the ears are white, but once cooked they turn black, and when dried they turn a gray-blue color.

¾ cup blue cornmeal (see Notes)
1 egg
¾ cup low-fat milk
1½ tablespoons vegetable oil
Salt to taste

Garnish:
¼ cup plain low-fat yogurt
Black, red, or golden caviar
Chopped fresh chives

1. Sift the cornmeal and set aside.
2. In a medium bowl whisk the egg with the milk and oil. Add the cornmeal and salt and continue to whisk until smooth.
3. Coat a large nonstick griddle or skillet with vegetable cooking spray and preheat.
4. Drop 2 tablespoons of the batter at a time, for each crepe, on the preheated griddle and cook for 1 to 2 minutes, or until light golden on one side. Flip the crepes and cook on the second side for an additional minute, or until cooked through. Continue preparing crepes, adding more vegetable cooking spray as needed. (Remember to always remove the pan from the heat before spraying.)
5. Smear 2 teaspoons plain low-fat yogurt on each crepe. Garnish with a pinch of black, red, or golden caviar, in the center, top with chives, and serve hot.

COOK NOTES: For longer storage, place the blue cornmeal in a sealed container in the refrigerator, or for short-term storage, keep in an airtight container in a cool place.

Blue cornmeal is available through the Williams-Sonoma catalogue or stores.

VARIATIONS:
* Yellow cornmeal can be substituted for blue cornmeal.
* The crepes can be topped with Baked Ratatouille (page 283) or other cooked vegetable dishes.

RICE

Brown Rice Baked with Vegetables and Tofu	SERVES: 6 CALORIES: 184 per serving PREPARATION TIME: 15–20 minutes COOKING TIME: 35–40 minutes

Tofu is a versatile and economical food that is low in calories, high in protein and nutrients, and has no cholesterol. This dish can be a side dish or served as a vegetarian main course.

1 tablespoon olive oil
1 medium onion, finely chopped
2 stalks celery, finely chopped
1 large zucchini, finely chopped
1 red or green pepper, seeded and finely chopped
2 cups cooked brown rice
2 cups crushed tomatoes packed in puree
2 tablespoons finely chopped fresh parsley
1 teaspoon finely minced garlic
½ teaspoon crumbled dried oregano
Salt and freshly ground pepper to taste
1 1-pound package Chinese (firm) tofu (see Notes)
2–3 tablespoons finely grated Parmesan cheese

1. Preheat the oven to 350°F. Spray a 2-quart baking dish with vegetable cooking spray.
2. In a large nonstick skillet heat the oil and sauté the onion, celery, zucchini, and pepper over medium heat for 7 to 8 minutes, or until softened, stirring often.
3. Place the cooked vegetables in a bowl with the rice, tomatoes, parsley, garlic, oregano, and salt and pepper and stir until well-mixed.
4. Drain the tofu between layers of paper towels and squeeze out the moisture. Dice into ½″ pieces, and gently fold into the mixture.

5. Pour the mixture into the prepared baking dish and sprinkle with Parmesan cheese. Bake for 25 to 30 minutes, or until hot and bubbling, and serve immediately.

COOK NOTES: Tofu is available in 1-pound or occasionally 14.2-ounce packages. Either size will work in this recipe.

If only Japanese or soft-variety of bean curd is available, you can press the water from the curds to make them firmer. To press, wrap each bean curd cake (or slice a whole cake into 2″ horizontal lengths) in cheesecloth and put in a large dish; place a 2- to 3-pound weight on top. A large book or several cans will do. After 1 hour, unwrap the bean curd and proceed with the recipe.

VARIATIONS:
* If tomatoes packed in puree are unavailable, use regular whole juice-packed tomatoes; chop, drain off most of the liquid. Return the tomatoes to the can and fill to the top with canned tomato puree.
* Additional vegetables such as diced mushrooms, broccoli, or chopped spinach can be added to the recipe if desired.

Brown Risi e Bisi	SERVES: 6 CALORIES: 202 per serving PREPARATION TIME: 15–20 minutes COOKING TIME: 55 minutes

Risi e Bisi is a Venetian specialty dish consisting of rice, peas, and prosciutto. This low-fat version contains a small amount of olive oil in place of lots of butter, and brown rice which is nutritionally superior and higher in fiber than white rice.

While brown rice does provide more nutrients than white rice, it is not a completely perfect food. It should not be eaten to the exclusion of other foods, which provide other essential nutrients needed by the body.

1 tablespoon olive oil
1 medium onion, finely chopped
1 cup brown rice
½ cup dry vermouth
3¼ cups boiling chicken broth
1 clove garlic, finely minced
1 10-ounce package frozen tiny peas
2 tablespoons finely chopped fresh basil
2 tablespoons finely chopped fresh parsley
Salt and freshly ground pepper to taste
2 tablespoons grated Parmesan cheese

Garnish:
Chopped fresh parsley

1. In a medium-sized nonstick saucepan heat the oil and sauté the onion over medium heat until soft, 6 to 7 minutes, stirring often.
2. Add the rice and continue to sauté, coating the rice with the onion. Add the vermouth and allow to boil for 2 minutes. Add the broth and garlic, bring to a boil, cover, reduce heat, and simmer for 35 minutes.
3. Add the peas, basil, parsley, and salt and pepper, stir to combine, cover, and continue to simmer for 10 minutes, or until the peas are cooked. (It may be necessary to add more broth if the rice is too dry.)
4. Stir in the cheese and serve hot, garnished with parsley.

COOK NOTE: Once opened store the unused raw brown rice in a sealed container.

VARIATION:
* If the peas are thawed, add after 40 minutes, and cook for only 5 minutes.

Lemon Brown Rice

SERVES: 4
CALORIES: 242 per serving
PREPARATION TIME: 10–15 minutes
COOKING TIME: about 1 hour

Brown rice is unpolished rice from which only the husks have been removed. It is nutritionally superior to white rice, richer in vitamins, minerals, and fiber. It also takes longer to cook than white rice because of the higher fiber and oil content of the bran layer. Brown rice has a shorter shelf life than white rice due to oxidation of the bran layer, so purchase it in smaller quantities.

1 tablespoon olive oil
1 onion, finely chopped
1 teaspoon finely minced garlic
1 cup brown rice
2¼ cups chicken or beef broth
¼ cup lemon juice
2 teaspoons grated lemon rind
Salt and freshly ground pepper

Garnish:
Chopped fresh parsley

1. In a nonstick saucepan heat the oil and sauté the onion and garlic over medium-low heat for about 6 to 8 minutes, or until soft. (Do not brown.)
2. Add the rice, stir to coat and add the broth, juice, rind, and salt and pepper. Bring to a boil, cover, reduce heat, and simmer slowly for 45 to 50 minutes, or until the liquid has been absorbed and the rice is fluffy.
3. Serve immediately, garnished with parsley.

VARIATION:
* Orange juice and rind can be substituted for the lemon.

Brown Rice Pilaf with Asparagus and Mushrooms	SERVES: 6 CALORIES: 174 per serving PREPARATION TIME: 10–15 minutes COOKING TIME: about 50 minutes

Serve this vegetable and starch course combined in one dish during the spring months when asparagus are plentiful. Out of season substitute broccoli florets or zucchini for the asparagus.

Asparagus are a good source of vitamin A and potassium, a fair source of vitamins B and C and iron, and are very low in sodium and calories.

1 tablespoon unsalted butter or margarine
1 small onion, finely chopped
½ pound mushrooms, wiped clean, thinly sliced
1 cup brown rice
2⅔ cups chicken broth
⅛ teaspoon grated nutmeg
Salt and freshly ground pepper to taste
½ pound asparagus, woody stalk parts removed, cut diagonally
*   into 1" pieces (see Note)*
2 tablespoons finely grated Swiss cheese

Garnish:
Chopped pimiento

1. In a medium-sized nonstick saucepan heat the butter or margarine and sauté the onion and mushrooms over medium heat for 7 to 8 minutes, or until softened, stirring often.
2. Add the rice and stir to coat; add the broth, nutmeg, salt and pepper, bring to a boil, cover, reduce heat, and simmer slowly for 35 minutes.
3. Stir in the asparagus, cover, and continue to cook for 5 minutes longer, or until the liquid is absorbed and the vegetables are tender.
4. Stir in the cheese and serve hot, garnished with chopped pimiento.

COOK NOTE: Select firm green asparagus spears with tightly closed heads and smooth skin. Keep asparagus refrigerated in a plastic bag; do not wash before storing. If possible, keep a wet towel around the base of the asparagus to keep them fresh.

VARIATION:
* Beef broth can be substituted for the chicken broth.

Dilled Rice with Leeks	SERVES: 4 CALORIES: 257 per serving PREPARATION TIME: 1–5 minutes COOKING TIME: about 35 minutes

Leeks are the sweetest and mildest members of the onion family and yet a whole bunch of leeks contains only 52 calories. In addition, leeks are richer in nutrients than other members of the onion family. Leeks contain a fair amount of vitamin C, calcium, and phosphorus, and are a good source of potassium.

2 medium leeks (see Note)
1 tablespoon unsalted butter or margarine
1 cup white rice
2 cups chicken broth
Salt and freshly ground white pepper to taste
1 tablespoon snipped fresh dill

Garnish:
Sprigs of dill

1. Cut the root ends off the leeks and cut off and discard the green upper leaves down to the point where the dark green begins to pale. Wash thoroughly, fanning out the leaves so the grit is easily removed. Thinly slice.
2. In a medium nonstick saucepan heat the butter or margarine and sauté the leeks over medium heat for 6 to 7 minutes, or until softened.
3. Add the rice and stir to coat. Add the broth and salt and

pepper, bring to a boil, cover, reduce heat, and simmer slowly for 25 minutes.

4. Remove the pan from heat, allow to rest for 5 minutes; add the dill, stir to combine, and serve hot, garnished with dill sprigs.

COOK NOTE: Select leeks with fresh green tops. The leeks should "give" a bit to the touch to assure their not being overly mature and woody on the inside.

Store the leeks unwashed with the roots attached; keep them dry or they will turn brown and begin to rot. Do not freeze.

VARIATION:
* Scallions can be substituted for the leeks.

Rice with Tomato and Basil Flavor	SERVES: 6 CALORIES: 140 per serving PREPARATION TIME: 10 minutes COOKING TIME: 30 minutes

It is usually pasta that is topped with tomato, basil, and garlic, but here rice is the ingredient that gets the honors.

1¼ cups chicken broth
¼ cup finely chopped onion
1½ teaspoons finely minced garlic
1 cup white rice
1 cup crushed tomatoes packed in puree
2 tablespoons chopped fresh basil, or ½ teaspoon crumbled dried
Salt and freshly ground pepper to taste

Garnish:
Chopped fresh basil or parsley

1. In a small nonstick saucepan heat the broth; add the onion and garlic and cook over medium heat for 5 to 6 minutes, or

until the vegetables are tender and the liquid has been absorbed.
2. Add the remaining ingredients, bring to a boil, cover, reduce heat, and simmer slowly for 25 minutes, or until the rice is tender and the liquid has been absorbed.
3. Place in a heated bowl and serve hot, garnished with chopped basil or parsley.

COOK NOTE: The reason it is best to place hot rice in a heated bowl is that if placed in a cold dish the rice that touches the dish tends to become gummy.

VARIATIONS:
* If tomatoes packed in puree are unavailable, use regular whole juice-packed tomatoes; chop, drain off most of the liquid. Return the tomatoes to the can, and fill to the top with canned tomato puree.
* The rice can be cooked in a 350°F. oven for about 25 minutes, or until the grains are tender.

Saffron-Flavored Rice	SERVES: 8
	CALORIES: 143 per serving
	PREPARATION TIME: 5 minutes
	COOKING TIME: 20–25 minutes

No butter or other fats are used in this saffron-flavored dish. Remember to refrigerate the canned broth before using so that the fat can be removed when chilled then discarded before adding to the rice.

2¾ cups chicken or beef broth
⅛ teaspoon powdered saffron, or ¼ teaspoon saffron threads
*   soaked in ¼ cup hot broth (see Note)*
1½ cups white rice
Salt and freshly ground pepper to taste

Garnish:
Chopped fresh parsley

1. Bring the broth to a boil, flavor with saffron, and add the rice; cover, reduce heat to very low, and cook undisturbed for 20 to 25 minutes, or until tender.
2. Serve hot, garnished with parsley.

COOK NOTE: Saffron, a very expensive spice, is the dried orange stigmas of the saffron crocus. Search for an East Indian grocery in your area where the spice is often sold less expensively, in smaller quantities and fresher, than at supermarkets or gourmet shops.

VARIATION:
* Brown rice may be substituted: increase cooking time to 40 to 45 minutes.

MAKE-IT-EASY TIP:
* If the rice must be held before serving, transfer to a colander set over a pot of simmering water, cover, and the rice will keep without overcooking for 30 to 60 minutes.

Curried Toasted Rice

SERVES: 4
CALORIES: 240 per serving
PREPARATION TIME: 10–15 minutes
COOKING TIME: 30–40 minutes

Toasting rice in a hot oven adds nutty flavor and crunchy texture without adding any extra calories.

1 cup rice (see Note)
1 tablespoon unsalted butter or margarine
1 small onion, finely chopped
2½ cups chicken or beef broth
2 tablespoons raisins
½–1 teaspoon curry powder or to taste
Salt and freshly ground pepper to taste

Garnish:
Sprigs of watercress

1. Preheat the oven to 400°F.
2. Pour the rice onto a baking sheet in a single layer and bake for 10 to 15 minutes, or until golden brown, shaking the pan occasionally. Allow to cool.
3. In a small nonstick saucepan heat the butter or margarine and sauté the onion over medium heat until golden. Add the rice and stir to coat with the mixture.
4. Add the broth, raisins, curry powder, and salt and pepper; bring to a boil, cover, reduce heat, and simmer slowly for 20 to 25 minutes, or until tender and the liquid is absorbed.

COOK NOTE: There is no reason to use instant rice, which has poor flavor and texture and represents little time-saving effort, considering that regular rice needs only an extra 10 minutes of cooking time.

MAKE-IT-EASY TIP:
* The rice may be toasted up to a week in advance and kept in a sealed container.

Basmati Rice with Orange Flavor	SERVES: 4 CALORIES: 196 per serving PREPARATION TIME: 5–10 minutes COOKING TIME: about 15 minutes

Basmati rice is a small-grained rice from India and Pakistan that has a wonderful texture and aromatic flavor (*basmati* translated means "queen of fragrance"). It is available in Asian and Middle Eastern markets as well as health food and specialty stores

1 cup basmati rice
1½ cups chicken or beef broth
¼ cup fresh orange juice (see Note)
1 teaspoon freshly grated orange rind
Pinch of grated nutmeg

Garnish:
Freshly grated orange rind
Chopped fresh parsley

1. Wash the rice thoroughly.
2. In a saucepan combine the remaining ingredients, add the rice, and bring to a boil. Cover, reduce heat, and simmer for 15 minutes, or until the grains have absorbed the liquid.
3. Serve hot, garnished with orange rind and parsley.

COOK NOTE: Thin-skinned oranges are usually the juiciest.

VARIATIONS:
* Plain white rice can be substituted for the basmati but cooked for 5 to 10 minutes longer.
* Brown basmati is basmati rice with the bran layer still attached, while calmati is brown basmati rice grown in California—either can be cooked using the same method as for white basmati rice.

Wild Rice Pilaf

SERVES: 4
CALORIES: 154 per serving
PREPARATION TIME: 10 minutes
COOKING TIME: 1¼ hours

Wild rice is not really rice. It is the seed of a grass that grows wild primarily in the Great Lakes region on lands held by native Americans who gather the crops. It is almost twice as expensive as paddy-grown rice because it is very difficult to harvest.

Because wild rice is low in fat, it has a longer shelf life than most grains and will not become rancid rapidly.

2 cups strong chicken broth
1 small onion, finely chopped
1 clove garlic, finely minced
1 teaspoon finely minced lemon rind
1 cup wild rice
2 tablespoons toasted sesame seeds

Garnish:
2 tablespoons chopped fresh parsley

1. In a nonstick medium saucepan heat ½ cup broth. When boiling, add the onion and garlic and cook until just softened.
2. Add the lemon rind and rice, stirring well to coat with the vegetables. Add the remaining 1½ cups broth, bring to a boil, cover, reduce heat, and simmer very slowly for 65 to 75 minutes, or until the rice is just tender.
3. Stir in the sesame seeds, place in a serving bowl, top with parsley, and serve immediately.

VARIATION:
* A julienned red bell pepper can be added along with the onion if desired.

OTHERS

Couscous with Stir-Fried Vegetables	SERVES: 8 CALORIES: 298 per serving PREPARATION TIME: 20−25 minutes COOKING TIME: 5−8 minutes

Couscous is a traditional Moroccan dish made with steamed grains of semolina. In this recipe the precooked medium-grain semolina is used.

1 14-ounce package precooked medium-grain couscous (Near East brand is good)
2¼ cups boiling chicken or beef broth (see Notes)
1 tablespoon unsalted butter or margarine
8 sun-dried tomatoes soaked in hot water for 20 minutes, (cellophane-packed, not oil-packed)
½ pound broccoli raab, rapini, or Chinese cabbage (see Notes)
1 3" piece of daikon, peeled and thinly sliced (see Notes)
2 large carrots, peeled and thinly sliced
2 zucchini, thinly sliced
2 yellow crookneck squash, thinly sliced
2 leeks, thinly sliced (white parts only)
2 tablespoons peanut oil
¾ cup chicken broth
2 tablespoons finely chopped fresh chives or scallion greens
1 tablespoon lemon juice
1 clove garlic, finely minced
Salt and freshly ground white pepper to taste

Garnish:
Pimiento slices

1. In a large bowl combine the couscous with the boiling broth and butter or margarine; cover and allow to stand for 5 to 10 minutes.

2. Drain the tomatoes and cut in half. Discard the tough stems of the broccoli raab and cut the leaves and stems into 2″ pieces. Place the tomatoes and broccoli raab along with the daikon, carrots, zucchini, squash, and leeks near the cooking area.

3. In a wok or large skillet heat the oil and add the leek. Stir-fry for 1 minute. Add the prepared vegetables and continue to stir-fry for an additional 2 minutes, or until the vegetables are crisp-tender. Add the remaining ingredients, stir, cover, reduce heat, and cook slowly for 1 to 2 minutes.

3. Arrange the couscous in a ring shape on a warm serving platter. Place the vegetables and sauce in the center and on the top of the couscous. Serve hot, garnished with pimiento slices.

COOK NOTES: Use chicken or beef broth depending on the main course.

Broccoli raab, or Italian turnip broccoli, is a distinctively flavored green, a relative of the cabbage family, that is used mainly for animal fodder in the United States. It is well-known in Italy, particularly in Rome, where it is called broccoli di rapa and is often smaller and less sharp in flavor. Select vegetables with fresh crisp-looking leaves and tiny yellow buds and store wrapped in paper towels in a plastic bag in the refrigerator. If unavailable substitute ½ pound broccoli florets.

Daikon, also called Japanese white radish, Oriental radish, and icicle radish, is a member of the turnip family and can be eaten raw or braised or stir-fried like a turnip. To store, wrap the daikon tightly in plastic wrap and place in the refrigerator. If unavailable, substitute ¾ cup sliced jicama, water chestnuts, or even turnips.

VARIATION:
* Any seasonal vegetables can be added or substituted in this recipe.

Carrot and Bulgur Pilaf	SERVES: 6 CALORIES: 156 per serving PREPARATION TIME: 10–15 minutes COOKING TIME: 50–55 minutes

Bulgur, also called bulgar, bulghul, or bulghur, is the staple of Middle Eastern cooking. It is cracked wheat that has been hulled and parboiled, a process that makes the grain easier to cook and gives a pronounced flavor and lighter texture.

1 tablespoon vegetable oil
1 small onion, finely chopped
4 medium carrots, peeled and finely chopped
1 cup bulgur (see Notes)
2 cups hot chicken or beef broth (see Notes)
1 teaspoon Worcestershire sauce
Salt and freshly ground pepper to taste
½ cup frozen tiny peas, thawed

Garnish:
Chopped fresh parsley

1. Preheat the oven to 350°F.
2. In a small nonstick ovenproof casserole, heat the oil and sauté the onion and carrots over medium heat until soft and golden, about 5 minutes.
3. Add the bulgur to the casserole, stir well, and add the hot broth. Bring to a boil, cover, and bake for 40 minutes.
4. Remove from the oven, add the peas, stir briefly to combine, cover, and return to the oven for 5 to 10 minutes, or until the peas are just heated through.
5. Serve the bulgur hot, garnished with parsley.

COOK NOTES: Bulgur is always cooked in the proportion of 1 cup grain to every 2 cups liquid. When cooked, it increases to 4 times its volume.

Select chicken or beef broth depending on the main course.

VARIATION:
* Bulgur can also be cooked on top of the range at a very slow simmer.

Curried Lentils	SERVES: 6 CALORIES: 149 per serving PREPARATION TIME: 10 minutes COOKING TIME: 55–60 minutes

Lentils are a good source of protein. Red and brown (or green or gray) lentils are among the few legumes that do not need any soaking before cooking because they cook so quickly and because soaking alters their texture and flavor.

3⅓ cups strong chicken broth
1 cup lentils
1 small onion, finely chopped
1 clove garlic, finely minced
2 teaspoons curry powder or more to taste dissolved in 1 table-
spoon lemon juice
½ teaspoon ground cumin
½ teaspoon chili powder
Salt and freshly ground pepper to taste

Garnish:
Chopped fresh parsley

1. In a medium saucepan bring the broth to a boil. Add the lentils, cover, reduce heat, and simmer slowly for 45 minutes, or until the lentils are tender.
2. Add the remaining ingredients, stir well, cover, and simmer for an additional 10 to 15 minutes.
3. Serve hot, garnished with parsley.

VARIATION:
* Chopped leeks or scallions can be substituted for the onion.

Mexican Bulgur	SERVES: 6 CALORIES: 182 per serving PREPARATION TIME: 10–15 minutes COOKING TIME: 25 minutes

The addition of peppers and spices transform the traditionally Middle Eastern bulgur into a Mexican side dish.

2 tablespoons unsalted butter or margarine
1 medium onion, finely chopped
1 green pepper, seeded and finely chopped
1 cup bulgur
2 cups chicken or beef broth (see Notes)
1 teaspoon chili powder
½ teaspoon ground cumin
Salt and freshly ground pepper to taste

Garnish:
Plain low-fat yogurt

1. In a large nonstick skillet heat the butter or margarine and sauté the onion and pepper over medium heat for 6 to 7 minutes, or until soft, stirring occasionally.
2. Add the bulgur and cook for 2 minutes, stirring to coat the grains.
3. Add the remaining ingredients, bring to a boil, cover, reduce heat, and simmer slowly for 15 minutes, or until the liquid has been absorbed. (Do not overcook.)
4. Serve the bulgur hot, garnished with yogurt.

COOK NOTES: Because bulgur has been precooked, it can be easily overcooked and will become mushy if too much liquid is added in proportion to the amount of grain.

Select chicken or beef broth depending on the main course.

ACCOMPANIMENTS:
Chopped tomatoes, chopped scallions, and Mexican Salsa served in separate bowls.

Toasted Barley and Dried Mushrooms Cooked in Broth	SERVES: 6 CALORIES: 154 per serving PREPARATION TIME: 10 minutes COOKING TIME: 20–25 minutes

Egg barley, also called farfel, are toasted noodles that are used in Jewish cooking. They can be added to soup or used here, cooked in broth, and served as a side dish.

2¼ cups chicken or beef broth
Salt and freshly ground pepper to taste
2 ounces dried French or Italian mushrooms soaked in hot water
   to cover for 20–30 minutes
1 7-ounce package toasted barley

Garnish:
Chopped fresh parsley
Grated lemon rind

1. In a medium saucepan bring the broth to a boil and season with salt and pepper.
2. Drain the mushrooms in a strainer and reserve the soaking liquid. Chop the mushrooms and add to the broth with soaking liquid.
3. Add the barley, bring the liquid to a boil again, cover, and simmer slowly for 15 to 20 minutes, or until the liquid is absorbed.
4. Serve the barley hot, garnished with chopped parsley and lemon rind.

VARIATION:
* If desired, ½ cup finely minced onions sautéed in a nonstick skillet with 2 tablespoons oil can be added with the mushrooms.

MAKE-IT-EASY TIP:
* Barley can be reheated in the top of a double boiler or in a low oven, but it may be necessary to add more liquid if the barley is quite dry.

Mushroom-Flavored Barley

SERVES: 8
CALORIES: 186 per serving
PREPARATION TIME: 15 minutes
COOKING TIME: about 1 hour 25 minutes

The barley we use for pilafs and other dishes is pearl barley, which has had the inner and outer husks, or the bran, removed and the grain is polished.

1 cup dried French or Italian mushrooms soaked in boiling water
*   for 30 minutes*
4 teaspoons vegetable oil
1 medium onion, finely chopped
¼ pound mushrooms, wiped clean, thinly sliced
1½ cups pearl barley (see Notes)
2⅓ cups chicken or beef broth (see Notes)
Salt and freshly ground pepper to taste

Garnish:
Chopped watercress

1. Preheat the oven to 350°F.
2. Drain the dried mushrooms through a strainer, slice into small pieces if too large, and reserve the soaking liquid, which should measure about ⅔ cup.
3. In a nonstick ovenproof casserole heat the oil and sauté the onion for 2 minutes over medium heat. Add the sliced raw mushrooms and continue to cook for an additional 5 minutes, or until the vegetables are soft.
4. Add the barley and cook, stirring to coat the grains. Add the reserved mushrooms, mushroom liquid, 1⅓ cups broth, and salt and pepper. Bring to a boil, cover, and bake for 45 minutes.
5. Add the remaining 1 cup broth, return to the oven, and cook for 20 minutes longer.
6. Serve hot, garnished with watercress.

COOK NOTES: Barley, like other grains, should be stored in un-opened packages in a cool dry area. Once opened, store the unused portion in a tightly sealed container.

Select chicken or beef broth depending on main course.

VARIATION:
* Barley can also be cooked on top of the range at a very slow simmer.

Asparagus Cooked in Foil

SERVES: 4
CALORIES: 19 per serving
PREPARATION TIME: 10 minutes
COOKING TIME: 20–30 minutes

Instead of topping with rich hollandaise sauce or melted butter, the asparagus in this recipe are baked in packets with broth and lemon juice and then served with the clear liquid.

1 pound asparagus, washed and trimmed
Salt and freshly ground pepper to taste
2 teaspoons lemon juice
¼ cup strong chicken broth

Garnish:
Chopped fresh parsley
Grated lemon rind

1. Preheat the oven to 400°F.
2. Place the asparagus in the center of a large sheet of aluminum foil in a baking pan with the edges folded up to keep the liquid inside.
3. Season with salt and pepper, sprinkle with lemon juice, and pour the broth over all.
4. Fold the sides over and seal. Bake for 20 to 30 minutes, or until the asparagus are al dente, just cooked.
5. Place the asparagus on a platter, pour the juices over, and serve immediately, garnished with parsley and lemon rind.

VARIATION:
* Beef or vegetable broth can be substituted for the chicken broth.

MAKE-IT-EASY TIP:
* If the asparagus stalks are thick, break off the tough woody stem ends and peel the lower sections up to the tenderer part with a vegetable peeler.

Crispy Onions	SERVES: 8 CALORIES: 76 per serving PREPARATION TIME: 10 minutes COOKING TIME: about 20 minutes

Instead of lots of oils or fats to sauté the onions, they are cooked in broth in a nonstick skillet and the results are crisp and grease-free.

¾ cup beef broth
6 large onions, thinly sliced

1. Heat the broth in a large skillet. Add the onions and cook over medium-high heat, stirring often, until the onions are golden, 15 to 20 minutes.
2. Serve hot.

COOK NOTE: Store onions in a well-ventilated dry area but not in piles. Single layers will ensure longer freshness of the onion.

VARIATION:
* Chicken broth can be substituted for the beef broth.

MAKE-IT-EASY TIP:
* The best way to keep eyes from tearing when slicing onions, by hand, or with a food processor, is by wearing workman's, ski, or swimmer's goggles.

Braised Artichokes with Vegetables	SERVES: 4 CALORIES: 216 per serving PREPARATION TIME: 20 minutes COOKING TIME: 55–60 minutes

Instead of dipping the artichoke leaves in gobs of melted butter, here they are braised and served with chopped vegetables in broth and wine. Serve the artichokes in soup bowls as an incredible first course.

4 medium to large artichokes (see Notes)
1 lemon, halved
1 tablespoon olive oil
2 medium onions, finely chopped
3 carrots, peeled and finely chopped
3 stalks celery, finely chopped
1 clove garlic, finely minced
2 tablespoons chopped fresh parsley
Salt and freshly ground pepper to taste
1 cup dry vermouth
2 cups chicken broth

1. Wash the artichokes. Slice off the stems 1″ from the base and remove all small bottom leaves. Cut off about 1″ from the top of the artichoke. Trim the tips of the leaves easily with a kitchen scissors to avoid prickles. Rub each cut side with a lemon half.
2. In a large stainless steel or porcelain-lined kettle or Dutch oven heat the oil and sauté the onions, carrots, and celery over medium heat until soft, about 5 minutes, stirring often. Add the garlic, parsley, salt and pepper, and vermouth, bring to a boil, and allow the wine to boil off for about 2 minutes. Add the broth.
3. Place the artichokes in the pan, pushing aside the vegetables so the artichokes will rest directly on the bottom of the pan. Bring to a boil again, cover, reduce heat, and simmer slowly for 45 to 50 minutes, or until the artichoke hearts are fork-tender.

4. Serve the artichokes in the center of a flattened soup plate, surrounded by vegetables and broth to be scooped up and eaten with the leaves.

COOK NOTES: Select artichokes with firm, solid heads and compact leaves. Size is not an indication of quality nor maturity; the larger artichokes grow at the top of the plant.

To improve the color, texture, and flavor of artichokes, try soaking them for 30 minutes, prior to cooking, in cold water to which either 1 tablespoon vinegar or 1 tablespoon lemon juice has been added.

Do not cook artichokes in aluminum or iron pots, which will discolor them and turn them grayish.

VARIATION:

* Artichokes can be blanched in boiling water for 10 minutes to easily remove the center leaves and chokes before braising. The vegetables can then be stuffed into the centers and braised as in step 3.

Puree of Cauliflower

SERVES: 6
CALORIES: 58 per serving
PREPARATION TIME: 15 minutes
COOKING TIME: 35–40 minutes

When cooking cauliflower avoid aluminum pots, which discolor the creamy white appearance.

1 head cauliflower, green leaves and heavy stem removed, washed, cut into florets
1 cup Light White Sauce (page 84)
2 tablespoons grated Parmesan cheese
2 teaspoons unsalted butter or margarine
Salt and freshly ground white pepper to taste

Garnish:
Cherry tomato halves

1. Drop the cauliflower florets into a large pot of boiling water, cover, and cook over medium heat for 10 minutes, or until very tender. Drain.
2. Preheat the oven to 350°F. Lightly spray a 1-quart soufflé dish or similar sized baking dish with vegetable cooking spray.
3. Place the drained cauliflower in a food processor or blender and process for 30 seconds; add the white sauce, cheese, butter or margarine, and salt and pepper and continue to process until smooth.
4. Place the puree in the prepared baking dish and bake for 25 to 30 minutes, or until heated through and lightly golden around the edges.
5. Serve hot, garnished with cherry tomato halves circling the edges.

COOK NOTES: Cauliflower is boiled covered to minimize the strong cooking odors.

Store cauliflower in an airtight container in the refrigerator and it will keep for about 5 days.

VARIATION:
* Bake the puree in 6 to 8 small ramekin dishes for 15 to 20 minutes.

MAKE-IT-EASY TIP:
* Boil 4 or 5 cloves and a cinnamon stick in a separate pot alongside boiling cauliflower, broccoli, cabbage, or other strong-smelling vegetables to keep the kitchen smelling sweet.

Broccoli with Sesame Flavor	SERVES: 6 CALORIES: 45 per serving PREPARATION TIME: 10 minutes COOKING TIME: 3 minutes

This member of the cabbage family is low in calories and high in nutrition, particularly when served simply, as below.

3 cups broccoli florets (reserve stems for another use) (see Note)
1 tablespoon reduced-sodium soy sauce
2 teaspoons toasted sesame oil
2 tablespoons toasted sesame seeds

1. Drop the florets into a large pot of boiling salted water and, when the water returns to a boil, cook, uncovered, for 2 to 3 minutes, or until just tender but still crunchy. Drain in a colander. (Do not overcook!)
2. Place on a serving platter, top with soy sauce and sesame oil, and sprinkle with sesame seeds. Serve hot or at room temperature.

COOK NOTE: Select broccoli heads with firm, compact bud clusters, which should be green or purple-green, depending on the variety. Stalks should be fresh and green. Avoid heads with open, yellow flowers or wilting leaves.

VARIATIONS:
* Asparagus can be substituted for the broccoli.
* The broccoli can be steamed if desired.

MAKE-IT-EASY TIP:
* Save the broccoli cooking water for use in cooked rice dishes or soups or stews.

Spicy Red Cabbage	SERVES: 8
	CALORIES: 65 per serving
	PREPARATION TIME: 15–20 minutes
	COOKING TIME: about 50 minutes

Red cabbage is an excellent source of fiber. When boiled, the red pigment anthrocyanin leaches during cooking and a blue color results. To stabilize the color, vinegar is added to the cooking liquid.

¾ cup strong chicken broth
1 medium onion, finely chopped
1 clove garlic, finely minced
1 2-pound head red cabbage, cut into strips, core removed (see Note)
1 tart apple, peeled, cored, and diced
¾ cup unsweetened apple juice
2 tablespoons apple cider vinegar
2 tablespoons lemon juice
1 tablespoon honey
1 teaspoon grated lemon rind
1 teaspoon caraway seeds
Pinch of ground cloves
Pinch of ground allspice
Salt to taste

1. In a pot bring the broth to a boil. Add the onion and garlic and cook, uncovered, over medium heat until soft, about 10 minutes.
2. Add the remaining ingredients, bring to a boil, reduce heat, cover, and simmer slowly for 40 minutes.
3. Serve hot.

COOK NOTE: Select heads of cabbage that are solid and heavy for their size.

VARIATION:
* A pear can be substituted for the apple.

MAKE-IT-EASY TIP:
* Red cabbage can be prepared a day or two in advance and reheated successfully.

Oven-Fried Potatoes	SERVES: 4 CALORIES: 134 per serving PREPARATION TIME: 10–15 minutes COOKING TIME: about 20 minutes

Instead of frying to obtain a crisp result, these potatoes are dipped in a light egg and mustard mixture and then broiled until golden brown, without fats or oils. Peeling potatoes is unnecessary and it removes a great deal of nutritional value that lies in or near the skin.

1 egg, lightly beaten
1 teaspoon Dijon mustard
¼ teaspoon paprika
Salt and freshly ground pepper to taste
4 medium potatoes, scrubbed, unpeeled, cut into 1"-thick steak
  fries

1. Preheat a broiler. Cover a broiling pan with aluminum foil.
2. In a bowl combine the egg with the seasonings and stir to combine.
3. Dip the potato pieces into the egg mixture and place on the prepared pan. Broil 4" to 6" from direct heat for 8 to 10 minutes per side, or until crispy on the outside and cooked through on the inside.
4. Serve hot.

VARIATION:
* For a spicy version, a pinch or two of cayenne pepper or even a shake of Tabasco can be added to the egg mixture.

Brussels Sprouts with Basil	SERVES: 4 CALORIES: 80 per serving PREPARATION TIME: 10 minutes COOKING TIME: 8 minutes

The fresh flavor of basil is important to this recipe. If fresh basil is unavailable, substitute fresh parsley or even fresh dill, and avoid dried herbs.

16–20 (1–1¼ pounds) small brussels sprouts, washed, wilted
 or damaged leaves removed (see Notes)
1 cup strong chicken broth
1 cup water
1 tablespoon unsalted butter
1 tablespoon chopped fresh basil
Salt and freshly ground pepper to taste

1. Cut off the bottom stems and any tough outer leaves of the brussels sprouts and make a tiny crosswise incision at the base to speed up the cooking process.
2. In an 8″ or 9″ skillet bring the broth and water to a boil, add the brussels sprouts, cover, reduce heat to medium low, and cook for 7 to 8 minutes, or until just tender.
3. Drain, toss with the remaining ingredients, and serve hot.

COOK NOTES: If possible, select brussels sprouts that are sold in bins rather than in packages, which often hide wilted or damaged sprouts. Choose the smallest, tightest heads that are the darkest shade of green.

Do not overcook brussels sprouts or they will become mealy in texture.

VARIATION:
* The sprouts can be steamed for 10 minutes in a vegetable steamer and then topped with butter, basil, and seasonings.

Puree of Carrot with Lemon Accent

SERVES: 4
CALORIES: 84 per serving
PREPARATION TIME: 10–15 minutes
COOKING TIME: 20 minutes

Carrots have such a sweet and naturally rich taste when pureed that they need little or no butter to make them wonderful. When cooked in broth they have extra added flavor and the broth can be used again to enhance soups, sauces, or other vegetables.

1 pound carrots, peeled and thickly sliced
Chicken broth to cover
1 tablespoon unsalted butter or margarine
2 teaspoons grated lemon rind
Salt and freshly ground white pepper to taste

Garnish:
Grated lemon rind and chopped fresh parsley combined

1. In a medium-sized saucepan place the carrots, cover with the broth, bring to a boil, cover, reduce heat, and simmer for 20 minutes, or until tender.
2. Drain the carrots (reserve broth for another use) and puree in a food processor or blender. Add the butter or margarine, lemon rind, and salt and pepper: continue to process until very smooth.
3. Place in a serving dish, garnish with the lemon rind and parsley mixture, and serve hot.

COOK NOTE: Do not store carrots with apples. Apples release a gas that gives carrots a bitter taste.

VARIATION:
* Orange rind can be substituted for the lemon rind.

Stir-Fried Kale with Garlic

SERVES: 4
CALORIES: 89 per serving
PREPARATION TIME: 10 minutes
COOKING TIME: about 9 minutes

Kale is a member of the cabbage family but unlike cabbage does not form a head but rather a bunch of frilly, heavy leaves on sturdy green stems.

1 pound kale (about 2 bunches), washed, stem ends removed (see Note)
1½ tablespoons peanut oil
2 teaspoons finely minced garlic
½ teaspoon sugar
Salt to taste
¾ cup chicken broth

1. Cut the kale leaves crosswise into 2" pieces.
2. Heat a wok or large skillet and add the oil. When hot, add the garlic and stir-fry for 20 seconds. Add the kale and continue to stir-fry for an additional 2 minutes. Add the sugar and salt, stir to coat, and finally add the broth.
3. Bring to a boil, cover, reduce heat to medium, and cook for 5 minutes, or until the greens are tender.
4. Serve hot.

COOK NOTE: Purchase kale in the winter months when it is plentiful and inexpensive. Store kale unwashed in a plastic bag in the refrigerator.

VARIATION:
* Other members of the cabbage family such as mustard greens, Swiss chard, broccoli raab, or spinach may easily be substituted.

Onions Baked in Their Skins	SERVES: 4 CALORIES: 141 per serving PREPARATION TIME: 5 minutes COOKING TIME: 1½–2 hours

Onions are flavorful simply baked in their own skins. It is important to line the pan with aluminum foil and spray with a vegetable cooking spray since the onions release a sticky syrup while baking.

4 medium to large yellow or sweet Bermuda onions (see Notes)
1½ tablespoons unsalted butter or margarine, diced
Salt and freshly ground pepper to taste

Garnish:
Sprigs of parsley

1. Preheat the oven to 375°F. Line a small baking pan with aluminum foil and spray with vegetable cooking spray.
2. Trim off the root ends of the onions but leave the skin intact. Place upright in the prepared pan and bake for 1½ to 2 hours, or until very tender.
3. Remove the skins and discard. Top each with melted butter or margarine, season with salt and pepper, and serve piping hot, garnished with parsley sprigs.

COOK NOTES: Do not store onions with potatoes. Onions will release a gas which hastens the spoilage of potatoes.

If an onion has a bad spot, toss it. Even if part of the bad onion can be salvaged, it always has a bad flavor.

VARIATION:
* Onions can be wrapped in foil and baked in the coals of an outdoor barbecue.

Creole Black-Eyed Peas

SERVES: 8
CALORIES: 90 per serving
PREPARATION TIME: 15–20 minutes
SOAKING TIME: 1 hour
COOKING TIME: 2 hours

Black-eyed peas, also known as cowpeas, crowder peas, or pea beans are neither a pea nor a bean. They belong to a subtropical group of legumes and are a staple to southern cooks, who refer to them simply as "peas."

2 cups dried black-eyed peas
3 cups chicken broth
2 cups crushed tomatoes packed in puree
1 large onion, finely chopped
2 stalks celery, finely chopped
3 teaspoons finely minced garlic
½ teaspoon dry mustard
¼ teaspoon ground cumin
¼ teaspoon ground ginger
¼ teaspoon cayenne
1 bay leaf
Salt to taste

Garnish:
Chopped fresh parsley

1. Place the beans in a medium-sized saucepan. Cover with 2 cups broth, bring to a boil for 2 minutes, cover, remove from heat, and allow to soak for 1 hour. Drain and discard the soaking liquid.
2. Add the remaining ingredients to the pan, including the remaining 1 cup chicken broth, bring to a boil, cover again, reduce heat, and simmer slowly for 2 hours, stirring occasionally; add water as necessary to keep the peas covered with liquid.
3. Remove the bay leaf, place in a serving bowl, and serve hot, garnished with parsley.

COOK NOTES: By bringing the peas to a boil and soaking for 1 hour as in step 1, the traditional 6 to 8 hours or overnight soaking time can be avoided. This method is also said to eliminate the gases in legumes. The soaking water is discarded to further aid in digestion.

The legumes must be softened before adding such acidic foods as tomatoes, which tend to slow down the cooking time.

VARIATION:

* If tomatoes packed in puree are unavailable, use regular whole juice-packed tomatoes; chop, drain off most of the liq-uid. Return the tomatoes to the can, and fill to the top with canned tomato puree.

MAKE-IT-EASY TIPS:

* The peas can be cooked earlier in the day or even a day in advance and reheated when ready to serve.
* Leftover cooked black-eyed peas freeze successfully.

Spaghetti Squash with Vegetable Topping	SERVES: 6 CALORIES: 79 per serving PREPARATION TIME: 20–25 minutes COOKING TIME: 1 hour 10 minutes

Spaghetti squash, also called vegetable spaghetti, is actually an edible gourd. It owes its name to the stringy texture of its flesh which, when cooked, turns into spaghettilike strands.

1 2-pound spaghetti squash
¾ cup strong chicken broth
1 medium onion, finely minced
2 carrots, peeled and finely chopped
1 clove garlic, finely minced
1 16-ounce can Italian tomatoes, well-drained, chopped
2 tablespoons chopped fresh parsley
2 tablespoons chopped fresh basil, or 1 teaspoon crumbled dried
Salt and freshly ground pepper to taste

Garnish:

2–3 tablespoons grated Parmesan cheese

1. Preheat the oven to 350°F.
2. Prick the squash all over with a fork; place on a rack in the oven and bake for 70 minutes, turning once during cooking.
3. In the meantime, in a medium-sized saucepan heat the broth and cook the onion, carrots, and garlic over medium heat, uncovered, until tender, about 10 minutes. Add the tomatoes and seasonings, reduce heat, cover the pot halfway, and simmer slowly for 20 minutes, stirring occasionally.
4. Split the squash in half horizontally, scoop out the seeds and discard. With a fork, string the fibers out of each half into a large serving bowl and toss with the cooked vegetable mixture.
5. Garnish with cheese, toss again, and serve hot.

COOK NOTE: Select oblong squash with rounded ends with either a bright yellow or whitish color and store in a cool, dry place for up to 1 month.

VARIATION:
* Cooked spaghetti squash can be tossed with Spinach Pesto (see Grilled Swordfish with Spinach Pesto, page 150).

MAKE-IT-EASY TIP:
* Spaghetti squash can be baked a day or two in advance as a time-saver. The recipe can then be assembled quickly and baked before serving.

New Potatoes with Dill	SERVES: 6 CALORIES: 154 per serving PREPARATION TIME: 5 minutes COOKING TIME: 30–40 minutes

It is a waste of both time and nutrition to peel potatoes. Much of the nutritional value of the potato lies in or near the skin. Really fresh new potatoes tend to cook faster than those potatoes that have been in storage for a while.

10 small new potatoes
1½ tablespoons snipped fresh dill
1½ tablespoons unsalted butter, diced
Salt and freshly ground white pepper to taste

Garnish:
Sprigs of dill

1. Scrub the potatoes, place in a medium-sized saucepan, and cover with water. Bring to a boil, cover, reduce heat, and cook until just fork-tender, 30 to 40 minutes. (Do not overcook.)
2. Drain the potatoes and toss in a bowl with the remaining ingredients.
3. Serve hot, garnished with dill sprigs.

COOK NOTES: Do not store potatoes in bright light or they can develop green spots which are bitter tasting and can be toxic. Store them in a cool, dark, and well-ventilated place.

Do not refrigerate potatoes. The starch in the potato converts to sugar in the refrigerator, creating an undesirable sweet taste.

VARIATIONS:
* Chopped fresh basil, parsley, rosemary, tarragon, or even mint can be substituted for the dill.
* The potatoes can be steamed for 30 to 40 minutes instead of boiled.

Stuffed Baked Potatoes	SERVES: 4 CALORIES: 151 per serving PREPARATION TIME: 10–15 minutes COOKING TIME: 15–20 minutes

Only recently has the potato's nutritional value become appreciated. It is a valuable source of amino acids and is high in potassium. Potatoes are low in calories, sodium, and fats, and high in fiber, especially if the skin is consumed.

Baked potatoes are given a lift here by stuffing with a mixture of part-skim ricotta, Parmesan cheese, and chives. The potatoes are rebaked until lightly golden on top.

2 large potatoes, baked (see Tips)
⅔ cup part-skim ricotta cheese
2 tablespoons grated part-skim mozzarella cheese
2 tablespoons grated Parmesan cheese
2 tablespoons finely chopped fresh chives
Salt and freshly ground pepper to taste

1. Preheat the oven to 400°F.
2. Slice the potatoes in half horizontally; carefully scoop out the flesh into a bowl, reserving the shells intact.
3. Combine the potato flesh with the remaining ingredients, stir until smooth, and divide among the 4 shells, piling high.
4. Bake the potato halves for 15 to 20 minutes, or until lightly golden on top.

VARIATION:
* If desired, ½ cup chopped spinach can be added to the potato filling.

MAKE-IT-EASY TIPS:
* To easily bake potatoes, scrub well, prick with a fork, and bake on the center rack of a 400°F oven for 1 to 1¼ hours, depending on size.
* To keep potato shells upright while baking, place in a giant muffin tin.

Braised Scallions

SERVES: 6
CALORIES: 54 per serving
PREPARATION TIME: 10–15 minutes
COOKING TIME: about 15 minutes

Scallions are braised in broth and a tablespoon of oil to bring out their subtle flavor, avoiding lots of butter and salt.

3 bunches scallions (see Note)
1 tablespoon olive oil
⅓ cup dry vermouth
⅔ cup chicken broth
1 teaspoon lemon juice
1 teaspoon Worcestershire sauce
Salt and freshly ground pepper

1. Trim off the root ends and wilted greens of the scallions and discard. Wash the scallions thoroughly.
2. In a large nonstick skillet heat the oil and sauté the scallions over medium heat, turning often, for 2 to 3 minutes, or until barely colored.
3. Add the vermouth and allow to boil about 2 minutes. Add the remaining ingredients; bring to a boil, cover, reduce heat, and simmer slowly for 5 to 10 minutes, depending on size, or until the scallions are tender.
4. With a slotted spatula or tongs, transfer the scallions to a warm platter. Thicken the pan juices by boiling over high heat until reduced and syrupy, about 2 minutes. Pour the juices over the scallions and serve hot.

COOK NOTE: Select young tender, clean scallions, with well-trimmed bulbs, firm, with fresh, bright green tops.

VARIATION:
* Whole peeled shallots can be substituted for the scallions.

Butternut Squash with Ginger Flavor

SERVES: 4
CALORIES: 115 per serving
PREPARATION TIME: 5–10 minutes
COOKING TIME: 1 hour

Butternut squash, also called Waltham squash, or African bell, has a thick bulbous neck and base resembling a light bulb. Banana squash, or any hard-shelled winter squash, can be substituted for butternut squash in this recipe. Most winter squash such as butternut are excellent sources of vitamin A. The more orange the flesh of the squash, the richer its supply of vitamin A. In addition, winter squash is low in both sodium and calories.

1 2-pound butternut squash (see Notes)
1 tablespoon unsalted butter or margarine
2 teaspoons grated fresh ginger
2 teaspoons grated lemon rind
Salt and freshly ground white pepper to taste

Garnish:
Grated lemon rind

1. Preheat the oven to 350°F.
2. Puncture a few holes in the squash, place on a baking sheet, and bake for 1 hour, or until the flesh is tender, turning once. Slice the squash in half, remove the flesh, and discard the seeds and peel.
3. Place the squash in a food processor or electric mixer, add the remaining ingredients, and process or blend just until combined.
4. Place the squash in a serving bowl, garnish with additional lemon rind, and serve immediately.

COOK NOTES: Butternut squash, like other winter squash, should be firm and heavy, but not shiny. Select squashes free from blemishes and scars and without blackened stems or rotten spots or pitting.

Store winter squash at room temperature or the starch will convert to sugar and affect the flavor.

VARIATION:
* The squash can be beaten by hand if desired.

Baked Cherry Tomatoes with Dill	SERVES: 6 CALORIES: 61 per serving PREPARATION TIME: 10 minutes COOKING TIME: 18–20 minutes

Cherry tomatoes seem to be available and tasty year-round when other tomatoes are hard and tasteless. It is easy to pop the tomatoes in the oven and bake them for a colorful and tasty side dish.

2 pints cherry tomatoes, washed, stems removed
2 tablespoons unsalted butter or margarine, melted
Salt and freshly ground white pepper to taste
4 teaspoons snipped fresh dill

1. Preheat the oven to 350°F. Generously coat with vegetable cooking spray a shallow baking dish that can accommodate the tomatoes in a single layer.
2. Place the tomatoes in the baking dish, drizzle with butter or margarine, and season with salt and pepper. Bake for 18 to 20 minutes, or until heated through, shaking the pan occasionally.
3. Toss with the dill and serve immediately.

VARIATIONS:
* The tomatoes can be sautéed in a nonstick skillet on top of the range.
* Chives, basil, or even tarragon can be substituted for the dill.

Stir-Fried Zucchini in Black Bean Sauce

SERVES: 4
CALORIES: 83 per serving
PREPARATION TIME: 15–20 minutes
COOKING TIME: 5–6 minutes

Fermented black beans, also called salted black beans, are small preserved soybeans that are extremely strong, pungent, and salty. They are generally used in conjunction with garlic as a flavoring. There is no substitute for these beans since their flavor is so unique. Salt should be added carefully, if at all, to any dish prepared with fermented black beans.

1 pound zucchini, scrubbed clean, cut into ¼″ circles (see Notes)
½ cup sliced water chestnuts
2 teaspoons fermented black beans, rinsed and patted dry
   (available at Chinese groceries and many supermarkets)
1 clove garlic, finely minced
1 teaspoon finely minced fresh ginger
1 tablespoon reduced-sodium soy sauce
1 tablespoon dry sherry
2 teaspoons arrowroot dissolved in 2 tablespoons chicken broth
1 tablespoon peanut oil

1. In a bowl combine the zucchini and water chestnuts and place near the cooking area.
2. Smash the black beans with the side of a Chinese cleaver or kitchen knife and combine with the garlic and ginger on a plate set near the cooking area.
3. In a cup combine the soy sauce and sherry and place along with the arrowroot in broth near the cooking area.
4. Heat a nonstick skillet or wok, add the oil and, when hot, add the garlic-bean mixture and stir-fry for 30 seconds. Add the zucchini and water chestnuts and continue to stir-fry for 3 to 4 minutes. Add the soy sauce mixture, stir to combine; add the arrowroot and broth and stir until the sauce slightly thickens.
5. Serve immediately.

COOK NOTES: Select small to medium firm zucchini with a tender rind that a fingernail can scrape away or puncture easily. Avoid larger zucchini, which tend to be watery and full of seeds.

Black beans are rinsed to remove excess saltiness.

VARIATIONS:
* Any other summer squash, broccoli, or asparagus can be substituted for the zucchini.
* For a spicier dish, add 1 teaspoon chili paste with garlic (available at Asian grocery stores) along with the soy sauce mixture.

Sweet Potato and Carrot Tzimmes	SERVES: 8 CALORIES: 140 per serving PREPARATION TIME: 20 minutes COOKING TIME: about 1 hour 10 minutes

Tzimmes is a traditional Jewish dish, a sweet combination of baked vegetables or meat and vegetables. According to Patti Shosteck in *A Lexicon of Jewish Cooking* (Contemporary Books, 1979): "The Yiddish word tzimmes comes from two German words, zum and essen, meaning 'to the eating.' So often did Jews go 'to the eating' and find a sweet vegetable or fruit stew on the table that the stew itself took on the name tzimmes and so did any mixed-up, troublesome, or messy situation."

6 pitted prunes soaked in ¼ cup boiling water for 30 minutes
1 cup strong chicken broth
1 small onion, thinly sliced
2 carrots, peeled and thinly sliced
1 tart apple, peeled and thinly sliced
2 pounds sweet potatoes, peeled and sliced ½" thick (see Note)
⅔ cup orange juice
2 tablespoons lemon juice
2 teaspoons honey
1 teaspoon grated orange rind
½ teaspoon ground cinnamon
¼ teaspoon grated nutmeg
Salt to taste

1. Remove the prunes from the water, slice them in half, and reserve the liquid.
2. Preheat the oven to 350°F. Lightly coat a 1½-quart casserole with vegetable cooking spray.
3. In a nonstick skillet heat ½ cup broth. Add the onion and carrots and cook over medium heat for 3 minutes. Add the apple, and continue to cook for an additional 3 to 4 minutes, or until the vegetables are soft. Place in a large bowl.
4. Add all the remaining ingredients, including the broth, prunes, and prune liquid to the cooked vegetables. Stir, pour into the prepared casserole, cover, and cook for 55 to 60 minutes, or until the vegetables are very tender.
5. Serve hot.

COOK NOTES: Technically, sweet potatoes are not yams. Yams are moist, starchy tropical vegetables of African origin that appear mainly in Latin markets. The vegetables labeled "yams" or "Louisiana yams" that you see at the supermarket are actually sweet potatoes.

Sweet potatoes can be divided into two types, moist-fleshed and dry-fleshed. The former convert most of their starches to sugar during cooking, becoming sweet and soft; they are a deep orange in color. The latter convert less starch upon being cooked, are less sweet and drier, and are light yellow. Regional preference is the deciding factor.

VARIATION:
* Apple juice can be substituted for the orange juice.

Tomatoes Baked with Spinach Pesto

SERVES: 6
CALORIES: 54 per serving
PREPARATION TIME: 5 minutes
COOKING TIME: 15–20 minutes

Both the colors and the flavors of tomatoes and spinach mesh together well. In this recipe, tomatoes are sliced in half, topped with spinach pesto, a flavoring mixture of spinach, Parmesan cheese, and garlic, and broiled until golden brown on top.

Since the tomatoes are to be cooked, it is not necessary to search for the best ripe tomatoes. This is one way to use those hard supermarket tomatoes and make them tasty.

6 small to medium tomatoes, washed
½ cup Spinach Pesto (page 150)
2 tablespoons grated Parmesan cheese

1. Preheat the oven to 400°F. Lightly coat with vegetable cooking spray a baking pan that can accommodate the tomatoes in a single layer.
2. Slice the tomatoes in half horizontally and gently squeeze out and discard the seeds. Place the tomatoes, cut side up, in the prepared pan and spread the tops with spinach pesto. Sprinkle each tomato with 1 teaspoon cheese.
3. Bake the tomatoes for 15 to 20 minutes, or until lightly golden on top, and serve hot.

VARIATIONS:
* Basil can be substituted for spinach in the pesto.
* Tomatoes may also be broiled 5″ to 6″ from the heat source for 5 to 8 minutes.

MAKE-IT-EASY TIP:
* To keep the tomatoes upright while baking, place the halves in a muffin tin.

Turnips au Gratin	SERVES: 8 CALORIES: 55 per serving PREPARATION TIME: 15–20 minutes COOKING TIME: 25–30 minutes

Turnips are an excellent source of potassium and are very low in calories, particularly when topped with béchamel sauce prepared with nonfat milk. Do not toss away the tender turnip greens, which are a good source of vitamins A and C as well as calcium and iron.

4 large turnips, peeled and sliced ¼" thick (see Note)
Salt and freshly ground white pepper to taste
1 cup Béchamel Sauce (page 85)
3 tablespoons grated Parmesan cheese

Garnish:
Chopped fresh parsley

1. Preheat the oven to 400°F. Lightly coat a 9"- × -12" or similar sized shallow baking dish with vegetable cooking spray.
2. Place a layer of overlapping turnip slices on the bottom of the pan, season with salt and pepper, and top with half the béchamel. Place the remaining turnips on top, season with salt and pepper, cover with the remaining béchamel, and sprinkle with Parmesan cheese.
3. Bake for 25 to 30 minutes, or until lightly golden on top and the turnips are tender.
4. Serve hot, garnished with parsley.

COOK NOTE: Select smooth, round turnips with purple-tinted white skin. There should be only a few scars at the top and fibrous roots at the base. If leafy tops are attached they should be fresh, green, and crisp. Avoid turnips that look shriveled or feel soft. Store turnips in a cold, humid environment such as the refrigerator.

VARIATION:
* Light White Sauce can be substituted for the béchamel.

Baked Ratatouille

SERVES: 8
CALORIES: 84 per serving
PREPARATION TIME: 20–25 minutes
COOKING TIME: about 35 minutes

A traditional ratatouille recipe involves sautéing salted eggplant and zucchini in lots of olive oil. By baking the ratatouille here, the oil is reduced to 1 or 2 tablespoons and the salt is added to taste. Ratatouille makes a wonderful vegetable accompaniment or can be used to fill calzone, top pizzas, or garnish an omelet.

1 medium eggplant, washed, dried, and sliced ¼" thick
1–2 tablespoons olive oil
6 ripe tomatoes
4 medium zucchini, washed and sliced ¼" thick
2 onions, thinly sliced
¼ cup chopped fresh parsley
1 clove garlic, finely minced
2 tablespoons fresh basil, or 1 teaspoon crumbed dried
2 teaspoons capers, drained
½ teaspoon crumbled dried oregano
Salt and freshly ground pepper to taste

1. Preheat a broiler. Coat a 7"-×-11" casserole or similar sized baking dish with vegetable cooking spray.
2. Brush the eggplant slices lightly with oil and broil for about 4 minutes on each side, or until golden. Stack the slices and cut into quarters. Reduce the oven to 350°F.
3. Cut the tomatoes in half crosswise and gently squeeze in your hand to remove the seeds and excess liquid. Slice.
4. In a large bowl place the vegetables and remaining ingredients and gently toss to combine. Put the ratatouille in the prepared casserole.
5. Cover the casserole and bake for 25 minutes, or until the zucchini and onions are tender.
6. Adjust the seasonings and serve hot, at room temperature, or cold.

VARIATIONS:

* Celery, yellow squash, or other seasonal vegetables can be added to this baked vegetable casserole.
* For a heartier casserole, sprinkle 2 tablespoons grated Parmesan cheese on top.

MAKE-IT-EASY TIPS:

* Squeeze the tomatoes over a sieve-lined bowl so that the juice can be saved for other cooking uses and the seeds can be easily discarded.
* In general, substitute 1 teaspoon dried herbs for every tablespoon of fresh herbs. In larger amounts, however, such as 2 tablespoons fresh herbs, cut down on the dried herbs. They can become overpowering and bitter in large quantities.

Mixed Vegetables Cooked in Lettuce Packages	SERVES: 4 CALORIES: 61 per serving PREPARATION TIME: 20–25 minutes COOKING TIME: 15–20 minutes

Any combination of seasonal vegetables can be used for filling the lettuce leaves. Follow the ingredients listed below or be creative and invent a combination of your own.

4 large iceberg lettuce leaves
½ cup strong chicken broth
1 large leek, finely sliced (white part only)
5–6 mushrooms, wiped clean, sliced
2 pattypan squash, washed and each cut into 4 triangles
1½ cups broccoli florets, washed
1 tomato, peeled, seeded, and roughly chopped
Salt and freshly ground pepper to taste

1. Preheat the oven to 400°F.
2. Drop the lettuce leaves into a pot of boiling water; when the water returns to a boil remove the leaves and drain on paper towels.

3. In a medium skillet heat ¼ cup broth and when boiling add the leek; cook over medium heat for 2 minutes. Add the remaining ingredients including the remaining ¼ cup chicken broth, bring to a boil, cover, reduce heat to medium low, and cook for 3 minutes. Allow to cool slightly.
4. Place a quarter of the vegetable mixture on each of the leaves, fold the edges over, and place the folded side down in a baking dish. Bake for 10 minutes.
5. Serve the packages hot and allow your guests to open them at the table.

VARIATION:

* A large zucchini or crookneck squash can be substituted for the pattypan squash.

MAKE-IT-EASY TIP:

* To easily remove lettuce leaves from the head, bang the core end down on a countertop. The core can be easily removed and the leaves readily pulled apart.

SALADS

Two-Lettuce Salad with Creamy Horseradish Dressing	SERVES: 6 CALORIES: 53 per serving PREPARATION TIME: 10 minutes

The creaminess of this wonderfully tangy dressing comes from low-fat yogurt, while the spiciness is a result of horseradish and mustard.

1 head each leaf and red leaf lettuce, washed and dried

Dressing:
½ cup plain low-fat yogurt
1 tablespoon mayonnaise
1 tablespoon finely chopped fresh chives
1 teaspoon grainy-style Dijon mustard
1 teaspoon white horseradish (see Note)
1 teaspoon capers
Salt and freshly ground white pepper to taste

1. Tear the lettuce into pieces and place in a salad bowl.
2. In a medium-sized bowl whisk the dressing ingredients together until smooth.
3. Place the dressing on the salad, toss well, and serve immediately.

COOK NOTE: It is best to use prepared horseradish that is preserved in vinegar for this recipe. If you do grate horseradish yourself in a food processor, make sure to stand back when removing the lid since the fumes are very strong.

VARIATION:
* The dressing can be used as a dip for crudités.

Fennel, Pepper, and Radish Salad with Lime Dressing	SERVES: 6 CALORIES: 59 per serving PREPARATION TIME: 15–20 minutes CHILLING TIME: 1 hour

Florentine fennel, also known as finocchio by Italian cooks, looks like a flattened bunch of celery with a bulbous base and feathery green leaves. It has a distinctive anise taste with a crunchy celerylike texture. The Greeks referred to fennel as the "diet vegetable" since it had so few calories, naming it "Marathon" from their verb *maraino* which meant "to grow thin." Fennel is also rich in vitamin A and is a good source of potassium and calcium.

1 fennel bulb
1 green pepper, seeded and cut into julienne strips
1 bunch radishes, thinly sliced

Dressing:
¼ cup lime juice
2 tablespoons olive oil
1 tablespoon orange juice
2 teaspoons grainy-style Dijon mustard
½ teaspoon sugar
Salt and freshly ground white pepper to taste

1. To prepare the fennel, cut off the feathery tops at bulb level. Remove the tough outer stalks, wash and drain the vegetable, cut off the hard base, and thinly slice with the grain.
2. In a salad bowl combine the fennel, pepper, and radishes.
3. In a small bowl whisk the dressing ingredients until smooth, pour over the salad, toss, and chill for 1 hour, or until ready to serve.

VARIATIONS:
* Lemon juice can be substituted for the lime juice.
* The salad can also be served at room temperature.

Arugula and Persimmon Salad

SERVES: 4
CALORIES: 140 per serving
PREPARATION TIME: 10 minutes

The juxtaposition of the tart arugula greens and the sweet persimmon fruit makes this salad so special. Serve it during the fall and early winter when persimmons are most plentiful. Use either the fuyu, the flatter-shaped applelike hard persimmon, which does not need to be ripe before eating, or the hachiya, the plum-shaped, slightly pointed, bright orange variety, which must be very ripe—I repeat, *very* ripe—before eating. The hachiya should be like a balloon about to burst before eating or you will "pucker up" from the astringency.

1 head Boston lettuce, washed and dried
2 small bunches arugula, washed and dried (see Notes)
2 ripe fuyu or hachiya persimmons (see Notes)

Dressing:
2 tablespoons walnut oil (see Notes)
1 tablespoon balsamic vinegar (see Notes)
1 tablespoon strong chicken broth
½ teaspoon honey
Salt and freshly ground white pepper to taste

1. Tear the lettuce and arugula and distribute among 4 salad plates.
2. Slice the fuyu persimmons (with peel) or spoon hachiya persimmon flesh (without peel) on top of each salad plate.
3. In a cup whisk the dressing ingredients together, sprinkle the dressing over each salad, and serve immediately.

COOK NOTES: Unripe persimmons make you pucker-up because of tannic substances that are transformed only with complete ripening. Persimmons reach full color before they are ripe. To be ripe, a persimmon must be as soft as a very overripe tomato. To ripen a persimmon overnight, wrap in aluminum foil and place in the freezer. Thaw at room temperature and use immediately.

Arugula is a tart salad green of the mustard family. Wrap washed greens in paper towels, place in a plastic bag, and store in the refrigerator for up to 3 days.

Walnut oil imported from France is expensive but, used in small amounts such as in this recipe, can be an essential taste enhancer. Purchase in small amounts and store in the refrigerator for up to 8 months. The domestic walnut oil, usually available in health food stores, is less expensive but does not have the flavor of the imported variety.

Balsamic vinegar, unlike other vinegars, is not made from wine but from the unfermented "must" of white grapes from Modena, Italy, that has been boiled down to a sweet concentrate. Beyond that, by law, balsamic vinegar must be aged for at least 10 years or more, during which time it derives its special flavor and aroma. The resulting product is a vinegar with about 6 percent acidity, highly aromatic, and a wonderfully sweet taste. The rule in Italy for balsamic vinegar is: "use it sparingly!"

VARIATIONS:
* Peanut or olive oil can be substituted for the walnut oil.
* Flavored vinegars such as raspberry, red wine vinegar, or cider vinegar can be substituted for the balsamic vinegar.
* Radicchio, dandelion greens, or other tart greens can be substituted for the arugula.

Mixed Green Salad with Light Vinaigrette	SERVES: 6 CALORIES: 71 per serving PREPARATION TIME: 10 minutes

This is a good basic salad that goes with almost every meal. Any type of seasonal greens can be added for taste and flavor such as tart arugula, radicchio, or endive. The light vinaigrette is zesty and flavorful and yet contains a limited amount of oil. Chicken broth is used to add flavor and substance to the dressing without extra calories.

1 head each romaine lettuce, Boston lettuce, and leaf lettuce, washed and dried

Vinaigrette:
¼ cup chicken broth
2 tablespoons olive oil
1½ tablespoons raspberry or red wine vinegar (see Note)
1 tablespoon lemon juice
1 tablespoon chopped fresh parsley
1½ teaspoons grainy-style Dijon mustard
Pinch of sugar
Salt and freshly ground pepper to taste

1. Tear the lettuce into pieces and place in a salad bowl.
2. In a small bowl combine the dressing ingredients and whisk until smooth.
3. Toss the lettuce with the vinaigrette and serve immediately.

COOK NOTE: Raspberry vinegar adds an additional sweetness to the dressing.

VARIATIONS:

* Minced garlic or shallots, chopped fresh herbs, diced capers, Worcestershire sauce can all be added to the vinaigrette if desired.
* For a thicker consistency the vinaigrette can be pureed in a food processor or blender until smooth.

MAKE-IT-EASY TIP:

* Lettuce can be washed and dried, the leaves wrapped in a tea towel or paper towels, and refrigerated until ready to serve.

Coleslaw with Sweet and Sour Creamy Dressing

SERVES: 6
CALORIES: 89 per serving
PREPARATION TIME: 10–15 minutes
CHILLING TIME: 2–3 hours or overnight

Coleslaw is traditionally prepared with high-fat mayonnaise dressing. Here the dressing is low-fat, prepared with yogurt and buttermilk.

1 head green cabbage, shredded (about 4 cups) (see Note)
2 large carrots, peeled and shredded

Sweet and Sour Creamy Dressing:
¾ cup plain low-fat yogurt
¼ cup buttermilk
2 tablespoons mayonnaise
1 tablespoon cider vinegar
1 tablespoon sugar
1 teaspoon Dijon mustard
½ teaspoon celery seed
Pinch of cayenne pepper
Salt and freshly ground white pepper to taste

Garnish:
Shredded carrots

1. Place the shredded cabbage and carrots in a salad bowl.
2. In a separate bowl combine the dressing ingredients and whisk until smooth, or prepare in a food processor or blender.
3. Toss the cabbage and carrots with the dressing and allow to marinate for 2 to 3 hours or overnight.
4. Serve chilled, garnished with shredded carrots.

COOK NOTE: Select a head of cabbage that is reasonably solid and heavy for its size, with green outer leaves.

VARIATION:
* The salad can be prepared with half green cabbage and half red cabbage.

Greek Salad with Lemon-Herb Dressing	SERVES: 6 CALORIES: 192 per serving PREPARATION TIME: 20 minutes

A traditional Greek salad has lettuce, cucumber, tomatoes, onions, Greek olives, and feta cheese with a dressing rich in olive oil. This light version has all the basics, but a dressing low in oil.

1 large head Boston lettuce, washed and dried
½ "European" hothouse cucumber, thinly sliced, or 1 regular
* cucumber, peeled, seeded, and sliced*
1 small red onion, thinly sliced
1 green pepper, seeded and thinly sliced
1 pint cherry tomatoes, halved
4 fresh basil leaves, shredded
8 sun-dried tomatoes soaked in hot water for 20 minutes, sliced
* (optional) (cellophane-packed not oil-packed)*
2 ounces feta cheese, crumbled

Dressing:
3 tablespoons olive oil
3 tablespoons lemon juice
1 tablespoon grainy-style Dijon mustard
1 teaspoon finely minced garlic
¼ teaspoon crumbled dried oregano
Salt and freshly ground pepper to taste

Garnish:
8 tiny niçoise olives
2 tablespoons chopped pimiento

1. Place the lettuce, cucumber, onion, pepper, cherry tomatoes, and basil in a bowl. Cover with paper towels and plastic wrap and chill until ready to use.
2. When ready to serve, distribute the sun-dried tomatoes, if desired, and the feta cheese over the greens.
3. In a small bowl combine the dressing ingredients, whisk until smooth, and pour over the salad.

4. Toss well and serve immediately garnished with the olives and pimiento.

VARIATIONS:
* The salad can be transformed into a main course by adding a 7-ounce can of water-packed tuna, drained and crumbled.
* Other ingredients can be added if desired: sliced mushrooms, water-packed or frozen artichoke hearts, zucchini, crookneck squash, broccoli or cauliflower florets, spinach leaves, and green beans.

MAKE-IT-EASY TIP:
* Greens can be washed and thoroughly dried, placed in paper towels, and refrigerated in a plastic bag for several hours in advance.

Romaine Lettuce and Grapefruit Salad with Red Onion	SERVES: 4 CALORIES: 107 per serving PREPARATION TIME: 10–15 minutes

The natural sweetness in this salad comes from frozen apple juice concentrate. The vinaigrette is light in oil and is made smooth in texture thanks to the addition of broth and grainy mustard.

1 head romaine lettuce, washed and dried
1 grapefruit (see Note)
½ red onion, thinly sliced

Dressing:
2 tablespoons vegetable oil
2 tablespoons strong chicken broth
2 tablespoons lemon juice
2 teaspoons frozen apple juice concentrate, thawed
1 teaspoon grainy-style Dijon mustard
Salt and freshly ground white pepper to taste

1. Tear the lettuce into small pieces. Peel the grapefruit using a sharp knife to remove all the outer white membrane. Cut each slice of grapefruit in between the inner membrane.
2. Place the lettuce in the bottom of a salad bowl or on individual plates, top with prettily arranged grapefruit sections, and finally place a layer of onion rings.
3. In a small bowl whisk the dressing ingredients until smooth.
4. Pour the dressing over the salad and serve immediately.

COOK NOTE: When selecting grapefruit, choose firm globes with smooth skin and a well-rounded or slightly flattened shape. A grapefruit should be heavy for its size, a good indication of high juice content. Avoid puffy-looking grapefruit with rough skin; they will probably lack flavor and juiciness.

VARIATION:
* Two heads leaf lettuce or Boston lettuce may be substituted for the romaine.

MAKE-IT-EASY TIP:
* To easily peel a grapefruit, cut a slice from the top and place on a cutting board, cut side down. With a sharp paring knife, cut off the peel in strips from top to bottom, making sure to remove the white membrane or pith as well.

Spinach Salad with Creamy Curry Dressing

SERVES: 6
CALORIES: 89 per serving
PREPARATION TIME: 10–15 minutes

Although it is true that spinach is not quite the ultimate food in terms of nutrition as we've been told for centuries, it is still high in iron, potassium, and vitamins A and C, and is a good source of fiber.

2 pounds fresh spinach leaves, washed and dried
1 tart apple, peeled, cored, and roughly chopped
3 scallions, finely minced (green and white parts included)

Dressing:
¾ cup plain low-fat yogurt
1½ tablespoons mayonnaise
2 teaspoons lemon juice
½ teaspoon curry powder or to taste
1 teaspoon Dijon mustard
Salt and freshly ground white pepper to taste

Garnish:
Toasted sesame seeds

1. Remove the tough stems from the spinach; tear the leaves into small pieces, and place in a salad bowl along with the apple and scallions.
2. In a small bowl combine the dressing ingredients and whisk until smooth.
3. Pour the dressing over the spinach leaves, toss well, and serve immediately, garnished with toasted sesame seeds.

VARIATION:
* ½ cup sliced water chestnuts can be added.

MAKE-IT-EASY TIP:
* An easy way to dry spinach is to wrap the leaves in layers of paper towels or tea towels, place in a plastic bag, tie up, and refrigerate for several hours. The spinach will be dry and crisp.

Watercress Salad with Orange and Red Onion

SERVES: 4
CALORIES: 154 per serving
PREPARATION TIME: 10 minutes

Watercress is incredibly low in calories, about 6 calories per cup —and in larger quantities is valuable for its source of vitamins A and C and calcium and iron. Topped with this low-fat dressing it is a perfect addition to a light meal.

2 bunches watercress, washed and dried
2 navel oranges, peeled, sliced, and cut into small pieces (see Notes)
½ red onion, thinly sliced

Dressing:
3 tablespoons olive oil
2 tablespoons raspberry or red wine vinegar
½ teaspoon Dijon mustard
Pinch of salt
Salt and freshly ground pepper

1. In a large salad bowl layer the watercress with the oranges and onions.
2. In a small bowl whisk the dressing ingredients until smooth.
3. Pour the dressing over the salad, toss well, and serve immediately.

COOK NOTES: Select firm and heavy oranges with fine-textured skin. A green skin color or russeting does not indicate poor quality.

When peeling an orange, make sure to remove all the white membrane, called the pith.

VARIATIONS:
* Sweet Maui onions can be substituted for the red onion.
* Tart apples, peeled and thinly sliced, can be substituted for the oranges.

Sashimi Salad

SERVES: 4
CALORIES: 145 per serving
PREPARATION TIME: 15 minutes

This salad combines the fresh taste of raw fish with the crispy texture of crunchy vegetables in a wonderful first-course or lunch dish. If raw fish is not your thing, by all means substitute cooked bay shrimp or crab for the fish.

The vegetables can be varied according to seasonality and preference for taste and color.

1 bunch red leaf, leaf, or Boston lettuce, washed and dried
¼ pound radicchio, washed and dried
1 cup shredded daikon radish
½ cup shredded carrots
¼ cup finely minced scallions (green and white parts included)
4 ounces very fresh Hawaiian tuna or yellowtail (or combination
  of both) (see Notes)

Dressing:
2 tablespoons toasted sesame oil
2 tablespoons reduced-sodium soy sauce
2 tablespoons Japanese rice or white wine vinegar
2 teaspoons sake (Japanese wine) or dry sherry
1 teaspoon sugar
Pinch of wasabi powder (Japanese horseradish)

Garnish:
Toasted sesame seeds
Pickled ginger

1. Arrange a bed of lettuce attractively on each of 4 plates; top with the radicchio, daikon, carrots, and scallions.
2. Pat the fish with paper towels, place on a cutting board, and with a very sharp knife slice into ¼"-thick slices or slightly thinner if possible, using smooth strokes.
3. Top each of the salads with fish slices artistically arranged on top of the greens.

4. In a small bowl whisk the dressing ingredients until smooth and pour over each salad.
5. Serve immediately topped with sesame seeds and a garnish of pickled ginger.

COOK NOTES: Since the fish is to be eaten raw, it must be *very* fresh! The fish should be sliced at the last possible minute, before serving.

Raw fish cut for sushi is very thinly sliced while fish cut for sashimi, as here, is cut slightly thicker.

VARIATIONS:
* Red cabbage can be substituted for the radicchio.
* Jicama or even sliced water chestnuts can be substituted for the daikon radish.
* A few shakes of Tabasco can be substituted for the fiery wasabi powder.

Warm Grilled Salmon Salad	SERVES: 4 CALORIES: 376 per serving PREPARATION TIME: 20 minutes MARINATING TIME: 1–2 hours COOKING TIME: 4–6 minutes

This is an adaptation of a dish served at the Neiman-Marcus restaurant in Beverly Hills, which features both spa and light-style cooking.

1 12-ounce salmon fillet

Marinade:
½ cup fresh lemon juice
3 tablespoons olive oil
3 tablespoons white wine
1 tablespoon chopped fresh basil
1 teaspoon fresh chopped rosemary
1 teaspoon chopped fresh thyme
Salt and freshly ground pepper to taste

1 head each Boston and red leaf lettuce, washed and dried
2 small bunches arugula, or similar bitter-flavored greens, washed and dried
1 10-ounce package frozen artichoke hearts, cooked according to package directions, cooled and halved, or 1 14-ounce can artichoke hearts, drained and halved
1 pint cherry tomatoes, washed and halved
⅔ cup frozen corn kernels, thawed
8 small pitted black olives, drained

1. Place the salmon in a glass or ceramic-coated dish.
2. In a small bowl combine the marinade ingredients, whisk until smooth, and pour half the mixture over the salmon, coating both sides. (Reserve half for the salad dressing and set aside.) Cover and allow to marinate at room temperature for 1 to 2 hours.
3. Preheat an outdoor or indoor grill or broiler.
4. Arrange the lettuces and arugula on 4 individual plates. Distribute the artichoke hearts, tomatoes, corn, and olives over each salad.
5. Remove the salmon from the marinade, drain well, and grill for 2 to 3 minutes per side, basting often. Slice the salmon thinly or cut into large chunks. Place the remaining marinade on top of the greens, top with warm grilled salmon, and serve immediately.

VARIATIONS:
* Additional vegetables such as steamed asparagus or string beans can be added to the greens if desired.
* If fresh basil, rosemary, or thyme are unavailable, substitute chopped fresh parsley or dill, which are more plentiful all year.

MAKE-IT-EASY TIP:
* A cast-iron pan with a grid on the bottom, coated before heating with vegetable cooking spray or a light rubbing of oil, provides an easy and quick method of grilling the salmon.

Gazpacho Salad

SERVES: 4
CALORIES: 111 per serving
PREPARATION TIME: 15–20 minutes
CHILLING TIME: 1 hour

Gazpacho is a chilled Spanish soup consisting of salad ingredients such as tomatoes, green pepper, onions, garlic, olive oil, and vinegar. This salad has all the ingredients but is served finely chopped with a low-fat dressing.

It is best to prepare this salad in the summer and early fall when tomatoes are at their ripest and most flavorful. In fact, this salad offers a good opportunity to use overripe tomatoes.

4 medium ripe tomatoes, roughly chopped
1 cup "European" hothouse cucumbers, roughly chopped
1 cup green or red pepper, roughly chopped
2 scallions, finely chopped (green and white parts included)
¼ cup red onion, roughly chopped

Dressing:
2½ tablespoons, red wine vinegar
2 tablespoons olive oil
2 tablespoons finely chopped fresh basil
1½ teaspoons finely minced garlic
1 teaspoon Dijon mustard
Salt and freshly ground pepper to taste

Garnish:
Chopped fresh cilantro (coriander)

1. In a large salad bowl combine the vegetables.
2. In a small bowl combine the dressing ingredients, whisk until smooth, and pour over the vegetables. Gently toss, cover, and chill for 1 hour.
3. Serve the salad chilled, garnished with chopped parsley.

VARIATIONS:
* Other chopped vegetables such as zucchini, leeks, or radishes can be added if desired.
* Do not substitute dried basil for fresh in this recipe. If fresh basil is unavailable, substitute chopped fresh parsley.

Sweet and Sour Chinese Cabbage	SERVES: 4 CALORIES: 104 per serving PREPARATION TIME: 15 minutes COOKING TIME: 5 minutes

This vegetarian dish is a favorite in Peking. It is wonderful served hot or cold the next day as a pungent salad. Celery cabbage, or napa cabbage, Peking, Shantung, Tientsin, chou de Chine, or pe-tsai, are really all Chinese cabbage, which has a compact barrel shape, uniform yellow-white color, and broadly ribbed leaf stalks with crinkled leaves.

1½ pounds celery cabbage
2 tablespoons reduced-sodium soy sauce
2 tablespoons orange juice
2 teaspoons sugar
Salt to taste
1½ tablespoons peanut oil
2–3 small dried whole red chile peppers
2 tablespoons Japanese rice vinegar

1. To prepare Chinese celery cabbage, wash well, particularly at the base. Remove the root and outer leaves from the cabbage and discard. Cut the inner leaves crosswise into 1½" pieces.
2. In a small bowl combine the soy sauce, orange juice, sugar, and salt; set near the cooking area.
3. In a wok or large skillet heat the oil and stir-fry the peppers over medium heat for 30 seconds, or until they darken.
4. Add the cabbage and stir-fry over medium heat for 2–3 minutes, stirring constantly to prevent browning. Add the

sauce and toss to coat. Add the vinegar and continue to stir-fry for 30 seconds.

5. Remove the peppers and serve warm or chill and serve cold.

COOK NOTE: Cantonese housewives sometimes leave celery cabbage out on the kitchen counter a day before use to allow its crisp leaves to sweeten as they wilt.

VARIATION:

* White vinegar can be substituted for Japanese rice vinegar.

Pasta and Chicken Salad with Hot and Sweet Mustard Dressing	SERVES: 4 CALORIES: 430 per serving PREPARATION TIME: 15–20 minutes COOKING TIME: 10–15 minutes

This is my favorite salad, light in oil, full of texture, and with a spicy sweet and sour mustard dressing.

2 whole skinless, boneless chicken breasts
2 tablespoons grainy-style Dijon mustard
1 tablespoon lemon juice
½ pound capelli d'angelo (angel hair pasta) or capellini
2 tablespoons chopped fresh parsley
2 tablespoons chopped fresh chives or scallion greens
2 teaspoons toasted sesame seeds

Hot and Sweet Mustard:
2 tablespoons rice vinegar
1 tablespoon corn oil
1 tablespoon grainy-style Dijon mustard
2 teaspoons toasted sesame oil
2 teaspoons honey
2 teaspoons reduced-sodium soy sauce
1 teaspoon dry mustard
1 clove garlic, finely minced

½ teaspoon grated fresh ginger, or pinch of ground
⅛ teaspoon red pepper flakes
Salt and freshly ground black pepper to taste

Garnish:
Chopped red preserved ginger or pimiento strips

1. Preheat a broiler or outdoor grill. Pound the chicken to uniform thickness between sheets of waxed paper, to ensure even cooking.
2. Grill the chicken for 4 to 5 minutes per side, or until just tender, basting with the mustard and lemon juice. (Do not overcook.) Cut into bite-sized pieces.
3. Cook the pasta in a pot of boiling water until just tender. Drain and cool. Combine with the chicken in a large salad bowl. Add the parsley, chives, and sesame seeds; toss again. Allow to cool thoroughly.
4. In a food processor or blender combine the dressing ingredients until smooth. Pour over the salad, toss and serve at room temperature or chill and serve cold, garnished with chopped ginger or pimiento strips.

VARIATIONS:
* Grilled shrimp can be substituted for the chicken.
* Regular Dijon mustard can be substituted for the grainy variety, but the latter adds texture and additional flavor to the recipe.

MAKE-IT-EASY TIP:
* Toasted sesame seeds are available at Asian markets or some supermarkets. If not available, toast regular sesame seeds in a nonstick pan for a few minutes, until golden.

Sunomono (Japanese Vinegared Salad)	SERVES 4 CALORIES: 67 per serving PREPARATION TIME: 10–15 minutes MARINATING TIME: 2–3 hours or overnight

Sunomono means "vinegared things," especially this low-fat salad, which includes no oil. If possible, use "European" hothouse cucumbers, which are easier to handle since they require no peeling or seeding.

1 large "European" hothouse cucumber, or 2 regular cucumbers, peeled and seeded, thinly sliced
1 teaspoon salt
½ cup Japanese rice vinegar
1½ tablespoons sugar
1½ tablespoons reduced-sodium soy sauce
Red leaf lettuce
6 ounces bay shrimp or small to medium shrimp, diced

Garnish:
2 scallions, finely chopped (green part only)

1. Place the cucumber slices in a colander, sprinkle with salt to release excess moisture, and allow to stand for 20 minutes. Rinse, pat dry to remove any water and excess salt, and place in a medium-sized bowl.
2. In a small bowl combine the vinegar, sugar, and soy sauce, stir and pour over the cucumbers. Toss well, cover, and allow to marinate for 2 to 3 hours or overnight.
3. Just before serving, drain the cucumbers from the marinade and arrange attractively on 4 lettuce-lined salad plates.
4. Toss the shrimp in the reserved marinade and place on top of the salads. Garnish with scallions and serve chilled.

VARIATIONS:
* White wine or even cider vinegar can be substituted for the Japanese vinegar.
* Crab, lobster, or other cooked seafood can be substituted for the shrimp.

Jicama Salad

SERVES: 8
CALORIES: 67 per serving
PREPARATION TIME: 15 minutes
CHILLING TIME: 1 hour

Jicama is a tropical root vegetable in the morning glory family that originated in Mexico. (The name literally means "edible storage root.") It resembles a giant turnip in shape and is brown like a potato on the outside. The taste is a cross between an apple and a fresh water chestnut.

2 medium jicama, peeled and grated (3 to 4 cups) (see Note)
5 scallions, thinly sliced
1 large green pepper, seeded and julienned
½ large "European" hothouse cucumber, or 1 large cucumber,
  peeled and seeded, julienned

Dressing:
3 tablespoons olive oil
2 tablespoons red wine vinegar
2 tablespoons grainy-style Dijon mustard
Salt and freshly ground pepper to taste

1. Place the vegetables in a large salad bowl.
2. In a small bowl combine the dressing ingredients and whisk until smooth.
3. Pour over the salad and allow to chill for 1 hour before serving.

COOK NOTE: Select firm jicamas. The vegetable is often quite large, but sections can be cut off, the cut side of the leftover piece covered with plastic wrap, and refrigerated for several weeks.

VARIATIONS:
* If jicama is unavailable substitute peeled celery root, sun-chokes, or even carrots.
* Balsamic vinegar, a beautifully aged and flavorful vinegar, makes a lovely addition to this salad. Balsamic vinegar is highly aromatic, with a sweet and intense flavor.

Mushroom Salad

SERVES: 4
CALORIES: 119 per serving
PREPARATION TIME: 10 minutes
CHILLING TIME: 1 hour

Unlike most salads, which are tossed at the very last minute to avoid sogginess, this mushroom salad should be allowed to marinate in the dressing for an hour before serving. The mushrooms should be tossed with the dressing immediately after slicing to avoid discoloration.

1 pound mushrooms, wiped clean, sliced

Dressing:
3 tablespoons chicken broth
2½ tablespoons olive oil
2 tablespoons lemon juice
1½ teaspoons grainy-style Dijon mustard
1 tablespoon capers, drained
Pinch of sugar
Salt and freshly ground pepper to taste

Garnish:
Chopped fresh parsley

1. Place the mushrooms in a bowl.
2. In a food processor or blender puree the dressing ingredients until smooth.
3. Immediately toss the mushrooms with the dressing, coating well; cover and refrigerate for 1 hour, or until ready to use.
4. Allow to sit at room temperature for 20 minutes and serve garnished with parsley and black pepper.

VARIATION:
* Minced garlic or shallots can be added to the dressing.

MAKE-IT-EASY TIPS:

* A mushroom brush, or similar style soft brush, dipped in lemon juice, is a handy tool for cleaning mushrooms without soaking them.
* Mushrooms are stored most successfully in a brown paper bag, which absorbs excess moisture.

Three-Pepper Salad with Oranges and Cumin-Flavored Dressing	SERVES: 6 CALORIES: 77 per serving PREPARATION TIME: 15 minutes

Low in calories—a medium pepper contains about 15—bell peppers are extremely high in vitamin C. In addition, 1 medium raw bell pepper provides more than the recommended daily allowance of vitamin C for an adult. It also supplies some vitamin A and a variety of other vitamins and minerals, plus fiber for good digestion. The dressing for the salad is made creamy with low-fat yogurt.

1 large green pepper, seeded and julienned
1 red pepper, seeded and julienned
1 yellow pepper, seeded and julienned
3 navel oranges, peeled, sliced, and slices cut into quarters
3 scallions, finely chopped (green and white parts included)
3 tablespoons chopped fresh cilantro (coriander)

Dressing:
¼ cup plain low-fat yogurt
2 tablespoons lime juice
2 teaspoons corn oil
1 teaspoon honey
¼ teaspoon ground cumin
Salt and freshly ground pepper to taste

1. Layer the salad ingredients in a large glass bowl.
2. In a small bowl whisk the dressing ingredients until smooth.
3. Toss the salad with the dressing and serve immediately.

VARIATIONS:
* If red and yellow peppers are unavailable or overly expensive, use only green peppers and garnish the salad with chopped pimiento for color.
* The salad can be chilled for 2 hours before serving.

MAKE-IT-EASY TIP:
* To peel an orange easily, cut a slice from the top and place on a cutting board, cut side down. With a sharp paring knife, cut off the peel in strips from top to bottom, making sure to remove the white membrane as well.

Chicken and Watercress Salad

SERVES: 6
CALORIES: 171 per serving
PREPARATION TIME: 15 minutes
COOKING TIME: about 20 minutes
MARINATING TIME: 4–6 hours or overnight

As with most ancient plants, many myths and legends became associated with watercress. The ancient Persians were advised to feed watercress to their children if they wanted to improve their growth. Since green leafy vegetables are an excellent source of vitamins and minerals, the advice was probably good.

The chicken is cooked by a Chinese method called "White-cut" style, which is a wonderful way to poach chicken to a velvety texture that is perfect for salads.

2 quarts water or broth
2 whole uncooked or cooked chicken breasts, skin and bones
  discarded
1 onion, sliced
1 carrot, sliced

Dressing:
¼ cup chicken broth
3 tablespoons lemon juice
2½ tablespoons olive oil
1½–2 tablespoons fresh snipped dill

1 tablespoon grainy-style Dijon mustard
1 clove garlic, finely minced
Salt and freshly ground pepper to taste

1 pound watercress (about 2 bunches), washed and broken into
  bite-sized pieces
1 "European" hothouse cucumber, thinly sliced
Salt and freshly ground pepper to taste

1. To cook the chicken for the salad (if you're not using leftover cooked chicken), in a pot large enough to hold the chicken breasts comfortably bring the water or broth to a boil. Add the chicken, onion, and carrot, bring to a boil again, cover tightly, reduce heat to medium, and cook without peeking for 15 minutes. Turn off the flame entirely and allow the chicken to cool in the cooking liquid in the covered pot for 20 minutes. Strain and reserve the broth for another use. Discard skin and bones, shred the chicken, and place in a large bowl. (If using cooked chicken, shred the meat.)
2. In a small bowl, combine the dressing ingredients, stir well, and pour over the chicken. Toss to combine, cover, and refrigerate for 4 to 6 hours or overnight.
3. Place the watercress and cucumber in a large bowl, top with the chicken and dressing, adjust the seasonings, toss, and serve chilled or at room temperature.

VARIATION:
* Spinach, basil, arugula, radicchio, or other greens can be substituted for the watercress.

Snow Pea Salad with Lemon-Ginger Dressing	SERVES: 6 CALORIES: 93 per serving PREPARATION TIME: 10–15 minutes CHILLING TIME: 2–3 hours or overnight

The pungent lemon-ginger dressing is low in oil but made thick and creamy with the addition of grainy-style Dijon mustard.

1½ pounds fresh Chinese snow peas, stringed (see Note)

Dressing:
3 tablespoons lemon juice
2 tablespoons grainy-style Dijon mustard
1 teaspoon fresh ginger
Salt and freshly ground white pepper to taste
2 tablespoons olive oil

1. Drop the peas into a pot of boiling salted water and, when the water returns to a boil, drain. Rinse under cold running water and drain again. Chill for 2 to 3 hours or overnight.
2. In food processor or blender, process lemon juice with mustard, ginger, and salt and pepper. While machine is running add oil through top opening and continue to process until smooth. Chill until ready to serve.
3. When ready to serve, arrange the snow peas on a serving platter, drizzle with dressing, and serve chilled.

COOK NOTE: Snow peas, also called edible pod, Chinese pea, or sugar pea, are edible pods essential to Chinese and, more currently, French cuisine. In France, they are called *mange-tout*, referring to the fact that you "eat it all," including the pod. Store snow peas sealed in a plastic bag to preserve moisture.

VARIATIONS:
* Broccoli or cauliflower florets blanched for 2 minutes can be substituted for the snow peas.

* Sugar snap peas, a variety introduced in 1979, can be substituted for the snow peas. This new variety, a cross between a garden pea and a snow pea, is round and fat like a green bean, and should be prepared in the same manner as a snow pea.

Chilled Chinese Bean Curd in Sauce	SERVES: 6 CALORIES: 111 per serving PREPARATION TIME: 10 minutes CHILLING TIME: 2 hours

Chinese or Japanese bean curd cakes, also called tofu, are a low-calorie source of protein. This recipe is like a salad with spicy dressing.

1 1-pound package Chinese bean curd (tofu), drained and cut
   into 1″ square pieces (see Notes)
2 scallions, finely chopped (green part only)
1 teaspoon finely minced fresh ginger

Sauce:
2 tablespoons reduced-sodium soy sauce
1½ tablespoons Japanese rice vinegar
1 tablespoon peanut oil
1 tablespoon toasted sesame oil
½ teaspoon sugar
Salt to taste

Garnish:
2 teaspoons toasted sesame seeds

1. Place the bean curd in a medium bowl and gently toss with the scallions and ginger.
2. In a small bowl combine the sauce ingredients and whisk until smooth. Pour over the bean curd, gently toss to coat, and chill for 2 hours.

3. Garnish with sesame seeds, toss, and serve the bean curd chilled or at room temperature.

COOK NOTES: Tofu is available in 1-pound or occasionally 14.2-ounce packages. Either size will work in this recipe.

If only Japanese or soft variety of bean curd is available, you can press the water from the curds to make them firmer. To press, wrap each bean curd cake (or slice a whole cake into 2″ horizontal lengths) in cheesecloth and put in a large dish; place a 2- to 3-pound weight on top. A large book or several cans will do. After 1 hour, unwrap the bean curd and proceed with the recipe.

VARIATION:

* Finely chopped cucumbers or radishes can be added for a crunchier texture.

Spaghetti Squash Salad	SERVES: 6 CALORIES: 81 per serving PREPARATION TIME: 10 minutes COOKING TIME: 1 hour 10 minutes MARINATING TIME: 30 minutes

Spaghetti squash, also known as diet spaghetti, is a large oval-shaped vegetable that owes its name to the stringy texture of its flesh which, when cooked, turns into spaghettilike strands. Spaghetti squash often contains a sticker explaining how to cut and steam it, but I have yet to find anyone who can cut through this gourd with anything less than a hacksaw. Baking or boiling whole softens the skin and makes cutting easier.

1 medium-large spaghetti squash
½ "European" hothouse cucumber, grated
2 scallions, finely chopped (green parts only)

Dressing:
2 tablespoons peanut oil
1½ tablespoons Japanese white vinegar
2 teaspoons reduced-sodium soy sauce
1 teaspoon finely minced garlic
½ teaspoon grated fresh ginger
Salt and freshly ground pepper to taste

Garnish:
2 tablespoons toasted sesame seeds

1. Preheat the over to 350°F.
2. Prick the squash with a fork all over and bake for 1 hour and 20 minutes, turning once. When cool enough to handle, split the squash in half horizontally, scoop out and discard the seeds. With a fork, string the fibers out of each half. Chill the cooked "spaghetti."
3. In a large bowl place the squash, cucumber, and scallions.
4. In a separate bowl combine the dressing ingredients, whisk until smooth, and pour over the squash mixture. Toss well, cover, and allow to marinate in the refrigerator for 30 seconds.
5. Top with sesame seeds, adjust seasonings, and serve chilled or at room temperature.

VARIATION:
* Zucchini can be substituted for the cucumber.

Brown Rice Salad with Crunchy Vegetables	SERVES: 6 CALORIES: 133 per serving PREPARATION TIME: 15–20 minutes COOKING TIME: 40 minutes CHILLING TIME: 4 hours or overnight

Brown rice is nutritionally superior to white rice and makes a delicious crunchy-textured salad when combined with vegetables and a low-fat dressing prepared with low-fat yogurt.

3 cups raw brown rice
3 cups water
2 large carrots, peeled and finely chopped
8 water chestnuts, finely chopped
2 scallions, finely chopped (green and white parts included)
1 stalk celery, finely chopped
1 cup Sweet and Sour Creamy Dressing (page 290)
Salt and freshly ground pepper to taste

Garnish:
2 tablespoons toasted sesame seeds

1. To cook the brown rice, place the water in a medium saucepan, bring to a boil, add the rice, but do not stir. Cover, reduce heat, and simmer slowly for 40 minutes, or until the liquid is absorbed and the grains are tender.
2. In a large bowl combine the rice with the remaining ingredients and stir until well-mixed. Place in a covered container and chill for 4 hours or overnight.
3. Season to taste with salt and pepper, top with sesame seeds, and serve chilled.

VARIATIONS:
* Other chopped seasonal vegetables such as zucchini, cucumber, or even tomato, can be added if desired.
* Cooked chicken, meat, or seafood can turn this recipe into a main-course salad.

Tabbouleh (Wheat Pilaf Salad)

SERVES: 6
CALORIES: 126 per serving
PREPARATION TIME: 1 hour
CHILLING TIME: 2 hours or overnight

Tabbouleh, or tabbouli, is a salad made with Middle Eastern bulgur, a cracked wheat, marinated with fresh mint, lemon juice, and spices. Tabbouleh is low in calories and high in fiber. For best results use a fine-grain bulgur.

1 cup fine-grain bulgur soaked in 2 cups boiling water for 1 hour
½ cup chopped fresh parsley
3 tablespoons finely chopped fresh mint leaves
2 scallions, finely chopped (green and white parts included)
¼ cup lemon juice
1 tablespoon finely grated lemon rind
1 teaspoon finely minced garlic
¼ teaspoon ground coriander
¼ teaspoon ground cumin
¼ teaspoon dry mustard
Pinch of paprika
Salt and freshly ground pepper to taste

Garnish:
Halved cherry tomatoes
Fresh sprigs of mint

1. When the bulgur wheat is light and fluffy, in a bowl combine the remaining ingredients, toss with the bulgur, and mix well; chill, covered, in the refrigerator for 2 hours or overnight.
2. Taste, adjust the seasoning with salt and pepper, and serve chilled, garnished with halved cherry tomatoes and fresh mint sprigs.

COOK NOTE: Coriander and cumin are two spices that are pungent on their own but especially flavorful when used together.

VARIATIONS:

* Seeded and roughly chopped tomatoes can be added if desired.
* Lime juice can be substituted for the lemon juice.
* Tabbouleh can be used as a filling for grape leaves and served as an appetizer.

Lentil Salad

SERVES: 6
CALORIES: 178 per serving
PREPARATION TIME: 10 minutes
COOKING TIME: 40 minutes

Lentils add an excellent source of protein to this salad, which can be served as a side dish or a main-course supper salad.

1 cup dried lentils
1 medium onion stuck with 2 whole cloves
1 small bay leaf
3¼ cups water
⅓ cup finely minced scallions (green and white parts included)
2 teaspoons finely minced garlic
2 tablespoons olive oil
2 tablespoons red wine vinegar
1 teaspoon Dijon mustard
½ teaspoon crumbled dried thyme
Salt and freshly ground pepper to taste

Garnish:
12 cherry tomatoes
2 tablespoons chopped fresh parsley

1. In a large Dutch oven or kettle place the lentils, onion, and bay leaf. Cover with the water, bring to a boil, cover, reduce heat, and simmer slowly until the lentils are just tender, 40 to 45 minutes. Do not overcook. If there's any excess liquid, drain off. Discard the onion and bay leaf.
2. Place the lentils in a large bowl, add the scallions and garlic, and gently toss.

3. In a small bowl whisk the remaining ingredients together, pour over the salad, and toss to combine the flavors.
4. Serve at room temperature or chill and serve cold, garnished with cherry tomatoes and chopped parsley.

COOK NOTES: Do not overcook lentils for salad or they will become mushy and have a disagreeable effect on the texture of the salad.

If serving the salad chilled, remember to adjust seasonings.

VARIATION
* Chopped green or red peppers can be added with the scallions.

Beet and Red Potato Salad with Mustard-Horseradish Dressing	SERVES: 4 CALORIES: 168 per serving PREPARATION TIME: 15 minutes COOKING TIME: 1¼ hours CHILLING TIME: 2–4 hours

An inch of the stem portion of the beet is retained to prevent "bleeding" of the color as well as the nutrients during cooking. Do not toss away the tops of the greens. Beet greens are an excellent source of vitamin A, potassium, and iron.

1 bunch fresh beets, rinsed
4 medium red potatoes
2 scallions, finely minced (green and white parts included)

Dressing:
2 tablespoons grainy-style Dijon mustard
1½ tablespoons olive oil
1 tablespoon red wine vinegar
1 teaspoon white horseradish
Salt and freshly ground white pepper to taste

Garnish:
Beet greens

1. Preheat the oven to 400°F.
2. Cut off the beet greens and reserve for garnish, retaining an inch of the stem portion. Leave the root end intact and wrap the beets tightly in aluminum foil. Bake for 1¼ hours, or until tender. Unwrap, peel, and cut off the stem and root ends. Cut into quarters.
3. In the meantime, scrub the potatoes, wrap in foil, and bake for 30 minutes, or until fork-tender. Unwrap and cut into quarters similar in size to the beets.
4. In a bowl combine the dressing ingredients together, whisk until smooth, and pour half over each of the vegetables. Toss separately and chill for 2 to 4 hours, or until ready to serve.
5. Arrange the beets and potatoes on a plate of beet greens and serve chilled or at room temperature.

VARIATION:

* Leftover meats or poultry can be added to turn this dish into a main-course salad.

MAKE-IT-EASY TIP:

* To avoid burning and staining the fingers, wear rubber gloves while peeling the beets.

Salad of Buckwheat Noodles with Crunchy Vegetables	SERVES: 8 CALORIES: 243 per serving PREPARATION TIME: 20 minutes COOKING TIME: 3–5 minutes

Japanese soba, also called buckwheat noodles, are actually made with a combination of wheat and buckwheat flours. They are available in many east Asian markets as well as health food stores.

1 14-ounce package soba (buckwheat noodles)
½ cup flaked crabmeat
1 3"-piece "European" hothouse cucumber, or 5" piece regular cucumber, peeled and seeded, julienned

3 carrots, peeled and cut into julienne strips
1 3"-piece daikon radish, peeled and cut into julienne strips
2 scallions, finely chopped (green parts only)
1 cup alfalfa or mung bean sprouts

Dressing:
3 tablespoons reduced-sodium soy sauce
2 tablespoons dry sherry
1 tablespoon toasted sesame oil
1 tablespoon peanut oil
½ teaspoon minced fresh ginger

1. Add the soba to a large pot of boiling water, stir, allow the water to reach a second boil, and cook over medium heat for 3 to 5 minutes, or until just tender. The buckwheat noodles cook very rapidly so watch carefully to avoid overcooking, which will result in a mushy texture. Drain well and run under cold water for several minutes to cool and prevent from sticking. Drain again.
2. In a large bowl combine the crab, cucumber, carrots, daikon, scallions, and sprouts.
3. In a bowl whisk the dressing ingredients together, pour over the noodles, and toss well.
4. Add the noodles to the crab mixture, toss well, and serve at room temperature or slightly chilled.

VARIATIONS:
* A new product called surimi, imitation crab, or sea legs, a combination of fish made to look like crab, can be substituted for the crab.
* Blanched snow pea pods, broccoli, or other vegetables can be added as desired.

Crab Salad with Sweet Peppers	SERVES: 6 CALORIES: 133 per serving PREPARATION TIME: 15–20 minutes CHILLING TIME: 2 hours

This light salad can be served as a supper for 4, a side dish for 6, and an appetizer for 8.

1 medium red pepper, seeded, finely chopped
1 medium yellow pepper, seeded, finely chopped
1 zucchini, finely chopped

Dressing:
2 tablespoons peanut oil
2 tablespoons Japanese rice vinegar
2 tablespoons reduced-sodium soy sauce
2 tablespoons finely chopped scallions
 (green and white parts included)
2 tablespoons finely chopped cilantro (coriander)
1 teaspoon finely minced garlic
Salt and freshly ground white pepper to taste
1 pound crabmeat, flaked (see Note)

Garnish:
Toasted sesame seeds

1. Place the peppers and zucchini in a large bowl.
2. In a small bowl whisk the dressing ingredients until smooth, pour over the salad, cover, and allow to marinate for 2 hours.
3. Add the crabmeat, toss, garnish with sesame seeds, and serve the salad chilled.

COOK NOTES: Always pick over crabmeat carefully to remove bits of cartilage, especially in the fresh variety.

Crab is added at the end because if marinated with the vegetables, it will lose its white color in the soy sauce.

VARIATIONS:
* Shrimp, lobster, or other seafood can be substituted for the crab.
* The vegetables can be julienned if desired.
* Green pepper can be substituted for the red and yellow peppers.

Spicy Shrimp Salad	SERVES: 4 CALORIES: 401 per serving PREPARATION TIME: 20 minutes COOKING TIME: 30–35 minutes CHILLING TIME: 3–4 hours or overnight

This rice salad needs little or no salt since it is full of hot peppers, pungent coriander, and lots of cider vinegar for flavor.

2½ cups strong chicken broth
1 onion, finely chopped
1 clove garlic, finely minced
1 jalapeño pepper, finely chopped
1 cup raw rice

Dressing:
¼ cup apple cider vinegar
2 tablespoons olive oil
Pinch of crumbled dried thyme
Pinch of cayenne pepper
Salt to taste

1 pound bay shrimp or small to medium cooked shrimp, diced
2 tablespoons red or green bell pepper, seeded and julienned
1 tablespoon chopped fresh parsley
1 tablespoon chopped fresh cilantro (coriander)

Garnish:
Cilantro
Cherry tomatoes

1. In a saucepan heat ½ cup broth and cook the onion, garlic, and jalapeño pepper over medium heat until tender, 5 to 10 minutes.
2. Add the remaining 2 cups broth and the rice, bring to a boil, cover, reduce heat, and simmer slowly for 25 minutes, or until the liquid is absorbed. Allow to cool.
3. In a large salad bowl whisk together the dressing ingredients.
4. Combine the shrimp, bell pepper, parsley, and cilantro, and toss with the dressing. Add the cooled rice, stir, cover, and chill for 3 to 4 hours or overnight.
5. Adjust the seasonings and serve, garnished with cilantro and cherry tomatoes.

COOK NOTE: Cilantro, also known as leaf coriander and Chinese parsley, is sold with the roots, which should not be removed until the leaves are used. Keep the root end in water in a jar, cover with a plastic bag tied at the top, and the herb will keep for a week.

VARIATIONS:
* Julienned zucchini or blanched broccoli florets can be added with the bell pepper.
* Cooked crabmeat, scallops, or squid can be substituted for the shrimp.

BREADS

The breads in this chapter consist of quick breads and muffins that require no rising time, popovers quickly prepared in a blender or food processor, and a whole-wheat dough that utilizes the combined talents of quick-rise yeast and a food processor, which results in a wonderful French bread in only a matter of minutes.

A few Make-It-Easy Tips to remember when preparing muffins:

- Muffins freeze successfully.
- Use an ice cream scoop to fill the muffin cups easily with the perfect amount of batter.
- Raisins and berries are coated with the dry ingredients to prevent them from sinking into the batter.

Whole-Wheat Popovers	YIELD: 6 CALORIES: 144 per popover PREPARATION TIME: 5 minutes COOKING TIME: 30–35 minutes

Popovers are crisp, light, hollow muffins made from a thin batter that puffs up over the molds in baking. Traditionally, popover muffin molds are well-greased and heated before adding the cold batter. Here the muffin molds are generously coated with vegetable cooking spray.

1 cup sifted whole-wheat flour
1 cup low-fat milk
2 eggs
2 teaspoons vegetable oil
½ teaspoon salt

1. Preheat the oven to 425°F. Generously coat 6 large or 8 small metal or glass muffin molds with vegetable cooking spray.
2. In a food processor, blender, electric mixer, or by hand combine the ingredients; mix or stir until the batter is smooth.
3. Place the sprayed muffin molds in the oven to preheat for 2 minutes.
4. Pour the batter into the preheated cups, filling two-thirds full; return to the oven and bake in the top third of the oven for 30 to 35 minutes, or until puffy and golden brown.
5. Serve immediately.

VARIATION:

* For extra flavor, 1 or 2 tablespoons chopped fresh chives, basil, or dill can be added to the batter.

MAKE-IT-EASY TIPS:

* The large metal popover pans, which are deeper and fuller than regular muffin tins, are best to use since they can be preheated and turn out larger, lighter, and airier popovers.
* The best volume is achieved if all ingredients are at room temperature when combined.

Applesauce-Bran Loaf	YIELD: 1 loaf, 10 slices per loaf CALORIES: 125 per slice PREPARATION TIME: 15 minutes COOKING TIME: 35–40 minutes

Bran is one of the sources of fiber in our diet. According to Jane Brody in *Jane Brody's Good Food Book:* "Adding fiber to the diet actually increases the amount of fat that you excrete, which may help to protect against heart disease as well as assist in weight loss. Fiber also helps to lower blood cholesterol and to maintain blood sugar on a more even keel." Ms. Brody continues, corroborating many recent scientific studies, on the virtues of fiber in preventing colon cancer as well.

This bread is high in fiber, low in fat, and contains only the natural sugar from the raisins and unsweetened applesauce.

1 cup whole-wheat flour
1 cup unprocessed bran
1 tablespoon baking powder
½ teaspoon ground cinnamon
¼ teaspoon grated nutmeg
Pinch of salt
3 tablespoons raisins
1 egg
¾ cup unsweetened applesauce
⅓ cup frozen apple juice concentrate, thawed
¼ cup nonfat milk
2½ tablespoons vegetable oil

1. Preheat the oven to 350°F. Coat an 8"-×-4"-×-2" loaf pan with vegetable cooking spray.
2. In a large bowl combine the dry ingredients; stir to blend. Add the raisins and coat with the dry mixture.
3. In a separate bowl whisk the egg and the moist ingredients; beat until smooth. Pour the mixture into the dry ingredients and stir until thoroughly combined.
4. Pour into the prepared pan and bake for 35 to 40 minutes, or until lightly golden on top and a knife inserted comes out clean.
5. Remove from the oven and place the pan on a rack for 10 minutes. Turn the loaf out onto the rack and cool before serving. (The bread is first cooled in the pan and then on the rack to prevent sogginess.)
6. Serve at room temperature.

VARIATION:
* The bread can be baked in 3 mini-loaf-sized pans for 25 to 30 minutes.

Whole-Wheat French Bread	YIELD: 2 loaves, 12 slices per loaf CALORIES: 103 per slice PREPARATION TIME: 15 minutes RISING TIME: 30–45 minutes COOKING TIME: 20–25 minutes

This easy and incredibly flavorful French bread contains no oils or fats. With the use of a food processor, the yeast requires only a quick proofing, the dough is kneaded for just 20 seconds, and with the aid of quick-rise yeast, a total of only 30 minutes is needed for it to rise and settle before baking.

The best part about this dough is that it can be used to make light pizzas and calzones with a variety of toppings and fillings.

1 packet (1 tablespoon) quick-rise or regular yeast
2 cups lukewarm water
2 tablespoons honey
2 teaspoons salt
3 cups white all-purpose flour
2 cups whole-wheat flour
1 teaspoon caraway seeds (optional)
1 egg white
1 tablespoon sesame seeds
1 tablespoon poppy seeds

1. Place the yeast in the bowl of a food processor. Add the water, honey, and salt. Pulse for 1 second and allow to sit for 5 minutes for quick-rise yeast and 10 minutes for regular yeast.
2. Add 2 cups white flour, the whole-wheat flour, and caraway seeds, if desired. Process for a few seconds until just combined. Add a quarter of the remaining white flour and process for a few seconds. Gradually add the remainder of the flour, ¼ cup at a time, until the dough is still sticky but smooth. Do not overprocess.
3. Turn the wet dough out on a floured board and knead for a

few seconds until it is no longer sticky, or until a finger inserted in the center springs back.

4. Coat a medium-sized bowl with vegetable cooking spray and place the dough in the bowl. Cover with a slightly dampened towel and allow to rise in a draft-free area for 15 minutes for quick-rise yeast and 30 minutes for regular yeast, or until doubled in size.

5. Preheat the oven to 375°F.

6. Form the dough into two long baguettelike shapes measuring about 16″ each and place on a nonstick baking sheet. Brush lightly with egg white, sprinkle with sesame and poppy seeds, and make cuts along the top of the dough at intervals with kitchen scissors (see illustration). Cover with the dampened towel and allow to rise an additional 15 minutes. Bake for 20 to 25 minutes, or until golden on top.

8. Serve hot or warm.

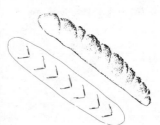

VARIATIONS:

* The dough can be cut into 20 rolls and snipped for a decorative effect. Rolls should be baked only 15 minutes or until golden.
* The dough can be used to make 4 medium-sized pizzas or 12 calzones.

MAKE-IT-EASY TIPS:

* The food processor enables you to proof and knead dough without the traditional time-consuming procedures associated with bread baking. It is important, however, never to overprocess dough in the food processor.
* Cut the dough with kitchen scissors to divide into loaf, roll, or other shapes to avoid unnecessary pulling of the dough.
* Dough freezes successfully.

Buckwheat and Bran-Apple Muffins	YIELD: 1 dozen CALORIES: 97 per muffin PREPARATION TIME: 15 minutes COOKING TIME: 15 minutes

These muffins are high in bran fiber, low in fat, and low in sugar.

¾ cup unprocessed bran
½ cup buckwheat flour (see Note)
½ cup whole-wheat flour
¾ teaspoon baking soda
¼ teaspoon salt
Pinch of ground cinnamon
Pinch of grated nutmeg
1 egg
1 cup buttermilk
2 tablespoons corn oil
2 tablespoons frozen apple juice concentrate, thawed
1 tablespoon honey
1 tart apple, peeled and finely chopped
2 tablespoons raisins

1. Preheat the oven to 375°F. Coat a 12-cup muffin tin with vegetable cooking spray or line with paper muffin cups.
2. In a large mixing bowl combine the dry ingredients; stir together.
3. In a separate bowl whisk the egg with the buttermilk, corn oil, apple concentrate, and honey. Add to the dry ingredients, mixing until the ingredients are just moistened.
4. Fold in the apple and raisins; fill the muffin tins three-quarters full, and bake for 15 minutes, or until a knife inserted comes out clean, and the tops are lightly golden.
5. Serve the muffins warm.

COOK NOTE: Buckwheat, also called groats or kasha, is a member of the grass family, not a part of wheat. The plant is related to rhubarb or sorrel. Buckwheat flour is most often a mixture of ground buckwheat seeds and white flour and is traditionally used in yeast-raised buckwheat pancakes called blini.

VARIATION:
* The batter can be poured into 3 mini-loaf pans and baked for 20 to 25 minutes.

Peach-Bran Muffins

YIELD: 1 dozen
CALORIES: 122 per muffin
PREPARATION TIME: 15 minutes
COOKING TIME: 15 minutes

Unsweetened frozen peaches are a timesaver in this recipe and, combined with bran and whole-wheat flour, are baked into flavorful and healthy muffins.

1¼ cups unprocessed bran
1 cup whole-wheat flour
¼ cup firmly packed brown sugar
1 teaspoon baking powder
1 teaspoon baking soda
½ teaspoon ground cinnamon
Pinch of salt
¼ cup raisins
1 egg
¾ cup buttermilk
¼ cup orange juice
2 tablespoons vegetable oil
2 tablespoons maple syrup
1 cup frozen unsweetened peaches, thawed, drained, and
   roughly chopped

1. Preheat the oven to 400°F. Coat a 12-cup muffin tin with vegetable cooking spray or line with paper muffin cups.
2. In a large mixing bowl combine the dry ingredients and stir

together; add the raisins and toss to coat with the dry ingredients.

3. In a separate bowl whisk the egg with the buttermilk, orange juice, oil, and syrup until smooth.

4. Add the wet ingredients to the dry; stir until just combined. Fold in the peaches, fill the prepared muffin cups three-quarters full, and bake for 15 minutes, or until golden.

5. Remove the muffins from the pan, allow to cool slightly, and serve warm.

VARIATIONS:

* If fresh peaches are in season, peel them easily by dropping into boiling water for 1 minute; then promptly remove the peel. Slice the peaches and proceed with the recipe.
* Blueberries, fresh or frozen and thawed, can be substituted for the peaches.

Branberry Muffins

YIELD: 1 dozen
CALORIES: 156 per muffin
PREPARATION TIME: 15 minutes
COOKING TIME: 15 minutes

These healthful muffins are high in bran fiber and low in calories. The blueberries add a natural sweetness to the muffins and are also a good source of fiber.

1½ cups whole-wheat flour
¾ cup unprocessed bran
¼ cup firmly packed brown sugar
1 teaspoon baking powder
1 teaspoon baking soda
½ teaspoon salt
Pinch of grated nutmeg
⅔ cup fresh blueberries or frozen blueberries, thawed and drained
1 egg

½ cup buttermilk
½ cup frozen orange juice concentrate, thawed
¼ cup vegetable oil
2 teaspoons grated orange rind
1 teaspoon vanilla extract

1. Preheat the oven to 400°F. Coat a 12-cup muffin tin with vegetable cooking spray or line with paper muffin cups.
2. In a large mixing bowl gently mix the dry ingredients with the blueberries to prevent the blueberries from sinking into the batter by coating them.
3. In a separate bowl mix the remaining ingredients. Whisk until smooth.
4. Add the wet ingredients to the dry, and stir until just combined but not overmixed, and fill the prepared muffin cups three-quarters full.
5. Place in the oven and bake for 15 to 20 minutes, or until golden.
6. Remove the muffins from the pan, allow to cool slightly, and serve warm.

VARIATIONS:
* Chopped strawberries can be substituted for the blueberries.
* If desired, 2–3 tablespoons raisins can be added.

Fluffy Corn Muffins

YIELD: 18 large
CALORIES: 186 per muffin
PREPARATION TIME: 15–20 minutes
COOKING TIME: 15 minutes

If possible, select stone-ground or water-ground cornmeal, which has a higher nutritional count than the "enriched" variety.

2 cups white all-purpose flour
2 cups yellow cornmeal
2 teaspoons baking soda
⅛ teaspoon salt
2 eggs
2 cups buttermilk
½ cup honey
¼ cup vegetable oil
1 medium apple, peeled and finely chopped

1. Preheat the oven to 400°F. Coat a 12-cup muffin tin with vegetable cooking spray or line with paper muffin cups.
2. In a large bowl combine the dry ingredients.
3. In a separate bowl whisk the eggs with the buttermilk, honey, and oil. Add the mixture to the dry ingredients, add the apple, and stir until just combined, but not overmixed.
4. Fill the prepared muffin cups three-quarters full, and bake for about 15 minutes, or until golden.
5. Remove the muffins from the pan, allow to cool slightly, and serve warm.

VARIATION:
* If desired, ⅓ cup corn kernels can be added.

MAKE-IT-EASY TIP:
* Commercially sold buttermilk is a cultured low-fat product, not the by-product of butter making. If you've run out of buttermilk, add 2 tablespoons vinegar or lemon juice to 2 cups low-fat milk and allow to stand and thicken for 5 minutes. This substitute for buttermilk should be used only for cooking.

Blueberry—Oat Bran Muffins

YIELD: 1 dozen
CALORIES: 151 per muffin
PREPARATION TIME: 15 minutes
COOKING TIME: 15–20 minutes

Oat bran is a wonderful source of fiber in the diet and is used here in a flavorful muffin.

2¼ cups oat bran
1 cup whole-wheat flour
4 teaspoons baking powder
Pinch of salt
1 cup fresh blueberries or frozen blueberries, thawed and drained
2 eggs
½ cup nonfat milk
1 ripe banana, mashed
½ cup frozen apple juice concentrate, thawed
3 tablespoons vegetable oil
2 tablespoons molasses

1. Preheat the oven to 400°F. Coat a 12-cup muffin tin with vegetable cooking spray or line with paper muffin cups.
2. In a large mixing bowl gently mix the dry ingredients with the blueberries, to prevent the blueberries from sinking into the batter by coating them.
3. In a separate bowl mix the remaining ingredients. Whisk until smooth.
4. Add the wet ingredients to the dry, stir until just combined but not overmixed, and fill the prepared muffin cups three-quarters full.
5. Place in the oven and bake for 15 to 20 minutes, or until golden.
6. Remove the muffins from the pan, allow to cool slightly, and serve warm.

VARIATION:
* Chopped strawberries can be substituted for the blueberries.

DESSERTS

Baked Fruit Compote

SERVES: 6
CALORIES: 146 per serving
PREPARATION TIME: 15 minutes
COOKING TIME: 25 minutes

This easily assembled dessert can be baked and served warm or chilled the next day. Additional seasonal fresh or frozen unsweetened fruits can be added as desired.

1 16-ounce package frozen unsweetened peaches, thawed and drained
2 navel oranges, peeled, white membrane removed, sliced
4 1"-thick slices fresh pineapple, cut into chunks
2 tablespoons brown sugar
1 teaspoon ground cinnamon
½ teaspoon vanilla extract
Pinch of grated nutmeg

Garnish:
Plain low-fat yogurt lightly sweetened with honey and a pinch of vanilla extract

1. Preheat the oven to 350°F. Lightly coat a shallow baking dish with vegetable cooking spray.
2. In a large mixing bowl combine the fruit and flavorings, stir, and place in the prepared dish.
3. Bake for 25 minutes, or until lightly golden on top.
4. Allow to cool slightly, then serve warm with a dollop of sweetened yogurt.

COOK NOTE: Since dairy products tend to absorb pineapple odors easily, cut pineapple should be stored in a well-sealed container in the refrigerator.

VARIATION:
* If desired, 2 tablespoons frozen orange juice concentrate, thawed, can be substituted for the brown sugar.

MAKE-IT-EASY TIP:
* It is easy to remove the peel and pits from the orange sections if the oranges are left in boiling water for 5 minutes before peeling.

Blueberries in Snow

SERVES: 4
CALORIES: 120 per serving
PREPARATION TIME: 5 minutes

This dessert is traditionally prepared with heavy whipped cream or sour cream. Here low-fat yogurt, very lightly sweetened with a minimal amount of sugar, makes a deliciously acceptable substitute.

It is best to use fresh, not frozen, blueberries for this dessert. The frozen blueberries will be watery and lose their texture.

1 pint fresh blueberries, washed and cleaned (see Note)
1 cup plain low-fat yogurt
2–3 tablespoons sugar
1 teaspoon vanilla extract
¼ teaspoon almond extract

1. Place the blueberries in 4 dessert dishes and chill until ready to serve.
2. In a small bowl whisk the yogurt with the sugar and extracts. Chill until ready to serve.
3. At serving time, place a dollop of the yogurt mixture on each blueberry dish and serve.

COOK NOTE: Blueberries are perishable so they should be used within a few days of purchasing. Refrigerate the berries without rinsing until ready to use.

VARIATION:
* Other fresh berries or sliced peeled peaches or nectarines can be substituted for the blueberries.

Apricot-Yogurt Swirl	SERVES: 8 CALORIES: 142 per serving PREPARATION TIME: 5 minutes

This light dessert contains no sugar. It is sweetened with an apricot spread which is prepared from dried apricots and unsweetened apple juice.

6 cups plain low-fat yogurt (see Note)
1 cup Apricot Spread (page 87)

1. Place the yogurt in a bowl and chill until ready to serve.
2. When ready to serve, top the yogurt with the apricot spread, swirl, and serve chilled.

<u>COOK NOTE:</u> Select cartons of yogurt that are tightly sealed and well-chilled. If a bit of cloudy water separates from the yogurt do not worry; pour it off before using the yogurt.

VARIATION:
* Apricot Spread can be prepared in advance and chilled until ready to use.

Basic Poached Fruit	SERVES: 8 CALORIES: 125 per serving PREPARATION TIME: 15–20 minutes COOKING TIME: see chart below

This is a basic recipe for all poached fruit. Check the time chart at the bottom for the exact timing of each individual fruit.

2 cups unsweetened apple juice
1 cup fruit-sweetened cranberry juice
1 cup water
2 tablespoons lemon juice
½ teaspoon ground cinnamon
½ teaspoon grated nutmeg
½ teaspoon ground cloves
Approximately 8 fruits

Garnish:
Plain low-fat yogurt with vanilla extract added

1. In a large deep skillet or saucepan heat the juices and spices until boiling. Add the fruit and simmer, uncovered, until tender.
2. Remove the fruit to a serving dish, increase the heat, and cook the juices until reduced by half and syrupy in texture, 15 to 20 minutes.
3. Serve hot, at room temperature, or chilled with a dollop of yogurt if desired.

Fruit	Cooking time
8 whole ripe Bosc pears, peeled	20 minutes
8 whole Rome Beauty apples, peeled and cored	20–25 minutes
8 whole navel oranges, peeled	15 minutes
8 whole peaches, peeled or halved	10 minutes
8 whole plums, unpeeled	8–10 minutes
1 quart whole berries	3–4 minutes

COOK NOTES: Fruits should be cooked but firm. Reduce the cooking times by one-third if cutting the fruit into smaller sections before poaching.

Reserve the poaching liquid to reuse with other fruits, adding more water and/or juice to get back up to 1 quart if necessary.

VARIATIONS:

* If unsweetened cranberry juice is unavailable, use 2 cups apple juice and 2 cups water or add a favorite unsweetened nectar or juice such as orange, apricot, pear, or even white grape juice.
* Spices or flavorings may be varied according to taste. Try whole stick cinnamon or nutmeg, cardamom, strips of lemon or orange rind, vanilla bean, ginger, or a touch of sherry or port wine.

Pears Baked in Nectar

SERVES: 4
CALORIES: 209 per serving
PREPARATION TIME: 10 minutes
COOKING TIME: 1 hour to 1 hour 10
    minutes

We are all accustomed to baked apples, but baked pears are just as flavorful, especially when baked in unsweetened juice.

4 Bosc pears, unpeeled, cored
¼ cup unsweetened apple butter or Apricot Spread (page 87)
1½ cups unsweetened pear nectar or unsweetened unfiltered
    apple juice
1 teaspoon ground cinnamon
½ teaspoon grated nutmeg
Pinch of mace

Garnish:
Plain low-fat yogurt
Sprinkling of ground cinnamon

1. Preheat the oven to 375°F.
2. Place the pears in a deep baking dish, fill each of the centers

with 1 tablespoon apple butter or apricot spread and pour the juice over.

3. Sprinkle the spices on top of each and bake for 60 to 70 minutes, or until soft.
4. Remove from the oven and serve warm or chilled in individual dishes, topped with a dollop of yogurt and a sprinkling of cinnamon.

COOK NOTE: Bosc pears are distinguished by their symmetrical body, long tapering neck, and slim stem. This winter pear is excellent for baking, broiling, and poaching. The pear should be slightly ripe before baking, meaning that it yields to gentle pressure at the stem end.

VARIATIONS:
* Apples can be substituted for the pears.
* Any naturally sweetened preserves, those sweetened with fruit juice concentrates or pureed fruits, can be used. They are readily available at health food stores and many supermarkets.

Frozen Pineapple Sherbet	SERVES: 6 CALORIES: 96 per serving PREPARATION TIME: 5 minutes FREEZING TIME: 3– 4 hours

To achieve a sherbetlike texture, without the use of an ice cream machine, frozen pineapple is crushed in a food processor with pineapple juice and buttermilk. The creamy results are totally low-fat and contain only 2 tablespoons of sugar in 6 servings. This sherbet must be eaten immediately or it will become watery on standing.

3 thick slices fresh pineapple
1 cup unsweetened pineapple juice
½ cup buttermilk
2 tablespoons sugar

Garnish:
Sprigs of mint

1. Cut the pineapple into 1″ pieces, wrap in a single layer in plastic wrap, and freeze for 3 to 4 hours, or until solid.
2. Place the pineapple and remaining ingredients in a food processor and puree just until smooth and creamy.
3. Serve immediately, garnished with mint sprigs.

VARIATION:
* Pineapple can be cut, frozen, and stored in the freezer until just before preparation.

Pineapple-Yogurt Refresher	SERVES: 6 CALORIES: 96 per serving PREPARATION TIME: 10 minutes CHILLING TIME: 2 hours

This combination of pineapple, crunchy carrots, and yogurt makes a perfect low-fat refresher to end a meal.

1 16-ounce can juice-packed crushed pineapple, drained
1 large carrot, finely grated
3 tablespoons sugar
1 teaspoon vanilla extract
1 teaspoon coconut extract
1½ cups plain low-fat yogurt

Garnish:
Unsweetened coconut

1. Place the pineapple, carrot, sugar, vanilla, and coconut in a large bowl; stir to combine. Add the yogurt and continue to stir until smooth. Place in a covered container and chill for 2 hours.
2. Serve dessert chilled garnished with coconut.

COOK NOTE: Store vanilla and other extract bottles in their boxes to protect against the light and excessive heat that can cause extract's deterioration.

VARIATION:
* Almond extract can be substituted for the coconut extract.

Fruits with Port	SERVES: 4 CALORIES: 193 per serving PREPARATION TIME: 15 minutes CHILLING TIME: 1–2 hours

The fruit for this compote can be sliced or cut into chunks. The oranges and pears can be marinated overnight, but the bananas should be added at the last minute to avoid discoloration.

2 oranges, peeled, white membrane removed, sliced
2 ripe Anjou, Comice, or Bartlett pears, peeled, cored, and
  sliced
2 tablespoons raisins
¼ cup fresh orange juice
2 tablespoons port
2 bananas, sliced

1. In a large bowl combine the oranges, pears and raisins.
2. Stir the orange juice with the port, pour over the fruit, toss well, and marinate for 1 to 2 hours.
3. Add the bananas, toss to coat, and serve chilled.

VARIATION:
* Madeira or Marsala can be substituted for the port.

MAKE-IT-EASY TIP:
* Avoid purchasing oranges in netted or large plastic bags. Often there is a spoiled orange lurking in the center which can damage several more surrounding the bad one.

Light Banana Freeze	SERVES: 4
	CALORIES: 163 per serving
	PREPARATION TIME: 10 minutes
	FREEZING TIME: 4–6 hours or overnight

This incredible frozen all-fruit treat tastes like rich, creamy ice cream. It is best eaten right away or it will lose its smooth consistency.

4 ripe bananas, peeled, cut into large chunks
3 tablespoons frozen orange juice concentrate, thawed
1 tablespoon honey or to taste

Garnish:
Thin slices of orange

1. Place the bananas in a freezer container. Immediately sprinkle with orange juice, seal the container, and freeze for 4 to 6 hours or overnight.
2. Just before serving, add the honey to a food processor bowl, drop the banana slices, a few at a time, into the bowl, and puree until the consistency of soft ice cream.
3. Serve immediately, garnished with thin slices of orange.

VARIATION:
* Fresh orange juice can be substituted for frozen concentrated.

MAKE-IT-EASY TIP:
* Cut bananas can be kept in a sealed container in the freezer for several weeks before using.

Frozen Strawberry-Banana Yogurt	SERVES: 8 CALORIES: 124 per serving PREPARATION TIME: 10 minutes FREEZING TIME: according to manufacturer's directions on your ice cream maker

This frozen yogurt can easily be prepared in an ice cream maker.

1 pint fresh strawberries, washed and hulled
½ ripe banana, peeled
½ cup frozen apple juice concentrate, thawed
¼ cup honey
2 cups plain low-fat yogurt

Garnish:
Strawberry halves

1. In a food processor or blender puree the strawberries and banana with the apple juice and honey until smooth. Place in a bowl.
2. Fold in the yogurt, stir until well-mixed, and freeze in an ice cream maker according to directions. If an ice cream maker is unavailable, place the mixture in a freezer tray, freeze until firm, pour into the food processor, process until just smooth, and serve immediately.
3. Serve scoops of the frozen yogurt topped with strawberry halves.

COOK NOTE: The longer yogurt is stored in the refrigerator the more tart the flavor. The liquid that separates from the solid yogurt as it is spooned out should be poured off and discarded.

VARIATIONS:
* Peaches, raspberries, blackberries, or any other variety of fruit desired can be substituted for the strawberries.
* Frozen unsweetened fruits can be substituted for the strawberries.

Hot Strawberry Soufflé

SERVES: 6
CALORIES: 99 per serving
PREPARATION TIME: 15 minutes
COOKING TIME: 10–12 minutes

This recipe is a light version of one served by my friend Jane Raidin. She used sugar-laden apricot jam in the recipe, which I replaced with fruit-sweetened strawberry preserves. Only egg whites are used, reducing both calories and cholesterol.

1 10-ounce jar fruit-sweetened strawberry preserves or conserve
1 tablespoon lemon juice
2 teaspoons grated lemon rind
8 egg whites, at room temperature
¼ teaspoon cream of tartar

Garnish:
Plain low-fat yogurt with vanilla extract added

1. Preheat the oven to 400°F. Generously coat a 2-quart soufflé dish with vegetable cooking spray.
2. In a large mixing bowl combine the preserves with the lemon juice and rind and mix well.
3. In a separate bowl whip the egg whites with the cream of tartar until soft peaks form. (See Notes.)
4. Gently fold one-quarter of the beaten whites into the preserve mixture to lighten it. Fold in the remaining whites until the mixture is blended, pour it into the prepared baking dish and smooth the edges with a rubber spatula.
5. Bake for 10 to 12 minutes, or until the top is golden. Serve immediately with a dollop of yogurt flavored with vanilla.

COOK NOTES: The egg whites are whipped at room temperature for greater volume.

Do not whip egg whites in an aluminum bowl; it will tint them slightly gray. Use copper, glass, china, or stainless steel. Plastic tends to retain moisture, which would prevent the egg whites from whipping properly.

If you overbeat the whites, you might be able to save them by adding another white and beating again.

VARIATION:
* Any type of fruit-sweetened or unsweetened preserves or jams can be substituted for the strawberry. Try apricot, pineapple, raspberry, blackberry, or whatever flavor desired. If using raspberry or other preserves with seeds, remember to put through a sieve before adding to the soufflé.

MAKE-IT-EASY TIP:
* This soufflé, unlike other soufflés, holds well and can be left in a turned off oven for up to 10 minutes after baking.

Raspberry Applesauce	SERVES: 8 CALORIES: 104 per ½ cup serving PREPARATION TIME: 15–20 minutes COOKING TIME: 25 minutes

6 apples (Golden Delicious, MacIntosh, Pippin, Granny Smith),
washed, cored, and sliced
⅔ cup raspberries, rinsed
⅓ cup frozen apple juice concentrate, thawed
½ teaspoon ground cinnamon

Garnish:
Plain low-fat yogurt

1. Place the apples in a deep saucepan with the raspberries, juice, and cinnamon. Bring to a boil, cover, reduce heat to medium-low, and simmer for 25 minutes, or until the apples are very soft.
2. Remove from heat and put the mixture through a food mill or strainer to remove the peels easily. Allow to cool, place in a covered container, and chill until ready to serve.
3. Serve chilled with a dollop of yogurt.

VARIATION:
* Frozen unsweetened raspberries can be substituted for the fresh raspberries.

MAKE-IT-EASY TIPS:
* Applesauce will keep for several weeks in the refrigerator.
* A gadget called an apple slicer cores and slices apples in one swift motion.
* Apples can be peeled first, sprinkled with lemon juice to prevent browning, and cooked until soft without straining.

Crisp Apple Tart

SERVES: 8
CALORIES: 142 per serving
PREPARATION TIME: 20 minutes
COOKING TIME: 50–55 minutes

This crisp apple tart uses phyllo pastry, which is used in many Greek recipes such as baklava or Hungarian recipes such as strudel. It can be purchased fresh or frozen at Middle Eastern groceries or many supermarkets. This light and crisp crust is lower in both calories and fat than a traditional butter or oil pastry and needs only a light brushing of butter or margarine.

Phyllo pastry tends to dry out quickly. Once opened, place the contents of the package on a dry flat surface and cover with plastic wrap and a dampened tea towel. In addition, do not open the package of phyllo until the filling is prepared, as the leaves will dry out and become difficult to work with.

4 tart apples (about 2 pounds), peeled and sliced
2 tablespoons lemon juice
3 tablespoons brown sugar
2 tablespoons raisins
1 tablespoon arrowroot
1½ teaspoons ground cinnamon
Pinch of grated nutmeg
Pinch of ground cloves
4 sheets of phyllo pastry
2 tablespoons unsalted butter or margarine, melted

1. Preheat the oven to 350°F. Generously coat a 9″ or 9½″ cake or tart pan, preferably with a removable ring, with vegetable cooking spray.
2. In a medium-sized bowl combine the apples with the lemon juice and toss well. In a small bowl combine the brown sugar, raisins, arrowroot, and spices, stir well, and toss with the apples.
3. Place the 4 sheets of phyllo pastry in the prepared pan, crisscrossing them on the bottom (see illustration on page 69) and brushing each lightly with some of the butter or margarine. Trim the overhanging pastry leaving a 2″ border all around.
4. Place the apple filling in the pan, roll the outer edges of the overhanging pastry toward the filling, tucking it in and rolling to create a rim. Brush the edges lightly with the remaining butter or margarine. (See illustration on page 69.)
5. Place the pan on a cookie sheet and then on the bottom third of the oven; bake for 50 to 55 minutes, or until golden.
6. Remove from the oven, allow to rest for 10 to 15 minutes, remove the ring, and serve warm, cut into wedges.

COOK NOTE: Unused phyllo leaves can be rerolled in waxed paper and replaced in the original plastic cover, sealed securely, and stored in the refrigerator. Once thawed, the leaves should not be refrozen or they will become crumbly.

VARIATION:
* Pears can be substituted for the apples.

MAKE-IT-EASY TIPS:
* If the phyllo is frozen when purchased, thaw overnight in the refrigerator prior to use. It is best to leave at room temperature for 1 to 2 hours before using.
* If the dough tears while rolling to form a rim, do not worry. Spray it with vegetable cooking spray and push it together with your fingers.
* A gadget called an apple slicer cores and slices apples in one swift motion.

Italian Lemon Cheesecake

SERVES: 10
CALORIES: 200 per serving
PREPARATION TIME: 15–20 minutes
COOKING TIME: 50–55 minutes
CHILLING TIME: 6 hours or overnight

Cheesecake does not appear to be a light dessert, but this creamy lemon-flavored cake is prepared with part-skim ricotta cheese. The pastry consists of a few sheets of phyllo leaves, which when very lightly brushed with butter or margarine, become a crisp and flavorful crust.

1⅓ cups part-skim ricotta cheese
4 ounces Neufchâtel or light cream cheese
⅓ cup sugar
2 eggs, separated
½ cup low-fat milk
¼ cup white all-purpose flour
2 tablespoons lemon juice
2 teaspoons grated lemon rind
1 teaspoon vanilla extract
4 sheets of phyllo pastry
1½ tablespoons unsalted butter or margarine, melted

Garnish:
½ cup Apricot Spread (page 87)

1. Preheat the oven to 325°F. Generously coat a 9″ pie plate with vegetable cooking spray.
2. In a food processor or blender process the cheeses, sugar, egg yolks, milk, flour, lemon juice, lemon rind, and vanilla until smooth. In a bowl whip the egg whites until stiff and gently fold into the mixture.
3. Place the 4 sheets of phyllo pastry into the prepared pan, crisscrossing them on the bottom (see illustrtion on page 69) and brushing each lightly with some of the butter or margarine. Trim the overhanging pastry leaving a 2″ border all around.

4. Place the filling in the pan, roll the outer edges of the over-lapping pastry toward the filling, tucking it in and rolling to create a rim. Brush the edges lightly with the remaining butter or margarine. (See illustration on page 69.)
5. Place the pan on a cookie sheet, put in the center of the oven. Place a baking pan with 2″ of water on the lower rack of the oven. Bake for 50 to 55 minutes, or until set. Remove from the oven and allow to cool on a rack. Chill for 6 hours or overnight.
6. Top with the apricot spread, if desired, and serve the pie chilled, cut into wedges.

COOK NOTES: See the Crisp Apple Tart recipe for information on the handling of phyllo pastry.

The water bath is set under the baking cheesecake to create a humid oven, which will prevent the cheesecake from cracking on top.

VARIATION:
* This pie can be baked without the crust as a pudding.

Yogurt Cheesecake

SERVES: 8
CALORIES: 180 per serving
PREPARATION TIME: 20 minutes
COOKING TIME: 35 minutes
CHILLING TIME: 6—8 hours or overnight

This recipe is a variation on one that accompanies a new gadget called a Really Creamy™ Yogurt Cheese Funnel which is manufactured by Millhopper Marketing, Inc. in Gainesville, Florida. The funnel is a plastic device into which plain yogurt is poured and the whey (liquid) is drained off overnight in the refrigerator yielding a pure, soft cheese that has 90 percent less fat than commercial cream cheese and contains only about 28 calories per ounce, depending on the type of yogurt used. In addition, nearly half the sodium is removed in the whey. Yogurt cheese is wonderful used cold in dips and spreads or on a baked potato but when cooking with the cheese, take care that it does not boil or it may separate.

If you cannot find this new kitchen device, place several layers of cheesecloth over a small rack or in a strainer set over a bowl, add the yogurt, and allow the whey to drain off into a small bowl. The longer you leave the yogurt to drain (8 to14 hours), the thicker the consistency of the cheese. It is recommended to use plain low-fat yogurt without gelatin or stabilizers.

Crust:
8 zwieback, crushed
2 tablespoons unsalted butter or margarine, melted

Filling:
2 eggs
1½ cups yogurt cheese, prepared with low-fat or nonfat yogurt
⅓ cup sugar
1 tablespoon lemon juice
½ teaspoon vanilla

Topping:
½ cup yogurt cheese
2 teaspoons sugar
1 teaspoon vanilla

Garnish:
Strawberries, raspberries, blueberries, or other cut-up seasonal
    fruits

1. Preheat the oven to 325°F. Lightly coat an 8″ pie pan with vegetable cooking spray.
2. In the food processor or by hand, crush the cookies, combine with butter, and press them firmly into the bottom and sides of the prepared pan.
3. In a separate bowl, whisk the eggs and combine with the remaining filling ingredients. Pour the mixture into the prepared pan and bake for 20 to 25 minutes, or until set in the center.
4. In the meantime, whisk the topping ingredients together, spread over the pie, and return to the oven for an additional 5 to 10 minutes, or until firm.
5. Cool slightly and then chill for 6 to 8 hours or overnight.
6. Serve chilled garnished with berries or cut-up seasonal fruits.

VARIATION:
* Honey graham crackers or other low-sugar cookies can be substituted for the zwieback.
* Recipe can be prepared in an 8″ springform pan.

Papaya Broiled with Orange-Ginger Glaze

SERVES: 4
CALORIES: 86 per serving
PREPARATION TIME: 5–10 minutes
COOKING TIME: 3–4 minutes

Papayas are a good low-calorie source of potassium and are high in vitamins A and C. Although papayas are available all year long, purchase them when in abundant supply at a reasonable cost, in the late winter and early spring.

2 ripe papayas, split, seeds removed (see Note)
¼ cup fresh orange juice
4 teaspoons grated orange rind
2 teaspoons grated fresh ginger

Garnish:
Orange slices

1. Preheat a broiler.
2. Place the papaya halves, cut side up, in a shallow baking dish. Sprinkle each with orange juice, orange rind, and ginger.
3. Broil 4″ to 6″ from heat, 3 to 4 minutes, or until lightly golden, basting once.
4. Serve hot, garnished with orange slices.

COOK NOTE: Papayas are ripe when they yield to gentle pressure. The skin coloring may range from green with yellow blush to half green, half yellow. Papayas usually turn more and more yellow as they ripen, but remember the key to ripeness is the softening, since it is possible to have a fully ripe green papaya. They must, however, have a little yellow "breaking" through or they will not ripen.

VARIATION:
* Broiled papaya can be chilled and served cold.

INFORMATION SOURCES

Center for Science in the Public Interest Nutrition Action Letter
1501 16th Street. N.W.
Washington, DC 20036

Tufts University Diet & Nutrition Letter
William White Publications
475 Park Avenue
New York, NY 10016

University of California, Berkeley, Wellness Letter
Health Letter Associates
P.O. Box 10922
Des Moines, IA 50350

American Cancer Society
National Headquarters
90 Park Avenue
New York, NY 10016
1 (212) 599-8200
Cancer Information Number: 1 (800) 422-6237
(Local chapters listed in telephone directory)

American Diabetes Association
National Service Center
1660 Duke Street
P.O. Box 25757
Alexandria, VA 22314
1 (800) 232-3472
(Local chapters listed in telephone directory)

American Heart Association
National Headquarters
7320 Greenville Avenue
Dallas, TX 75231
1 (800) 527-6941
(Local chapters listed in telephone directory)

National Arthritis Foundation
1314 Spring Street N.W.
Atlanta, GA 30309
1 (404) 872-7100
(Local chapters listed in telephone directory)

Food & Nutrition Information Center
National Agricultural Library Building
10301 Baltimore Boulevard, Room 304
Beltsville, MD 20705
1 (301) 344-3719

The Nutrition Foundation Inc.
1126 Sixteenth Street N.W., Suite 111
Washington, DC 20036
1 (202) 872-0778

INDEX

ABOUT THE AUTHOR

Cooking is one of the many interests of Laurie Burrows Grad, author of *Make It Easy in the Kitchen* and *Make It Easy Entertaining*. She has also written numerous magazine pieces and is the resident chef on "Hour Magazine." She lives in Los Angeles.